Schooling as Uncertainty

Also available from Bloomsbury

Teacher Agency, Mark Priestley, Gert Biesta and Sarah Robinson
Peace Education, edited by Monisha Bajaj and Maria Hantzopoulos
Educational Privatization in Latin America, Africa, and Southeast Asia,
D. Brent Edwards Jr.

Schooling as Uncertainty

An Ethnographic Memoir in Comparative Education

Frances Vavrus

BLOOMSBURY ACADEMIC

LONDON • NEW YORK • OXFORD • NEW DELHI • SYDNEY

BLOOMSBURY ACADEMIC
Bloomsbury Publishing Plc
50 Bedford Square, London, WC1B 3DP, UK
1385 Broadway, New York, NY 10018, USA
29 Earlsfort Terrace, Dublin 2, Ireland

BLOOMSBURY, BLOOMSBURY ACADEMIC and the Diana logo are trademarks of
Bloomsbury Publishing Plc

First published in Great Britain 2021

Cover design: Charlotte James
Cover image © Edwin Remsberg / VWPics/Universal Images Group via Getty Images

A catalogue record for this book is available from the British Library.

A catalog record for this book is available from the Library of Congress.

ISBN: HB: 978-1-3501-6448-2
         PB: 978-1-3501-6449-9
       ePDF: 978-1-3501-6450-5
      eBook: 978-1-3501-6451-2

Typeset by Integra Software Services Pvt Ltd.
Printed and bound in Great Britain

To find out more about our authors and books visit www.bloomsbury.com
and sign up for our newsletters.

To Gus, Oscar, and Amina
Your story, my story, our story

Contents

Figures[1]

Acknowledgments

The Swahili proverb *mtu ni watu*—a person is people—reminds us that the accomplishments by which we define ourselves are the result of collective efforts. This book is no exception, and I am grateful to the many people who have helped bring it to fruition. Some have provided food and friendship; others have given valuable feedback on the chapters; and a few have walked beside me during the moments described therein and added joy to the journey.

First and foremost, my family has been with me nearly every step of the way. My sons, Gus and Oscar Leinbach, and their father, Tim, profoundly shaped this story through their presence at most of the major junctures in Tanzania and the United States. I am grateful for the support and insights they provided, even when the boys were too young to realize their comments were valuable social commentary. My parents, Gus and Hallie Vavrus, and siblings, Steve and Mary Vavrus, also supported me in innumerable ways during the thirty years recounted in this book and the twenty-five years preceding it. Their aerograms in the days before cell phones kept me connected to home when I was in Tanzania, and they buoyed me during the difficult periods recounted in the chapters to follow as well as the many left untold. Steve's avuncular presence in Madison, Wisconsin, kept my spirits high and his nephews entertained as I finished my dissertation, and his wise counsel over the years has helped to make my research possible. Although she has not yet been to Tanzania, Mary's manifestation in this work can be seen on nearly every page. She commented on the book proposal, carefully read each of the chapters, and provided advice whenever a personal or professional crisis emerged, as she has been doing for as long as I can remember.

Three friends, Stacie Colwell, Lesley Bartlett, and "Amina Omari," have become like sisters over the years and have played critical roles in the completion of this project. Stacie, with whom I was living when I began to study Swahili and went to Tanzania for the first time, encouraged me to take intellectual risks when I was timid about doing so and helped me to secure the postdoctoral fellowship at Harvard that enabled the longitudinal research project described in the second half of the book. Lesley, who has been my academic partner for nearly two decades, has given generously of her time in commenting on every chapter—and often on multiple drafts—and inspired me to finish this project when I seriously considered giving it up. And Amina, whose story appears on many of the pages to follow, has deepened my understanding of Tanzania at every turn and has helped me to become a better researcher, mother, and friend. The phone calls, text messages, and visits from each of these three close friends still arrive magically when they are most needed and have enabled me to stay strong through the completion of this book.

I also owe an unrequitable debt of gratitude to colleagues and former students at the University of Minnesota who have become even closer friends during the many years I have worked on this project. A number of them also provided support from their units that allowed me to gain critical feedback on the book from new audiences. Karen Brown, Greta Friedemann-Sánchez, Deborah Levison, and M. J. Maynes have worked with me on several projects supported by the University of Minnesota's Interdisciplinary Center for the Study of Global Change (ICGC), including a trip to, and subsequent course on, Cuba and a forthcoming book, *Children and Youth as Subjects, Objects, Agents: Innovative Approaches to Research Across Space and Time.* The feedback from participants at ICGC's Youth as Subjects, Objects, Agents writing workshop and the Department of History's Workshop on the Comparative History of Women, Gender, and Sexuality proved especially valuable, and I thank Emily Bruce, Elisheva Cohen, Kelly Condit-Shrestha, Joan DeJaeghere, Elisabeth Lefebvre, Emily Morris, Richa Nagar, Roozbeh Shirazi, and Laura Willemsen, in particular, for their helpful comments. A fellowship from the University's Institute for Advanced Study granted me a semester for writing and discussing this work with an insightful group of scholars, and the research workshop in my academic home, the Department of Organizational Leadership, Policy, and Development, also generated useful feedback. I thank the Chair, Ken Bartlett, my colleagues, and a special group of former students who have supported this work in various ways: Richard Bamattre, Kristeen Chachage, Ferdinand Chipindi, Peter Demerath, Anna Farrell, Michael Goh, Amina Jaafar, Chris Johnstone, Anna Kaiper, Christina Kwauk, Acacia Nikoi, Tom Ojwang, Rebecca Ropers, Maurice Sikenyi, Casey Stafford, and Elizabeth Sumida Huaman. Matthew Thomas, in particular, worked closely with me at Teachers College and the University of Minnesota during the years in which we developed the Teaching in Action program. I have learned a great deal about teaching and mentoring from him, and his invitation to serve as a Visiting Scholar at the University of Sydney and keynote speaker at the Oceania Comparative and International Education Society as I was refining the latter chapters proved invaluable.

Beyond the University of Minnesota, I received support from a host of colleagues whose invitations to their institutions enabled critical feedback on this project: Fida Adely at Georgetown University; Supriya Baily and Noah Sobe at the 2017 CIES Fall Symposium at George Mason University; Lesley Bartlett at the Autonomous University of Madrid; Kara Brown, Payal Shah, and Doyle Stevick at the University of South Carolina; Halla Holmarsdottir at the Oslo and Akershus University College of Applied Sciences; Sonia Metha at Macalester College; John Mugo at Twaweza; Karen Mundy and Carly Manion at the University of Toronto; and Bethany Wilinski at Michigan State University. I also received support from a number of institutions at different stages that made this work possible: Andrew W. Mellon Foundation Post-Doctoral Fellowship and Takemi Program in International Health Fellowship at the Harvard School of Public Health; the Fulbright Program through the Fulbright-Hays Group Project Abroad, Fulbright Doctoral Dissertation Fellowship, and Fulbright Scholars Fellowship; McKnight Presidential Fellowship at the University of Minnesota; and the Tanzania Commission for Science and Technology, which has reviewed my work on multiple occasions and provided instructive comments on the research that comprises this volume. I especially want to thank Mark Richardson, my editor at Bloomsbury, for his enthusiastic support of this project and his assistance in seeing it to its conclusion.

Finally, I wish to thank some of the many friends and family members in Tanzania and the United States who have provided advice, encouragement, and needed distraction to help me keep this project in its rightful perspective: Monisha Bajaj, Barbara Baron, Linda Beck, Monica Berendt, Amber Cordes-Eklund, Helen Desforges, Martin Desforges, Marc Dissell, Jean Gorman, Marianna Houston, Chuck Jahn, Alex Juffer, Nancy Kendall, Deb Kern, Helen Kinsella, Sarah Kwayu, Ulla Larsen, Jenny Leinbach, Nancy Leinbach, Phil Leinbach, Agnes Loeffler, Jasmin Makindara, Sheila Makindara, Christine Marsick, Bette Merchant, Michael Moses, Bertha Moshi, Charles Moshi, Goodiel Moshi, Zaina Mshana, Jeanne Mugge, Simon Mtuy, Tara Mtuy, Nick Neeb, Yemama Omer, Betsy Parks, Gary Powell, Rakesh Rajani, Lisa Richey, Allen Rugambwa, Victorini Salema, Ashley Shuyler and AfricAid, Brian Singer and Project Zawadi, Marni Sommer, Aleesha Taylor, Godfrey Telli, Philbert Vumilia, Dierdre Williams, and Andria Wisler.

Glossary

Swahili	English
Baba	Father
Bibi	Grandmother
boma	headquarters
Chama cha Mapinduzi	Party of the Revolution
changamoto	challenges
choo	toilet or feces
duka	shop
Dada	older sister
Habari (gani)?	a greeting similar to "How are you?"
Haki ya Mungu	For the love of God
hii	this
Hodi	a greeting used to announce one's presence at the door
Hongera	Congratulations
kanga	bright cloth frequently worn over women's clothing
kihamba (vihamba, plural)	family homestead
kitenge	wax print fabric
kuhakikisha maisha	to make life certain
kujisaidia	literally "to help myself"—a euphemism for using the toilet
kulogwa	to be possessed or enchanted
Lete fimbo	Bring me a stick
maandazi	sweet, fried dough similar to doughnuts
Mama mlezi	a term identifying the woman who helped to raise someone if not the biological mother
Mama mkubwa	a term identifying a mother's older sister
maisha mazuri	a good life
maisha ni magumu	life is difficult

maji maji	chronic leaking of the umbilical cord stump
Marahaba	a response to *Shikamoo* given by an older person to a younger person
mbege	home-brewed beer made of banana or millet
mchicha	sautéed greens with onions
mchoyo	selfish person
mfadhili (wafadhili, plural)	sponsor
mganga	traditional healer
mitumba	used clothing
mkorofi	a rude, unpleasant person; a troublemaker
mlevi (walevi, plural)	an alcoholic
mpango wa Mungu	God's plan
mtoto yatima (watoto yatima, plural)	an orphan
Mungu akipenda	God willing
mzungu (wazungu, plural)	white person or foreigner
Nitakuchapa	I will hit you
Njoo	come here
nyonyo	breast
Nzuri	a response to *Habari?* and meaning "I'm fine"
pilau	a dish of spiced rice, beef, and vegetables served on special occasions
profesa msaidizi	professor's assistant
shamba	family farm
Shikamoo	a polite greeting from a younger person to an older person
tamaa	desire
tabia	a person's character
Uchagga	land of the Chagga
ugali	stiff porridge
ugonjwa huo	"that disease" in reference to HIV/AIDS
ujamaa	familyhood; form of socialism developed by President Julius Nyerere
ujamaa vijijini	rural socialism
uji	thin porridge

Map of Tanzania and the Kilimanjaro Region

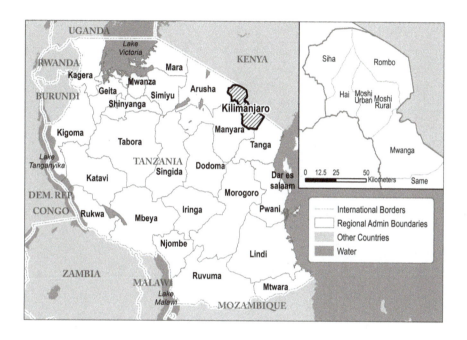

Introduction

The story of my family can be summarized in a single tale of our beloved Uncle Joe overcoming the odds to secure a library card for Gus, his younger brother and my father. Seven years his senior, it fell to Joe to teach Gus the ways of the new country where their immigrant family had landed so that Gus could eventually show the siblings to follow how to succeed among the Americans. My grandparents were born in Austria-Hungary, and, though neither one had gone to school beyond third grade, they both knew how to read and greatly valued education. As the First World War approached, my grandfather fled to the United States because, as a Slovak, he refused to fight for his arch-enemies, the Hungarians and the Huns. He left his new wife and baby—Uncle Joe—and did not return until after the war. My father was born in 1920 in the new nation of Czechoslovakia, and, later that year, they departed for America, eventually settling into a poor immigrant neighborhood on the south side of Chicago. My grandparents knew no English and understood little about this strange new land. Thus, it was Joe, the seven-year-old, who had to figure out the school system, learn the language, and ensure the educational success of his little brother. By the time Gus was ready to start school, Joe's education was about to be sacrificed because the growing family needed his income, and strapping eighth grade boys could easily find work in the "City of the Big Shoulders" (Sandburg 1916/1992).[1]

Joe sensed that if he could get his brother a library card of his own, then Gus might get hooked on reading and succeed in school. So off the boys went to the Chicago Heights Free Public Library, and the handsome Joe Vavrus used his charm to persuade the skeptical librarians to entrust his brother, a six-year-old wearing tattered shoes and well-worn knickers, with borrowing privileges (see Figure 1). Joe's sacrifice was Gus's salvation: My father never stopped reading, and he told my brother, sister, and me many times that it had saved his life. When he was drafted at the outset of the Second World War, his high score on the IQ test was his ticket to studying German while his high school classmates—immigrants all—were shipped off to the front line to become "cannon fodder," as he used to say.

Gus spent the final year of the war in Paris comfortably ensconced at an Allied post on the Champs-Élysées, intercepting German radio signals by day and learning French from his Parisian girlfriend after hours. Once the war ended, my father qualified for the GI Bill, which enabled him to study linguistics at Columbia University and the University of Chicago, where he eventually earned a PhD. And although he was the only one among his brothers and sisters to complete a doctoral degree, six of Gus's seven siblings who lived to adulthood finished college, and four of them received master's degrees. Joe's determination to set his brother on the path of literacy, and my father's subsequent counsel to his younger siblings to "get an education," form the storyline of my family narrative, a classic American immigrant tale in which schooling enabled the newcomers to secure a good life.

Given this context, it may come as a surprise that *uncertainty*, rather than the certainty of schooling, forms the central thesis of this book. A useful anthropological definition of the term suggests that uncertainty is "the limited ability to predict even the immediate future—that is, to engage it prudently and with foresight" (Calkins 2016: 3). Stories of people enacting their dreams for the future upon obtaining a high school diploma or a college degree are well known, and they abound among my relatives. They are especially important to highlight at this time when severe cuts to public education have become the norm in many countries, including the United States.

Figure 1 The Vavrus family with Joe in the back row and Gus in the front, *c.* 1926.

Yet my interest lies in the stories that hide in the shadows, in the uncomfortable accounts of times when schooling did not enable the future one predicted or when it was still insufficient to combat the social forces that can disrupt lives, especially the lives of women. A master's degree did not keep my aunt from a back-alley abortion in the years before the procedure was legal, and college did not lead to happy marriages among my relations or the economic freedom for the womenfolk to leave troubled relationships. In more recent years, I have observed cousins—male and female—with advanced degrees but without steady employment and have witnessed the ways that student loan debt compounds precarity over the course of decades. Without question, schooling has the potential to mitigate uncertainty, but it is not always a reliable prophylactic; instead, schooling can become a source of uncertainty itself.

If we ignore the Janus-faced nature of schooling, we also brush aside the cultural, political, and economic forces that greatly affect how it can be used, and by whom, to make life safer and more secure. The result, as we see today, is a narrow focus on the cognitive aspects of schooling—on learning—as though mastering phonics and multiplication tables could, in and of themselves, guarantee a good life. Without a doubt, learning the basics, and beyond, matters a great deal; however, "learning equity" remains elusive, as Daniel Wagner pointed out, because "opportunities for learning are not equally distributed" (2018: 2, 249).

Similarly, the current focus in the fields of education, economics, and international development on noncognitive skills, such as determination, persistence, and grit, identifies an important set of attributes for success in schooling (Duckworth 2016; Heckman 2013; Tough 2016). Nevertheless, the acquisition of these skills alone cannot fully compensate for the inequality of opportunity that lies beyond the school doors for low-income and minoritized youth. An affordable college education and a full-time job with adequate benefits, including for college faculty, are dwindling opportunities in many countries, and the United States is no exception. When individuals seek post-secondary schooling and stable employment—and I acknowledge some have largely given up on both—they do so in the hopes of establishing a sense of certainty in a world of tremendous unpredictability (Morris 2018). As I seek to show in the chapters to follow, these goals are still attainable for some, or at least temporarily, but we ought to be far more skeptical about cognitive and noncognitive skills as the primary engines producing certainty through schooling. Gender, race, nationality, and social class continue to matter no matter how gifted or gritty one may be.

*****

The Quest for Certainty

My family has informed the stories in this volume in many ways, but the plot primarily reflects my varied experiences as an educational anthropologist, comparative education researcher, and development studies scholar working in the United Republic of Tanzania for more than twenty-five years, a period that spans nearly half my lifetime. From this vantage point that crosses both time and space, I have come to see schooling as far more precarious and contextualized than many researchers and policy makers admit (Bartlett and Vavrus 2019). The anthropological imperative to develop an understanding of other ways of life through extended periods of fieldwork often heightens one's awareness of the inconsistencies and uncertainties of everyday existence, which, in turn, calls into question widely held views about institutions like schooling as a panacea for social ills (Vavrus 2003). I have certainly developed heightened cognizance as a result of research that has sought to develop trust and understanding over time through ongoing engagement in the Kilimanjaro Region of northern Tanzania.

Nearly ninety years ago, John Dewey, the renowned philosopher and education scholar, gave a series of lectures entitled *The Quest for Certainty*. In them, Dewey warned against "the separation of intellect from action," fearing that intellect—meaning abstract knowledge, theory, and thought—had become divorced from the actions and activities of everyday life (1929: 5). Dewey argued, "The distinctive character of practical activity, one which is so inherent it cannot be eliminated, is the *uncertainty* which attends it … Through thought, however, it has seemed that men might escape from the perils of uncertainty" (1929: 6; emphasis added). Critical of this view, Dewey dubbed the attempted escape from the uncertainty of action by way of the intellect "a spectator theory of knowledge" (1929: 23). In other words, what "spectator scholars" believe they know about a phenomenon is not derived from messy engagement with it in specific circumstances; instead, their knowledge precedes or presumes interaction with the phenomenon because their goal is to describe it in broad, immutable terms, believing that experiences, processes, and states of being are universal rather than context specific.

Despite Dewey's eloquent critique of nomothetic, decontextualized knowledge, we find ourselves today inundated with research and policy to enhance learning and teaching as though they connote identical forms of human activity the world over. In my view, too many researchers and policy makers have lost sight of the fact that these are highly contextualized forms of social practice. The principal actors are children, each one unique and delightfully unpredictable, and teachers, who recalibrate their practice to meet the needs of their students and appropriate policy as they see fit.

Ample research has demonstrated that the very concept of childhood varies widely around the world (Gottlieb and DeLoache 2017; Katz 2004; Lancy 2015), and so, too, the qualities of a good teacher (Schweisfurth 2013; Vavrus and Bartlett 2013). Therefore, the global dissemination of a set of "best practices" for learning and teaching ought to be treated with a degree of skepticism (Klees et al. 2020; Steiner-Khamsi 2013; Tikly 2004; Vavrus 2016b). There are certainly lessons to be learned through comparative educational research, but this is a different approach than one where generic assessments and scripted lessons serve as the cornerstones of efforts at "scaling up" from local to international levels (Agarwal and Satish 2017; World Bank 2013). I contend that many scholars of schooling have too tightly embraced a belief in the certainty of educational "science," especially educational psychology, to find cognitive and behavioral solutions to the problems confronting contemporary society. By scaling up of successful policy and programs in one setting, it is thought that what has worked well in one community will necessarily hold elsewhere.

There are voices in the field who question such certainty, most notably critical scholars in comparative education, international development, and educational anthropology. Fred Erickson, as one of the latter, recommended an alternative paradigm:

> The future continues to be original, the local refuses to hold still. General prescriptions for practice do not fit the circumstances of specific situations ... [W]e all must give up on the grandiosity of the current worldview—the paradigm of "scaling up" and "best practices" and "high fidelity implementation." A much more modest approach is necessary—scaling down expectations for what research can do, and for how school improvement can take place.
>
> (2014: 3)

In a similar vein, comparative education scholar Keita Takayama (2020) has recently called for "negative comparative education," which draws on concepts from Zen Buddhism and scholarship in the Japan Comparative Education Society to reconceptualize the certainty of "positive" education and research. Negation, in this sense, rejects the view of education as primarily a process of mastering established knowledge, skills, theories, and methods, and then applying to one's research in a deductive, top-down manner. Instead, negativity identifies the "sense of confronting the limits of previous knowledge and opening oneself up for new ways of knowing and being" (90). According to Takayama, it insists that researchers adopt a very different stance, one that may be disorienting and difficult because it requires humility in listening and learning from others "as a source of theoretical and philosophical insights" (93).

If my experience during the past few decades has taught me anything, it is that the fields of education and development studies need to reject the hubris of "positive," and positivist, research that too often treats theory and methods emanating from the West as universal (Chakrabarty 2000; Chen 2010; Takayama 2020; Vavrus 2016b). As students, scholars, and practitioners, we ought to consider how uncertainty and its concomitant discomforts constitute "ontological, epistemological, and methodological work" that impels us to become more than spectators in generating meaningful social theory (Thomas and Vavrus 2019: 4; see also Pillow 2003; Takayama 2020). It calls on us to be critical, comparative scholars "with our feet on the ground" as we try to make sense of new experiences and understandings (Brice 2017, question 2).

To this end, I offer a reflexive account of schooling as uncertainty that explores a series of particular circumstances as they unfolded over time in Tanzania and the United States, and helped me to think analytically about their imbrication. In this book, there is no methods chapter interrupting the flow of the narrative, and I have relegated theoretical analysis to the background even though I fully acknowledge the omnipresence of theory as it undergirds action, discourse, and thought.[2]

My primary sources are my headnotes—noteworthy remembrances and reflections—and letters to my parents, along with reams of field notes, student essays, household surveys, and interview transcripts. My mother meticulously maintained my correspondences, from the first aerogram sent home in 1990, when I participated in a Swahili language program in Tanzania, to the final weeks of a year-long sabbatical in 2007 in the town of Moshi (Kilimanjaro Region) with my family. Regrettably, the advent of the cell phone meant the demise of my letter writing, but I continued to take ample field notes from 2008 to 2017 as the coordinator of a teacher education program and a longitudinal research project in the Kilimanjaro Region (see Chapters 10, 11, and 12).

From these many notes, letters, interviews, and observations, I have identified a recurrent theme that opens up new analytical possibilities in the study of education, development, and uncertainty. *Kuhakikisha maisha*, a Swahili phrase that literally means "to make life certain," draws attention to the ways that people seek to employ schooling to create certainty about their futures in highly volatile places and periods. I do not dispute the data showing that people with higher levels of education are typically healthier, report higher levels of satisfaction with their lives, and earn more over the course of their careers in Tanzania, the United States, and other countries (Grossman 2005; Hanushek and Woessman 2015; Vandemoortele and Delamonica 2000). Yet this effort to make life more certain through schooling is repeatedly foiled for many people owing to economic, political, and social forces that limit their odds of having a stable life.

Theorist Lauren Berlant (2011) coined the term "cruel optimism" to describe the fantasy of a good life that many in Europe and the United States hold dear, even as their likelihood of securing such a life continues to slip away. She argued that optimism turns cruel when clinging tightly to it becomes "an obstacle to your flourishing" (1). The widespread attachment to schooling in Tanzania as the primary means of securing a good life appears similarly cruel in that completing college, or even primary school in some communities, is a virtual impossibility due to structural forces that prevent poor families from paying requisite fees and forgoing their children's labor. Under these circumstances, the longing for ever more schooling can become an impediment to young people's well-being because they hook their hopes for the future on a possibility they are highly unlikely to realize. The profound disorientation when schooling is severed evokes not merely disappointment but intense uncertainty about one's identity and the resources that will be available going forward to secure *maisha mazuri*, a good life, in both cultural and material terms.

The conditions of poverty in Tanzania, a country of approximately 54 million people (National Bureau of Statistics 2019), are much starker than in the United States. It has a per capita gross national income hovering around $1,020 per year (World Bank 2018); high youth unemployment in the formal, wage-earning sector (DeJaeghere 2017); and a very young population in which 63 percent of the country is under the age of twenty-five (Central Intelligence Agency 2018). Moreover, most parents of the students with whom I have worked during the past two decades did not attend secondary school themselves. Less than 15 percent of the population in the 1990s had completed post-primary education (Ministry of Education and Vocational Training [MOEVT] 2014; Vavrus 2003), which meant that the majority of secondary school students depended on their teachers rather than parents to provide the academic support they needed to have a fighting chance at economic stability in the future.

In addition, my longitudinal research showed that only about 20 percent of youth who completed primary school in the early 2000s had the opportunity to study in secondary school, even in the Kilimanjaro Region, which is known for its relative abundance of schools and widespread support for formal education (Vavrus 2016a). Although the gross enrollment rate for secondary school now stands at approximately 30 percent (UNESCO 2018), this expansion has left many people uncertain about education quality and relevance in a country where two-thirds of the population is still engaged in subsistence agriculture (Deloitte 2016).

Yet the attachment to schooling as a mode of certainty feels as strong today as it did decades ago, when there were far fewer secondary school graduates and greater prestige in completing an A-level degree.[3] When I was new to this environment, such certainty surprised me because daily life *in school* was strikingly unpredictable, and the education students received was often of low quality. Thus, those who succeeded somehow had to master both the formal curriculum—in English, a foreign language—and the "hidden curriculum" aimed at producing disciplined youth who accepted the regime in school and could adjust to the frequent changes in policy and practice at the local and national levels (Apple 1990; Bourdieu and Passeron 1990).

The chapters that follow illuminate this precarity in many ways, such as the capriciousness of corporal punishment and the fickleness of the examination system (see Chapter 6), and the recurring shifts in education policy that left students struggling to pay fees in the middle of the year and pre-service teachers without sufficient classroom preparation (see Chapters 2 and 10). Moreover, I heard and saw repeatedly how moving to the next level in the education system or getting a good job depended on "who knows whom, not who knows what," which led me to wonder what, exactly, schooling was supposed to make so certain.

Recent work by anthropologists on the concept of uncertainty suggests that it has too often been conflated with danger, risk, and misfortune, each of which is a well-established area of research in the social sciences but with its own particular domains of analysis (e.g., Beck 1992; Douglas and Wildavsky 1982; Luhmann 1993; Whyte 1997). Instead, this new approach calls on researchers to decouple these concepts and consider uncertainty as generative in contemplating the future rather than only in explaining past calamities. Sandra Calkins (2016), for one, contended that examining how people act amid uncertainty reveals "a type of anticipatory knowledge production" (Chapter 1, Location 1153). Similarly, Samimian-Darash and Rabinow (2015) insisted that anthropologists should consider experiences:

> as objects of research and analysis and ask how they emerge in response to the
> problem of uncertainty: What kinds of truth claims are advanced about the

future, what kinds of interventions are considered appropriate, and what modes of subjectivity are produced within this problematization?

(4)

This recent work on the anthropology of uncertainty has helped me make sense of the arguments of my Tanzanian interlocutors about the benefits of schooling when the utility of the official curriculum often struck me as highly irrelevant for the lives of the vast majority of graduates. These young men and women talked far less about the acquisition of skills in mathematics, reading, science, or farming as the primary benefit of spending years in the classroom, even though they clearly valued this knowledge. Instead, they generally viewed schooling as critical to the credentialing and social networking essential for managing the many sources of uncertainty they anticipated in the future. In other words, schooling was a potent response, an appropriate intervention, for dealing with the anticipated risks of the labor market, the challenges of marriage, and the vagaries of farming.

Despite this view about schooling and preparedness for the future, there exists for some in Tanzania an alternative to the disappointment at the center of Berlant's notion of cruel optimism. When schooling *was* the source of their uncertainty, their disappointment was often tempered by a belief that God had an alternative path for them as captured in the oft-heard phrase *mpango wa Mungu* (God's plan).[4] In my interviews with youth a decade after most of them had failed the Primary School Leaving Exam (PSLE) at the end of Standard 7 or had dropped out of secondary school for lack of funds, they did not seem unduly surprised that their lives were not turning out as they had intended; they assumed there was a higher reason for this turn of events that they may not yet, or ever, understand (see also Calkins 2016). Thus, I witnessed many creative efforts on the part of young people to make their lives more certain, to prepare as well as they could for the future by obtaining as much schooling or vocational training as possible. At the same time, there was an acceptance that certainty is an elusive goal when families are financially strapped, when the quality of education is wanting, when a parent dies of AIDS, and when changes in policy disrupt schooling, all of which are themes taken up in the following chapters.

My doctoral research, conducted in 1996 and discussed most directly in Parts II and III, focused solely on the educational experiences and views of the future held by youth, teachers, and community members in Old Moshi, a community of some 20,000 people on the slopes of Mount Kilimanjaro in the Kilimanjaro Region (Moshi Rural District) of northern Tanzania. Though it was a qualitative study, I was decidedly absent in the dissertation beyond a brief section on reflexivity.

Yet in reading my journals and letters from this period some twenty year later, it is evident that I was drawn to questions about education and *kuhakikisha maisha* owing to circumstances in my own life. My motivations for ever more schooling were remarkably similar to my Tanzanian students' even though the material conditions of our lives and the absolute degree of uncertainty we faced were vastly different. This revisiting of my younger self through a re-reading of these texts has led me today to "[take] uncertainty as an anthropological mode, through which the inquirer is not external to the inquiry but rather changed by it" (Samimian-Darash and Rabinow 2015: 207).

*****

Producing Ethnographic Knowledge

Although I have revisited field notes, interview transcripts, and other material in writing this book, the project is not an ethnographic revisit in the classic sense of the term, whereby an anthropologist returns to her earlier field site many years later (e.g., Geertz 1995) or to the site of someone else's seminal work to consider it in a new light (e.g., Freeman 1983; Hutchinson 1996). Instead, I conceptualize this work as a longitudinal study of a Tanzanian community and the school, Njema Secondary School, which has long defined and shaped local views on education, gender, and development.[5] Moreover, this project is a reflection on how my own life has changed during this same period of time, in large part because of the myriad experiences I have had in this community as a teacher, researcher, parent, and friend.

Between 1990 and 2020, the year in which I conclude this book, I have made nearly twenty-five trips to Tanzania, most lasting between one month and one year and with most of my time spent in the Kilimanjaro Region. This process of ongoing engagement and observation has resulted in my personal and professional life becoming closely intertwined with several people with whom I lived and worked most extensively. This includes Mr. James Mweka, a respected teacher at Njema whom I met in 1993, and Ms. Amina Omari, a young woman who lived next door to my family in 1996 and has since become like a sister.[6] My goal was never to replicate studies of the Chagga, the major ethnic group in the region, carried out by earlier researchers (Moore 1986; Raum 1940; Rogers 1972) or by contemporary anthropologists (Setel 1999; Stambach 2000) to determine whether their findings in one part of Kilimanjaro held in Old Moshi.

Instead, I have returned repeatedly to this community to advance a different approach to knowledge production that unfolds over an extended period of time, acknowledges the researcher's role in producing such knowledge, and reflects on how she herself has been affected by the experience. Michael Burawoy (2003), in his analysis of revisits, made a compelling argument about the kind of "revisited" ethnographic research in which I have been engaged:

> Where *replication* is concerned with minimizing intervention to control research conditions and with maximizing the diversity of cases to secure the constancy of findings, the purpose of the *revisit* is the exact opposite: to focus on the inescapable dilemmas of participating in the world we study, on the necessity of bringing theory to the field, all with a view to developing explanations of historical change ... [To] place the revisit rather than replication at the center of ethnography is to re-envision ethnography's connection to social science and to the world it seeks to comprehend.
>
> (647; emphasis in the original)

From this perspective, the "inescapable dilemmas" of everyday life that confront researchers who participate in the communities they are studying serve to enrich social research because these dilemmas generate a productive sort of friction as they rub up against existing social theory (Tsing 2005). For instance, the theories of childrearing I considered universal as a young mother led to clashes with my Tanzanian neighbors regarding my apparent negligence in caring for my infant son, Gus (see Chapter 5). Additionally, my dilemma about how to respond to frequent corporal punishment at Njema Secondary School, and my changing views on this matter over time, led me to rethink theories of child development and global declarations about children's rights (see Chapter 6). Despite their significance, these sorts of predicaments that play out over years of engagement often remain absent from the researcher's analyses of historical change, reported, if they ever are, in memoirs or auto-ethnographies divorced from the broader phenomena in the world that the researcher has devoted her life to understanding. The co-construction of the narratives of the researcher and those with whom she has lived is rarely acknowledged or appears tangentially in academic texts when, in many cases, an analysis of such interconnections could be intellectually productive (Collins and Gallinat 2010; Inayatullah 2011).

I, too, have largely divorced my life writing and my academic writing but now seek to bring them together in this book. The longer I teach, the more I see this interplay as a potential source of knowledge about my fields of study and about the conduct of research itself to benefit the next generation of scholars. I now consider this separation of spheres to be a lost intellectual opportunity because the two are, so often, inextricably interconnected. Furthermore, the decision to present our lives as markedly separate and distinct from those who participate in our research fuels a sense that we *are* markedly different, denies our shared humanity, and obscures the fact that, in many cases, the conditions of our own lives are linked to the conditions of theirs. It has taken nearly two decades for me to recognize that both my Tanzanian interlocutors and I have been on similar quests to make life more certain through schooling, and we have succeeded at times and failed miserably at others. The different, though not incommensurable, conditions of uncertainty we have encountered along the way have served as an opportunity for deeper inquiry in my research and personal life.

As I detail in Part I, I began teaching in Tanzania only a few months after marrying Tim, a fellow graduate student I had met during a Swahili language program two years earlier. Still very much in the process of self-formation as a 25-year-old who had recently completed her master's degree, I nonetheless conceived of my future as one in which marriage to a man who shared my interests in Tanzania would enable me to fulfill my aspirations as an educational anthropologist focused on Africa. Leery about marriage after many painful years watching my parents' relationship dissolve, I wagered that Tim's pursuit of a PhD involving fieldwork in Tanzania meant he would, as a spouse, support my own academic pursuits. I was adamant about eventually becoming a professor because I sought the security of tenure, the special status of a job for life that university faculty enjoy (though not nearly as widely today). I did not want to relive my mother's fate of remaining in a marriage due to financial dependence on a spouse, and tenured professors were the most secure professionals I knew. Well aware of the uncertainties of married life, I sought a doctoral student for a spouse and ever more schooling for myself as means of preparing for what an unpredictable future might hold.

Looking back at the interviews I conducted with young women in 1996 as part of my doctoral research, it's apparent how they also sought to make their lives more certain by marrying men who had finished secondary school (at a minimum) and by completing as much schooling as they could. At the time, though, I was surprised by how many of these female students told me they wanted to stay in secondary school not for the sheer satisfaction of learning but primarily because it would enable them to marry educated men with the desirable qualities they sought, most notably men who wanted no more than two or three children and would not become *walevi*, drunkards. They knew marriage was expected of them unless they opted for the convent, and they also believed that men who had completed more schooling were more likely to support family planning, women's rights, and the use of both parents' earnings for the betterment of the household. More schooling, they repeatedly reported to me, would help them secure a life without the burdens of large families, without domestic abuse, and without the heavy weight of poverty so often associated with many children and an alcoholic spouse.

Exploring uncertainty through the domain of schooling encompassed stories like these from youth in secondary school who believed, as I did, that additional academic degrees and an educated partner might minimize economic and social risk. I continued to wonder, though, why many social scientists had stepped back from focusing on the social context of schooling, particularly the social inequities that make life more certain for some and far less so for others. Why have they become, instead, deeply attached to the notion that learning both cognitive and noncognitive skills is the overriding factor in determining whether a young person's life will unfold as anticipated?[7] The parallel question in the narrative about my life asks why the social, political, and economic contexts of higher education do not receive more attention in explaining the unequal distribution of uncertainty in the academy. Surely, cognitive deficiencies or the absence of resoluteness cannot explain the small percentage of women who become full professors and the even smaller numbers of students from racially minoritized groups who enter graduate school in the first place.

My goal is to explore these questions using a narrative approach that portrays the closely interconnected lives of a number of people, including myself, whose experiences enable an analysis of schooling as uncertainty. These accounts reveal how formal education can serve as a buffer against precarity as well as the ways in which schooling itself, through its attendant policies and practices, may compound vulnerability. My intersubjective experience as subject and witness is part of the larger story, and it would be a less trustworthy account if I omitted my own intimate, embodied knowledge. I have drawn on a vast amount of "data" in the form of field notes, interviews, and surveys in constructing this account as accurately as possible, but it is ultimately my interpretation, my memory, and my pen that are responsible for it.

Narrative and Memoir in Ethnographic Research

If you're passionate about your research, at some point you'll recognize that it's meaningful on a personal level because you're researching yourself. Only you've externalized the questions.

—Joel Dinerstein 2011: 122

The term *narrative* encompasses a number of different genres united by the qualities they share with storytelling. Memoir is one of these genres, but ethnography and life history could also be included as they tend to evidence a temporal sequence of events, a compelling plot, and a defined cast of characters (Franklin 2009; Karr 2015; Riessman 2008). Jerome Bruner (1991), in his foundational work on narrative, argued that a narrative way of knowing "brings profoundly into question not only the universality of knowledge from one domain to another, but the universal translatability of knowledge from one culture to another ... knowledge is never 'point-of-viewless'" (3).

While Bruner's bounded notion of culture is anachronistic, his ten characteristics of narrative address contemporary concerns about the limitations of cognitive and behavioral research on learning and teaching that assume universal applicability and scalability. For instance, Bruner noted the importance of exploring events as they unfold over time, or what he called "narrative diachronicity" (6); the significance of verisimilitude and descriptive detail of particular settings; and the strategy of "narrative accrual" or "coherence by contemporaneity" (18–19), by which he meant that any single event is connected to others and often at multiple scales. This aspect of accrual can be seen in Chapter 8, where I recount the stories of grandparents in Old Moshi who were raising their grandchildren in the mid-2000s, a situation that cannot be understood without considering the concomitant national and international HIV/AIDS crises. Similarly, the tale I tell of coaxing Gus to sleep alone when he was a toddler in Tanzania is inextricably linked to contemporaneous child-rearing expertise (see Chapter 5). By using narrative as a way to recount events in my life and in the lives of others, I seek to advance a form of knowledge production that retains its specificity to time and place without losing its contribution to our understanding of broader cultural, economic, and political forces.

*****

[N]o anthropologist can afford to omit consideration of the possibility that they may themselves be their own, intimate informants.
— Peter Collins and Anselma Gallinat 2010: 17

Many researchers who chose education as their field of study identify with its perils and promises in very personal ways. Some have deep scars from being placed in special education programs or from harassment and violence due to gender, race, sexual orientation, or social class. Others seek to explore an institution—the school—where they excelled and felt accepted for their love of reading or science when others in their lives did not understand or appreciate such passion. Many of my colleagues and students have had transformative experiences as teachers in the Peace Corps or on study abroad programs that have enabled them to infuse their reading of education and development theory with personal insights. Others have come to the United States to study from their home countries and have become astute observers of the cultural politics of American education through their experiences with a foreign system. Nevertheless, their perspicacity is constrained because memoir and other forms of autobiographical writing are not widely accepted in the social sciences, especially for graduate students, though these ways of producing knowledge are increasingly common in cultural anthropology and qualitative feminist scholarship.

This tendency to bracket one's own experience in academic writing creates the illusion that researchers rarely struggle with ethical dilemmas, familial disputes, or periods of profound disappointment when they conduct their work. Thus, I am not surprised when students ask me how I so easily adjusted to living in a rural African community or skillfully handled research and parenting, mistakenly believing I did. They have never heard or read otherwise, except in doctoral seminars when we occasionally put down our methods books and discuss the uncertainty of the "practical activity" of longitudinal, ethnographic research (Dewey 1929: 6).

In a groundbreaking volume entitled *Autobiographical International Relations: I, IR*, Inayatullah (2011) made a case for alternative forms of writing in political science, a discipline that has long embraced the distinction between self and object of research, which is a defining feature of positivism. He explained that the essays reflect the authors' academic location within IR; the intersection of their historical and cultural experiences with broader international forces; and how "theoretical decisions emerge from theorists' needs and wounds" (6). The volume is intended to nudge IR as a field "towards greater candidness about how personal narratives influence theoretical articulations" (Inayatullah 2011: 6).

It is my objective to move the fields in which I work in a similar direction, guided by a narrative approach that illustrates the potency of storytelling in generating new theories and ways of conceptualizing research relationships. Narratives can engage readers in the intellectual *and* affective lives of researchers, ideally generating greater understanding of the conditions in which knowledge is produced. Storytelling is also central to ethnographic writing that is attentive to the ways research participants make meaning of their lives and the broader social field in which this occurs. Through reflection over many years on the "braided worlds" that my Tanzanian interlocutors and I inhabit (Gottlieb and Graham 2012), I endeavor to generate a different kind of knowledge than a spectator embracing nomothetic social science might produce (Dewey 1929).

******

Conceptualizing Coevalness

The dominant forms of academic writing in the social sciences, including in education and development studies, rarely admit there is an author who selectively surveys the existing literature, designs the study, interprets the data, and makes recommendations based on a partial perspective on the world. Thus, there is limited examination of the intersubjective nature of knowledge production and the commingling of the lives of the researcher and community members. In other words, the "co-temporality" (Fabian 2014: 205), the sharing of the present moment in each other's lives, seldom becomes a salient aspect of inquiry. This leads to what anthropologist Johannes Fabian termed the "denial of coevalness" (2002: 25).

Coevalness, according to Fabian, "aims at recognizing co-temporality as the condition for truly dialectical confrontation between persons as well as societies" (2014: 205). Such recognition can be partially, if never fully, achieved through writing that reflects the shared exchanges and experiences, in both time and space, of researchers and their interlocutors. Fabian (2002) argued that such texts must reject temporal and spatial representations that position researchers in a modern, dynamic present and "natives" as suspended in a traditional, static past.

There are not many examples of how researchers might write about the profound intersubjectivity of fieldwork that attends to the temporality of their own lives, both the academic aspects and the personal domains that bear on it. How does one "braid" the strands of our own lives that grow during fieldwork with those of the families, friends, and institutions whose changing circumstances are the focus of our research (Gottlieb and Graham 2012)? This question begs an answer because many researchers, myself included, begin fieldwork as doctoral students in their late twenties and early thirties, a period when their lives are often altered by marriage, childbirth, or heightened responsibility to care for aging parents—obligations that shape in many ways what we study and how we study it. Our research projects are often intensely affected by these milestones, and their analytical absence diminishes the possibility of coevalness in our interactions with others and in our writing about the phenomenon at the center of our inquiry.

Despite my view that co-temporality ought to inform more ethnographic writing, I remain attentive to critiques of this form of reflexivity, especially by sociologist Pierre Bourdieu (Bourdieu and Wacquant 1992). He insisted that interpretation must remain focused on the different social locations of researchers and research participants, and I do not seek to downplay the distinct differences between Moshi and Manhattan, where I lived during most of the events recounted in this book. Bourdieu was especially insistent on examining the impact of a researcher's discipline, which establishes the categories of analysis guiding the conduct of inquiry and the theories employed to interpret the findings.

Although Bourdieu's admonishment is essential, his categorical rejection of this sort of intersubjective reflexive practice has always struck me as extreme. It suggests that the only source of knowledge affecting a researcher's interpretation is her discipline, not any other community—scholarly or otherwise—with which she has sustained engagement. Fabian's notion of coevalness, in contrast, is far more intersubjective, and it is evident in the writing of other anthropologists whose work has influenced my own (Behar 1991; Calkins 2016; Rabinow 1977; Rosaldo 1989). For instance, Meneley and Young proposed a process of reflexivity cognizant of the different structural conditions of researchers and interlocutors while simultaneously broadening the scope of the forces that affect the research imagination: "The point is not, simply, to position oneself within the text ... but to engage in a critical reflection on one's relationships with others, as circumscribed by institutional practices and by history, both within and outside the academy" (2005: 7). Such reflection can remain attentive to the ways that researchers are disciplined by the academic fields in which they are located while also considering how our past experiences, intersectional identities, and relationships with others in different domains of life can affect the inquiry process.

*****

Entangled Chapters

This book could be described in the terms Paul Rabinow used to introduce his slim volume, *Reflections on Fieldwork in Morocco* (1977). He stated simply, "The book is a reconstruction of a set of encounters that occurred while doing fieldwork" (6). Yes, this it is, but he accomplished much more as we, the readers, are drawn into Rabinow's reflections on the discipline of cultural anthropology through the vivid stories of his experiences and exchanges with people living in the town of Sefrou at the end of the 1960s. He aimed to reconsider how experience and relationships are translated into ethnographic knowledge.

My goal is similar in that I have reconstructed paired sets of encounters—one focused on the autobiographical "I" and the other on the ethnographic "Other"—set in the same temporal period and often, but not always, in the same space in Tanzania. The juxtaposition of these encounters is intended to illustrate how uncertainty manifests itself in different ways in different lives, disrupting and altering educational trajectories and the economic and social certitude that particular paths were thought to assure. These paired chapters also seek to highlight, to the extent one is ever able, the epistemological assumptions and taken-for-granted categories I have brought to my practice over the years as a scholar in three overlapping fields—anthropology of education, comparative education, and development studies.

Throughout, Bourdieu's rejection of intersubjective reflexivity serves as a counterweight to naïve similitude: My interlocutors and I may have had similar concerns, disappointments, and fears regarding the twists in our trajectories, but we approached them from very different subject positions, not only intellectually but also materially and spiritually. The greater economic certainty in my life and in the lives of my family members should always be understood in absolute and not relative terms. The potential loss of a professorial position in the United States, for instance, may invoke a similar sense of fear as someone who might lose her spot at the market selling chapati and tea, but in one case the consequences may be a loss of status or a temporary period of unemployment; in the other, it is likely to lead to hunger and children's expulsion from school for lack of fees.

Ruth Behar used the phrase "entangled stories" to describe writing that emerged from the simultaneous experiences of losing her grandfather in the United States and conducting fieldwork in Spain, which included research on rituals of death. Stressing the importance of connections across experiences and sites, she explained:

In writing *Death and Memory*, I mixed together levels of experience that are not usually mixed: ethnographic stories of death in rural Spain, which required my objective presence as an ethnographer, and my grandfather's death in Miami Beach, which had taken place in my pained absence. This convergence was a counterpoint, a surrealist moment, when incongruous experiences joined together to bring about an unexpected awareness, a form of knowing and feeling that put vulnerability at the center of ethnographic practice and ethnographic writing.

(Kenner 1991: question 5, paragraph 3)

Borrowing the term "entangled" from Behar (1991), an anthropologist who has also engaged with the concept of coevalness in her writing, the chapters that follow are arranged chronologically with each of the six parts organized as two entwined episodes wrapped around a common theme related to uncertainty. In addition, I share Behar's commitment to admitting vulnerability and making it a focal point in ethnographic writing so as to dispel the notion that our research can be fully shielded from the tumult in the other realms of our lives. To that end, I have expanded on Behar's (1996) mode of writing as a "vulnerable observer" and included excerpts from letters, journals, and field notes written during my first years in Tanzania that reveal the static notions of social relations I harbored, despite my best efforts to suspend them.

As an older and, I hope, wiser observer of my younger self, it pains me to reread some of these missives because they expose racialized assumptions that I would prefer not to examine. They also lay bare how gender, class, and academic disciplining have marked my work in ways that have often been uncomfortable to admit. These shortcomings have become even more apparent during the months in which I made final revisions to this manuscript as they coincided with the COVID-19 pandemic and the murder of George Floyd, an African American man, by a white police officer in Minneapolis a few miles from my home. The striking racial differences in deaths from the disease and from police violence in the United States forced me to realize that I had paid insufficient attention to white privilege and racial injustice in my work (Edwards, Lee, and Esposito 2019; Ford, Reber, and Reeves 2020). In part, this is due to very different racial histories in Tanzania and the United States, which, for instance, is evident in the Swahili term *mzungu* that means both white and foreigner. This conflation of whiteness and foreignness speaks to the vestigial relations of colonialism in Tanzania and to the necessity of intersectional analysis in which race may be one of several salient identities along with nationality, gender, age, marital status, and social class (DeJaeghere, Josić, and McCleary 2016; Hancock 2016; Stacki and Baily 2015).

At the same time, this historical moment has impelled me to ponder the centrality of gender, educational status, and nationality in my analysis and to consider questions about race that I would ask of my Tanzanian interlocutors if I were beginning my research today. Admitting this reconsideration of priorities at this point in my career may make me more susceptible to criticism for not having explored racial politics more fully in the past (see also Sriprakasha, Tikly, and Walker 2020). This is an apt critique, but one of the pedagogical purposes of this book is to illustrate for new and more established scholars how one learns over time and in vulnerable spaces through intersubjective encounters with others, including with one's present and past selves. It is through these experiences and the "inescapable dilemmas" they pose for researchers that knowledge of a different sort is produced from that which can be obtained through positivist social science (Burawoy 2003: 647).

Part 1, *Shaky Beginnings*, introduces the setting in Tanzania as I encountered it in 1992–1993, when Tim and I returned to the country as a newly married couple for his doctoral research and eventually began teaching at Njema Secondary School. Chapter 1 explores the uncertain state of our nascent nuptial union and my wavering commitment to living in Tanzania owing to the physical and psychological challenges for which I was woefully underprepared. Chapter 2 traces the transition from this period of existential angst to the adjustments of living in Old Moshi and teaching at Njema during a period of financial and managerial crisis at the school. The stories in these two entangled chapters invite readers to engage conceptually with the questions of what constitutes crisis, and for whom, and at what point are people willing to take extreme action when confronted with a sense of abandonment by those they thought would help make their lives more certain.

Part II, *Precarious Parenthood*, focuses on child birth and child death, and the precariousness of everyday life in countries like Tanzania where infant, child, and maternal mortality rates remain stubbornly high. Chapter 3 has two foci: first, the counsel I received in 1993 from well-meaning neighbors in Old Moshi about how to become pregnant when they perceived an undue delay in my childbearing, and, second, the complications that ensued when I gave birth to Gus in 1995. Chapter 4 begins as Gus, Tim, and I return to Old Moshi in 1996 for my doctoral research, and it recounts several instances of children's deaths in the community that would likely have been prevented with minimal improvements in health services. These experiences, especially the death of a fellow teacher's daughter, challenge the view that an advanced education can somehow supplant the material circumstances in which we find ourselves when most in need of care.

Part III, *Fallible Expertise,* explores the deeply held views on childrearing of my Tanzanian neighbors and fellow teachers that conflicted with my own, and how these views affected the ways we defined appropriate discipline and punishment. Elaborating on the year of fieldwork in 1996, Chapter 5 recounts how neighbors responded with alarm to our attempts to "discipline" Gus by teaching him to sleep in his own bed, leading me to question the certitude of my views on this practice and others. Chapter 6 expands on this theme by documenting my initial indignation at the use of corporal punishment at Njema Secondary School and the limits of coevalness when one holds strong views opposed by colleagues. It also illustrates how my views on teacher-centered instruction and corporal punishment shifted during the year as I adapted somewhat to the views and practices of my fellow teachers. This chapter concludes with an interview with a veteran teacher at the school who helped me to frame pedagogy and punishment within a broader postcolonial, post-socialist context.

The Interlude takes the narrative from the end of my doctoral research in Tanzania in 1996 to the beginning of my career as an assistant professor in New York City in 2000. There are stops along the way for job interviews, a postdoctoral fellowship, and the initiation of a twelve-year longitudinal research project in Old Moshi.

This section moves directly into Part IV, *AIDS and Uncertainty,* which takes the analysis of the political economy of Tanzania a step further by applying Berlant's concept of "crisis ordinariness" to the HIV/AIDS epidemic as it unfolded in the country during the 1990s through the mid-2000s (2011: 10). Chapter 7 recounts the experiences of several former Njema students following the death of a relative helping with their school expenses and the effect this had on their futures. Chapter 8 describes a summer when my family—now with the addition of a second son, Oscar—lived on Mount Kilimanjaro while I began a study of grandparents caring for their orphaned grandchildren. It recounts the grandparents' evocative stories to show how the HIV/AIDS crisis intensified existing struggles to feed, clothe, and educate children and grandchildren. Together, these chapters make the point that AIDS is not a singular crisis but one layered on top of extant ones in poor households.

Part V, *Policy Arbitrariness,* asserts that policy, whether intended for a single institution or an entire country, always contains an aspirational element alongside the inevitable uncertainty of implementation. This combination belies the promise of predictability that detailed policy guidelines and procedures suppose. Chapter 9 explores this argument in relation to the tenure review process, specifically my own, a daunting period in the personal and professional life of a faculty member as internal and external experts assess the previous six years of one's scholarship as a precondition of a job for life. Chapter 10 illustrates the arbitrariness of national policy by showing how it is profoundly affected in low-income countries by the global political economy and international development institutions, and how policy arbitrariness affects the aspirations for equality of citizens in these countries. The chapter centers on a dramatic shift in pre-service teacher education policy in Tanzania that was announced in October 2006, during the academic year I spent with my family at Badiliko Teachers College in Moshi. In these stories and others recounted in Chapters 9 and 10, I seek to show how the certainty of schooling is often undermined by the very policies that aim to systematize it.

Part VI, *The Social Life of Certainty*, considers how certainty is socially constructed and unevenly distributed across space, race, class, and gender. Chapter 11 builds on the previous one in addressing the themes of aspirations, knowledge production, and the certainty of development "experts" regarding their own expertise. By looking reflexively at my own role as a putative educational development expert in Tanzania, I show how even long-term engagement in a community does not ensure understanding and well-informed programs aimed at improving the quality of schooling. Chapter 12 highlights the limitations of the cognitive and noncognitive skills argument in the field of education by considering the lives of four youth from the longitudinal study I conducted in Old Moshi between 2000 and 2012. The chapter explores how family wealth and status, geography, and gender influenced youths' ability to build social capital they could later convert into the social connections and financial capital necessary for bright, determined young people to make their lives more certain through schooling.

The book concludes with an Epilogue that returns to the key places and persons discussed throughout the book. It also serves as a reflection on the uncertainty in my own life and in the lives of several former colleagues and neighbors as it intensified during the period in which this book was written. As a counterweight, the story ends with Amina, my fictive sister, who has managed to make her life ever more certain despite the tremendous odds against her. She asked that her words be used to conclude the book, so it is her story, entangled as it is in mine, that brings this period of our lives to a close.

Part One

Shaky Beginnings

1

Marital Misgivings

The Dobermans came racing down the driveway without warning, each one grabbing one of my calves with its sharp teeth and biting deep into my flesh. Tim's screams and my own alerted Anthony, the dogs' owner and my good friend from college, that something serious had happened in front of his house. Anthony and his wife, Joy, ran out the door and found me in the road, bleeding onto the shopping bags containing the food for our Christmas Eve meal that evening. Owing to the holiday, the clinics had already closed, but Joy's aunt was a nurse, and they quickly called her and pleaded for assistance in treating my wounds. They whisked me to the aunt's clinic, where she gently dressed my legs, gave me ample doses of painkillers and Valium for my nerves, and sent me home with a bag full of gauze bandages and antiseptic cream.

This was not exactly how our Christmas vacation in Zimbabwe was supposed to begin. It had been a whirlwind of a year: Deciding to get married in May (1992); moving in June from Minnesota, where Tim was finishing his doctoral coursework, to Wisconsin and starting my PhD program before deferring for a year; getting married at the beginning of September; and departing for Tanzania two weeks later for Tim's year of fieldwork. Then there were the adjustments to married life, the challenges of living in economically strapped Dar es Salaam, and the scouting of suitable sites for Tim's research in the Kilimanjaro Region of northern Tanzania. When Anthony invited us to spend Christmas with his family in Zimbabwe, we jumped at the chance for a leisurely holiday in a more "developed" country. Instead, I had canine bites on my legs and blood on my shopping bags.

*****

December 27, 1992

> *Dear Mom and Dad and any stray siblings around,*
>
> *How do you like these fancy aerograms from Zimbabwe? These scenes of Harare look quite different from our pictures of Dar, don't they? I still can't get over the stark contrast between these two capitals given that they are practically neighbors.[1] Harare, with its money-mover machines [ATMs] and six-lane highways; Dar, with its banks without electricity and dusty roads. I guess National Geographic isn't interested in running specials on take-away restaurants or pothole-free roads in "modern" Africa—huts and scruffy children get more viewers, I'm afraid …*
>
> *Today the bruising on my legs looks like it is going away, and I'm able to get around a bit better, but I'm still limping when I stand up from sitting or lying down and need to use a cane. Tomorrow I go back to the clinic so that the nurse can make sure the wounds are healing properly and that there is no infection … I do hope the rest of our stay here is less eventful.*

*****

Despite the dog bites, I reveled in the two weeks in urban Zimbabwe, soaking up the luxuries of constant electricity, potable tap water, riding buses with breathing room, and eating an abundance of familiar foods at the restaurants in Harare and Mutare. I had not tasted pizza or a tossed salad since we left the United States four months earlier, and I set aside my vegetarian principles for an afternoon and devoured a burger at Wimpy's, a popular fast-food chain. Zimbabwe had only gained independence in 1980, following a fifteen-year period marked by violence after the Unilateral Declaration of Independence from Britain by the white Rhodesian government of Ian Smith. Thus, racial tensions were still acutely felt in 1992, unlike our experience in Tanzania whose transition to independence from the UK in 1961 was notably free of such turmoil. Zimbabwe in the early 1990s still had a strong economy and vibrant agricultural sector, but this would change by the end of the decade when President Mugabe, the leader of the country from 1980 to 2017, made a series of decisions aimed at bolstering his position within the party rather than ensuring economic stability.

Returning to Tanzania after the New Year, I was confronted with an existential crisis that had been building for some time though with a temporary reprieve while on holiday in Harare. I had come to Tanzania with Tim without any particular purpose other than to be a supportive spouse while he conducted his doctoral research and to work on my Swahili skills in the hopes of returning to the country in a few years for my own research. Yet I was beginning to recognize that I was harboring a false sense of certainty regarding our marriage, thinking that the joining of two aspiring academics would mean adjusting in similar ways to living in a radically different environment and becoming partners in the research process itself. Whatever Tim might need to succeed, I assumed I could provide it as we were a young couple in love and cultivating academic careers. However, the first few months in Tanzania severely tested these assumptions because we responded very differently to the surroundings, and we did not, I discovered, hold the same convictions regarding a future as professors.

I had been drawn to Tanzania initially as an undergraduate student at Purdue University, where, during my senior year in the mid-1980s, I had the good fortune to study with Manning Marable, the noted scholar of African and African American history. Professor Marable introduced me to the work of Julius Nyerere, the first president of independent Tanzania[2] and a champion of socialist development for Africa. I became captivated by Nyerere's efforts to build unity across this country of more than 100 ethnic groups by promoting Swahili as the national language and prioritizing primary and adult education so that every citizen received a basic education.

Professor Marable encouraged me to apply to master's degree programs where I could study Swahili, African history, and educational language policy. This seemed like an ideal complement to my plan at the time of becoming a certified English as a second language (ESL) teacher and spending my twenties traveling the world teaching English. I had been teaching ESL for the past three years in an adult education program at Purdue and had found it intensely gratifying. As my senior year in college concluded, I received an offer from the University of Illinois at Urbana-Champaign in their noted master's program in teaching ESL and supported by a three-year fellowship to pursue Swahili and African studies.

The period at Illinois was a turning point not only for the intellectual stimulation the university provided but also for the unusual group of housemates I encountered during the years of living in the rambling dwelling we named the Big Yellow House. Many of the women and men who lived in the house for months or years at a time were students in the university's ambitious MD/PhD program, meaning they intended to complete three degrees—MA/MS, PhD, and MD—when most people can barely imagine finishing one. My closest friend and roommate, Stacie, developed her own interest in Tanzania and stayed with us in 1996 in Moshi to carry out archival research on colonial public health programs (see Chapter 4). These friends and my sister, Mary, who by 1992 was living in the Big Yellow House as she pursued her doctoral degree, had hosted our modest wedding reception in the living room and had bid Tim and me farewell as we departed for Tanzania a couple of weeks later.

It was these friends and my sister to whom I turned when the doubts about my purpose in Tanzania and my worth as a future scholar overwhelmed me. Tim had been listening to me for weeks as my uncertainties grew regarding my physical and psychological preparedness for the harsher conditions of his fieldwork that lay ahead once we left Dar. It had been hard enough to cope with water rationing in the city that followed no particular pattern and with navigating the city on buses that frequently broke down or in pick-up trucks loaded down with squawking chickens and ripe produce. And I was finding the sudden shift from doctoral student to housewife very disorienting. The most basic certainties regarding my health and physical needs had been stripped away; my strong network of family and friends could not support me from thousands of miles away; and my identity as an aspiring scholar whose prospects were as promising as my spouse's was slowly slipping away as I spent my days getting clean water and putting food on our table while Tim immersed himself in his research at the University of Dar es Salaam.

Intellectually, I knew these daily domestic tasks served as ideal language-learning opportunities. On the days when transport, shopping, and afternoon visits from the girls in the neighborhood proved entertaining and enlightening, I was able to revel in these "ethnographic moments" and felt that I might, indeed, turn out to be a decent educational anthropologist after all (see Figure 2). However, when the water truck that was supposed to arrive each morning left us dry, or when I knew I was being cheated at the market but didn't have the vocabulary to respond, or when a man would wildly scream "*mzungu*" at me through the bus window, I began to doubt whether I could handle eight more months of life in Tanzania. It was as though the intellectual life that had begun to blossom for me, and which I had anticipated bearing even more fruit during Tim's fieldwork, had withered away, leaving me with only a grim set of domestic duties from which to derive a sense of self. I could feel myself shriveling up like the passion fruit in the corner of our kitchen, its smooth golden rind now pockmarked and purple.

My sense of inadequacy was compounded by Tim's opposite reaction to the conditions in which we were living. He seemed completely unfazed by these difficulties and by the repeated bouts of typhoid and amoebas that plagued both of us. Rather than being discouraged, he thrived as he confronted new challenges and adjusted to our new surroundings with great aplomb. The physical setting was a good match for his minimalist sensibilities, and his passion for running marathons meant that he flourished amid intense physical challenges and had the mental fortitude that most people, myself included, were missing. It seemed

Figure 2 A neighbor and I practicing Swahili in our house in Dar es Salaam, 1992.

as though his doctoral research was a secondary consideration relative to the thrill of putting himself, and by extension me, through more intensive trials of material deprivation. As a newly married person, I did not yet realize how deeply these differences between us would define our relationship. At the time, they only compounded my feelings of inadequacy.

My doubts about fieldwork and marriage crystalized during my first visit to the field site Tim was contemplating on the dry, dusty plains below Mount Kilimanjaro. It was the site of one of the last remaining socialist villages called Chekereni, which had been established during the *ujamaa vijijini* (rural socialism) period of the 1970s. Tim's dissertation research in the field of cultural geography sought to investigate how people had come to reside in Chekereni and the extent to which the principles of *ujamaa* (African socialism) still governed its social and economic life. It was an ambitious project involving archival research in Dar es Salaam, which he had by then completed, as well as interviews and observations over many months in this *ujamaa* village.

I arrived in the middle of December, the season of confirmation parties and weddings, and was warmly welcomed by the residents of Chekereni. That first evening I sat alone on the porch of the small house that we were to share with Tim's primary informant, Ronald, as well as a teacher and her two children. The house was a tiny, unfinished structure with interior walls that did not extend to the ceiling and without electricity or piped water. The outhouse and space for bathing sat in a separate structure behind the main building. We had one of the bedrooms, Ronald had another, and the teacher with her two kids occupied the third bedroom. There was a storeroom for keeping bags of rice and flour as well as a small common area where we could eat our meals. The plan was for the four adults to share in the cooking, with Ronald on the roster for this particular evening.

No sooner had I gotten comfortable on the porch than two women from the shop across the way came over to find out why I was sitting by myself. They insisted I join them on the bench in front of the three shops that comprised "downtown" Chekereni, and we spent an hour or so exchanging stories about our families until Tim appeared. This initial conversation with two engaging neighbors reinvigorated my interest in learning more about how schooling affects women's lives, and I began to imagine the questions I might ask to gain insights into *ujamaa*, gender, and education.

At this point, Ronald, our housemate, arrived to tell us that he would cook dinner for all of us after a quick visit to the *mbege* bar down the road. *Mbege*, home-brewed beer made of banana or millet, is typically purchased for a pittance and served in large plastic tumblers at benches set up under an awning or tree. Knowing from experience in Dar that visits to *mbege* bars are rarely speedy affairs, Tim and I retired to our semiprivate room in the house and entertained ourselves in the darkness by making shadow figures with our hands and a flashlight beaming the figures against the bare cement wall.

Despite a few pangs of hunger, I was content to wait for Ronald to return while the flashlight illuminated our fanciful creatures. Yet at one point, my hand slipped, and the flashlight lit up the floor below our bed, revealing a crowd of cockroaches scurrying across the cement. Upon further inspection, I spotted a few more climbing up the wall on the other side of the room and quickly lost any interest in stepping out from underneath the mosquito net tucked tightly below our mattress. But at 9:30 p.m., Ronald called for us to join him for a dinner of rice and *mchicha*, one of my favorite dishes of sautéed greens with onions. Hunger turned me into an intrepid warrior, and I bravely donned my flip-flops and strode out to the common area to eat with the others. However, I succumbed to my fear of large insects by brushing my teeth and peeing in the grassy area next to the house rather than going into the outhouse, which Tim had vividly described to me as the epicenter of evening activity for the roaches.

Once we were back in bed again with mosquito netting all around as a precaution against malaria, I became aware of the lack of padding below my hips. Although Tim was told at the shop that he was purchasing a deluxe foam pad to serve as our mattress, I barely felt anything between my hips and the wooden boards holding up the thin pad. I eventually fell asleep until my bladder beckoned at 3:00 a.m., when I foolishly decided not to brave the bugs outside to relieve myself. This meant spending the next three hours trying unsuccessfully to go back to sleep as the urge to pee grew greater and the scratching of cockroaches below the bed intensified.

Groggy and grumpy when dawn finally came, I helped with breakfast preparations and then got ready for services at the Catholic and Lutheran churches in Chekereni. Tim had told me about the dual services that would include a wedding and confirmation ceremonies, but little did I appreciate how involved these events would be because we had been guests of a Muslim family in Dar and had not gone to church services. I assumed they would last about the same time as a service in the United States—an hour or so—and then we would move on.

The Catholic service began at 9:00 a.m. and ran a mere one hour and fifteen minutes, giving us time to get to the Lutheran service shortly after it began at 10:00 a.m. The intense December heat and the absence of fans in the Catholic church made sitting inside the crowded sanctuary an exercise in endurance as I forced my heavy eyelids to stay open. Thus, it was a relief to see people standing outside of the overflowing Lutheran church when we arrived because it meant we could sit under a shady tree with other latecomers and catch a cool breeze. We found a few empty spots on a bench in the shade and began listening to the sermon as the pastor's words wafted out of the open windows.

No sooner had we settled in comfortably than we began to hear murmurings from some of the women sitting near us who decided that it was not proper for Tim and me to be sitting outside. As the only white folks for miles around, they assumed we must be guests of the couple getting married or of one of the families whose children were being confirmed. Despite our protestations to stay put, they insisted that we be taken inside and given seats of distinction. This meant escorting us through the packed church to the very front pew, where those already seated pushed themselves even closer together to make room for two more bodies. Embarrassed by this unwarranted treatment based on racial privilege, I hesitantly whispered "*Habari?*" (How are you?) to the woman on my right, who was now pressed even more tightly against her large, matronly neighbor so that I could have a seat. The woman nonetheless smiled warmly, responded "*Nzuri*" (Fine), and placed her baby in my lap. After little Neema stared intently for a few minutes at the *mzungu* holding her, she and I both turned our attention to the long parade of girls and boys taking their first communion.

The transformation in these children, some of whom I had seen the day before playing in a vacant lot, was remarkable. Yesterday, the shoeless boys wore soiled, tattered T-shirts as they kicked a homemade soccer ball made from plastic shopping bags held together with bits of string; today, they were spotless, from the starched white collars under their suit jackets to their well-polished Black shoes. The day before, the girls had on oversized dresses with ruffles coming loose at the seams while this morning they looked like little brides in their white satin dresses and, in a few cases, with matching white lace gloves. These rambunctious children who had been running through the fields of Chekereni when I first encountered them were now standing silently, obeying every command the minister put forward. They stood, they recited solemnly, and they stood some more before they were officially confirmed into the church.

It was well past 1:00 p.m. when the service finally ended, and I was drenched from sitting on the crowded pew for nearly three hours with Neema's warm body on my lap. Ronald had offered to be our escort for the second half of the day, which involved attending several confirmation celebrations to which we had been invited and doing so in a way that would allow us to leave our gifts, eat a plate of *pilau* (a dish of spiced rice, beef, and vegetables served on special occasions), drink a soda, and move on to the next party. Ronald did a fine job at first of getting us seated, fed, and out the door within forty minutes, a feat I only appreciated years later when we had no one to help us negotiate these events and ended up for hours at a single party with plate after plate of *pilau* sent our way. Yet at the home of the local chairman of the ruling party, the *Chama cha Mapinduzi* (Party of the Revolution), our movement came to a grinding halt. This party was part celebration of the chairman's son's confirmation and part political rally, which meant there was plenty of *mbege* to be drunk before the food was served. Ronald was going nowhere, and he gestured for us to make ourselves comfortable for the long bout of drinking and eating ahead.

Already stuffed to the point of bursting, my mind turned to the churning and sharp pains developing in my gut, a telltale sign of a night of gastrointestinal adversity to follow. This golden anthropological moment that combined "culture"—as I understood it at the time—and politics was lost to the percolations in my digestive tract and to thoughts of cockroaches scurrying across my feet during a night in the outhouse. I convinced Tim that we should try and hitch a ride from Chekereni to Moshi and spend the night at the YMCA, my go-to place to stay whenever I had an overnight in town.

It was at the Y, a spartan but very clean and inexpensive hostel, where my most serious doubts about the months ahead resurfaced. It was four days before we were to depart for Zimbabwe, so I initially tried to push these thoughts aside and focus on the upcoming holiday in Harare. Yet my reaction to the weekend in Chekereni made it clear that we had to confront the very real possibility that I would not live with Tim while he conducted the rest of his research.

It was difficult for me to tell whether Tim was disappointed in me for not being made of stronger stuff or whether I was projecting my sense of shame and disappointment in myself onto him. We had already considered this option of living separately when we met with the education secretary for the Lutheran diocese schools in Kilimanjaro regarding my teaching English at a high school about fifteen miles away from Chekereni on the slopes of the mountain. One option was for me to stay at the house near the school during the week, which was by comparison quite luxurious, and Tim could come for the weekends. However, the secretary was also keen to have Tim teach mathematics as secondary schools were always short on teachers for this subject, and Tim had sufficient qualifications with his bachelor's degree in computer science and economics.

This option had appeal to both of us because Tim had begun to express increasing doubts about whether he wanted to become a professor after all, and this led to a questioning of the purpose of continuing with his research in Chekereni. Tim had found his doctoral program to be intellectually stimulating, but he didn't care for the one-upmanship of the seminars and dreaded entering the competitive academic job market that would follow the completion of his PhD. He was also finding that doing interviews with neighbors in Chekereni changed his relationship with them, from one of nascent friendship and coevalness to one in which he was extracting knowledge for a purpose that would produce no tangible benefits for these subsistence farmers. Although Tim had expressed these doubts already, my concerns about staying in Chekereni only heightened his misgivings and led us both to wonder about our immediate and long-term futures.

In my case, these uncertainties were especially distressing because I had convinced myself before we left the United States for Tanzania that my great appreciation for the country's socialist experiment would enable me to live like one of the people in an *ujamaa* village. This intellectual certainty did not allow me to consider how ill prepared I was for the myriad physical and psychological adjustments required of someone whose previous experience in Tanzania had been limited to a well-organized language study program.

I also felt uncertain about my preparation as I looked back on class discussions a few years earlier with my African studies professors at the University of Illinois. They were either Africans themselves from relatively privileged backgrounds or had spent many years on the continent and spoke in their anthropology, history, and linguistics lectures about hardships only as entertaining illustrations of larger theoretical points. Now, though, I longed to know how they had dealt with the challenges of fieldwork: Were their malaria-induced hallucinations as epiphanous in the moment as they seemed in their recounting to us in class, or were these, in fact, frightening experiences that led some of them to question their chosen profession? Had they ever worried about their safety or been attacked, as another female student and I had been during the Swahili language program in 1990 by three men wielding machetes? Did they ever feel ashamed because they could not cope in the moment with the physical hardships that the people around them had to deal with every day? I was only now, three months into our stay in Tanzania, slowly beginning to adjust to the challenges of our neighborhood in Dar es Salaam, and it was a far more comfortable place than rural Chekereni. What would my former professors have done, or was I simply not made of the same stuff as them? A gnawing voice kept taunting me, "You are bourgeois, baby," and I could not reconcile how this could be when I had long clung to the fantasy of myself as a tough, politically-committed researcher.

*****

Journal Entry: January 4, 1993, Dar es Salaam

Today I actually made my decision to leave quite final. I went first to the KLM office to see about leaving from Kilimanjaro, but they said it wouldn't be possible because of restrictions on my ticket. So I went to Air France to see about their next flight, which happened to be tonight! I thought this would be a bit too sudden, so I went for the Saturday [January 9th] option … Now that my ticket is in hand, I guess I'll let the ball roll in the direction of returning to the US. This means trying to really absorb everything in Dar es Salaam, from the bus rides to the heat to the language for I'm not going to be having any such experiences for a while. More importantly, though, it means coming to terms with the impending separation from Tim and trying to answer that question I am already starting to dread, "Why did you go home?"

As Susan [an American friend from the 1990 Swahili program conducting research in Tanzania] said today at lunch, she felt much more culture shock coming here the second time because we had been so sheltered as students. I fear this was a large part of my frustration: Because I had enjoyed myself so much then, I assumed it would be similar this time, even though I knew it would be somewhat more difficult. Susan also suggested that I may have found Tanzania harder to accept because I had just returned from Zimbabwe, where conditions are so much easier. That is certainly a factor, especially since the people we interacted with in Harare voiced my feelings about life with no electricity, regular water, hazardous transport, etc. That these Africans admitted they too could not live under those conditions may have allowed me to begin to accept my personal limitations ...

I want at this moment to put aside any guilty feelings or shame that I have about my decision. I've had four months here of very educational experiences—I simply think I have had enough for now.

*****

Arriving at O'Hare Airport in the middle of January was a shock to the system, with snow swirling across the runway and fellow passengers pulling down coats and hats from their carry-on bags. I, in contrast, had no winter clothes with me at all, only my cane from Zimbabwe that I needed to keep me steady as I walked slowly down the aisle. I had left the United States in September and planned to return in June, escaping the cold months altogether. Fortunately, I had been able to make a quick call to my parents before leaving Dar, telling them that I was coming home and asking whether anyone from the Big Yellow House could drive up from Urbana and meet me in Chicago with a coat and mittens. Sure enough, Mary and Stacie were waiting for me at the airport with curious expressions on their faces, delighted by our unexpected reunion but profoundly concerned as to why I had come back to the United States. This unexpected event had made for great speculation among the housemates, with some wondering whether Tim and I were splitting up and others convinced I must be pregnant. My answer fell far flat of their riveting speculations: I had reached a breaking point, and I needed a pause from the material conditions in Tanzania and the uncertainties I felt about my future with Tim.

The huge dining room table at the Big Yellow House was an ideal spot for long, leisurely meals shared by the roommates and their boyfriends. The house was always well stocked with food and drink, and the more wine we consumed, the more advice I received. Mary, Stacie, and the rest of the gang could offer a perspective on the situation that I had been unable to see in Tanzania. Unlike Tim, who preferred physical challenges and novelty more than the comfortable and familiar, the Big Yellow House gals immediately rallied to my side and advised me to ease up on myself. As anthropologists and historians themselves, they convinced me that many a scholar before me had drawn the line at conditions far better than I had described and had still written brilliant books about their research. They welcomed me to stay in their loving sororal care for as long as I wished, but I felt the urge to return to my parents' home in Indiana and consider my next steps.

The opportunity to talk, cry, rest, and laugh with my easy-going and remarkably nonjudgmental parents created an ideal space for the reflection I needed but had not been able to find in Tanzania. During this period, I wrote incessantly, to Tim and to myself in my journal, with words like "depression," "feeling crappy," "purposeless," and "failing confidence" repeating themselves with disturbing regularity. I could still recall the full force of the pain I was feeling at this time when I reread the journal twenty-five years later in the writing of this book. I realized that, in the years after this episode, I had constructed a narrative about myself as a confident, purposeful scholar, and I had buried this period of great doubt deep inside of me, just as I had concealed the journal itself in a box filled with mementos from happier times.

In addition to my doubts about conducting fieldwork in the future, and what this might mean for my career path, the journal revealed the extent to which I questioned my mental state and what I should do about it. When I was in high school in the early 1980s, my mother explained that she wanted Mary, our brother Steve, and me to know about a chronic illness that had long plagued her side of the family: depression. My mother, born in Texas in 1924, grew up in a very troubled time for her family and the nation. Her father, my grandfather, who died before I was born, had been a relatively successful salesman of oil-drilling equipment in Louisiana and Texas until the Great Depression hit in the late 1920s. He had had some bouts of depression as a young man, but the severe economic crisis meant that few people could purchase the equipment he was selling. His increasingly erratic behavior and suicide attempts resulted in repeated institutionalization at a time when treatment for depression meant electroshock therapy and rest in a sanatorium.

My grandmother was in no position to care for her two daughters—my mother and her younger sister—as she had always been "frail." This term captures a racially-toxic era, when frail was frequently ascribed to white middle- and upper-middle-class women who spent considerable time resting in bed while being tended to by Black domestic workers. We don't know whether our grandmother also suffered from depression, though the history on her side of the family included many troubled characters, from swashbuckling settlers of the Republic of Texas to opium addicts and alcoholics.

What my mother wanted her children to know was that she had inherited this illness and had been treating it successfully with medication. She was not ashamed of depression, even though few people in the 1980s would admit to being afflicted by it. The disease was still widely considered to be a flaw of one's character and not an illness to which one could be genetically predisposed. Mom wanted us to know that we were more likely to become depressed just as children in families with high rates of cancer or heart conditions might be afflicted by them. Yet it was not until this period of self-doubt in Tanzania that I began to wonder whether I, too, suffered from depression like many in my mother's clan.

In an era before the internet, I turned to the public library for sources about depression and spent several afternoons back in one of my favorite childhood haunts reading through medical journals about the disease. I certainly had some of the symptoms—sadness, bouts of tearfulness, and blaming myself for my failed attempt at living in Tanzania—but I did not have most of the others. My appetite was robust, as usual; I did not have difficulty sleeping; and I had no thoughts of injuring myself or others. This knowledge proved comforting as it appeared that my feelings were episodic rather than chronic, clearly connected to this difficult and tumultuous period.

As I continued to read and write during the weeks at my parents' home, the tone in my journal began to change. Revisiting these pages, I can now appreciate how they document the ways that a person can get through a sorrowful period and come through stronger and more sagacious on the other side. On one page, for instance, I discussed an insightful conversation with Stacie about keeping this period of my life in perspective, as I had given myself only a few months to make a number of significant life transitions—moving, marriage, starting a PhD program, and leaving family and friends far behind. On another page, I reflected on Mary's candid assessment of my unrealistic expectations about the exciting, romantic life of a trailing spouse and how it was time to be more pragmatic about what the future might hold if I decided to return to Tanzania, and to my marriage. Tim had now officially put his doctoral research on hold and was teaching at Njema Secondary School and living at the house near the school with two young British teachers. And in several sections of the journal, I repeatedly recorded sensible remarks from my parents about the inevitable difficulties that new identities and new surroundings present to us—difficulties they had experienced numerous times as they started new lives in new places during their forty years of marriage.

Slowly, my confidence in myself and my marriage returned, and I was now ready to make something of the time that remained before resuming my doctoral studies in Wisconsin in the fall. So, scraping together the remaining funds from my savings account, I bought a return ticket to Tanzania and to Tim.

*****

February 21, 1993

Dear Mom and Dad,

I can't believe that I'm actually at the Moshi YMCA again. Nothing much has changed here: The employees are still friendly and helpful, Mount Kilimanjaro still stands gloriously on the horizon. The only thing that has changed since my last stay is perhaps me. I feel much more content and excited about being here than I did before, probably because I am still full of the confidence that you sent me away with. I needed a lot of confidence to get here in one piece, although I should not have worried so much because Tanzanians do take care of their guests.

As soon as I arrived in Dar, I ran to see about the morning flight to Kilimanjaro that I had booked. Well, no such flight exists now that Air Tanzania's "spare plane" crash landed two weeks ago, as Tim had written in a letter. The only plane that day, an 18-seat special flight, was leaving at 5:00 p.m. I was able to change my ticket for this flight and settled in for an all-day wait at the airport. But when I went to check in at 3:00 p.m., I was told that the flight was full and my ticket was actually only for stand-by! I must have looked pretty pathetic at this point because the Air Tanzania manager came out and somehow arranged for me to get on that plane.

Knowing Swahili and something about Tanzania came in handy [when I landed in Kilimanjaro] because I spotted a nun coming out of the terminal and asked her if she and her sisters were returning to Moshi. They were not, but she put me in touch with a policeman who handed me over to a friend of his from a safari company. Sure enough, this kind Maasai driver brought me to the YMCA. The Y was already locked up, but since the guards knew me, they woke up the receptionist and I got a room. I slept very soundly, needless to say. Now it is Sunday morning, and I'll try to get a taxi to Old Moshi, hoping that Tim and his housemates will be there. More soon.

2

Spoons, Strikes, and Schooling

I stood at the buffet table in the YMCA's cavernous dining room, stirring another heaping teaspoon of instant Africafe into my steamy mug of milk and looking out at snowcapped Mount Kilimanjaro to the north. The sparkling glacier protruded from the clouds that shroud the 19,000-foot mountain, but they would soon lift as the sun rose higher in the sky, revealing settlements like Old Moshi across the mountain's lower slopes. After the long journey back to Tanzania, I felt relieved to be back in the familiar atmosphere of the Y and in the embrace of "Mother Kipoo," the maternal moniker for Kibo Peak (Ngatara 2001; see also Dundas 1924). Moshi seemed most welcoming, and I decided to take a stroll through its quiet Sunday morning streets before heading up the mountain. I knew transport would be limited anyway at this early hour, and a walk would allow me to mail the aerogram to my parents at the post office.

The relationship between "new" Moshi, the town at the base of the mountain, and Old Moshi, the community on the mountain slopes, had intrigued me since I first visited the Kilimanjaro Region a few months earlier. I did not yet know much about the intertwined history of Moshi Town and Old Moshi, but I had learned that the latter had once been the seat of German colonial rule in northern Tanganyika, a period that lasted from the late 1880s through the First World War. However, Old Moshi began to lose its political stature due to German alliances with other chiefdoms and, in 1911, with the extension of the railroad from the Indian Ocean coast to "new" Moshi at the base of the mountain (Iliffe 1969). Today, with a population of approximately 157,000, Moshi has blossomed even though it is not as large as the other large city in the north, Arusha, which has grown to more than 341,000 in the past few decades (Worldometer 2020).

The double road through the heart of Moshi hums with banks, shops, and businesses that cater to the thousands of tourists who arrive to climb Mount Kilimanjaro and go on a safari.[1] However, Moshi is most widely known within Tanzania for "chalkboards, clinics, and coffee," as a longtime resident once told me.

The Moshi Urban and Rural Districts have some of the highest adult literacy and school attendance rates in the country as well as an outsized number of colleges and universities relative to the rest of Tanzania (Vavrus 2016a) (see Figure 3). The Kilimanjaro Christian Medical Center (KCMC), a hospital founded in the early 1970s by an alliance of the Anglican, Lutheran, and Moravian churches, lies on the outskirts of town and has a sprawling campus comprising teaching, research, and clinical facilities unlike any other institution in a town of its size (KCMC 2017). And Arabica coffee, grown largely as a cash crop for export, has long enabled the Chagga to use the profits from its sale as capital for private ventures as well as for contributions to the establishment of churches, clinics, and schools (Vavrus 2003).

The YMCA is one of the most well-known institutions in Moshi, catering to domestic and international travelers seeking low-cost accommodations; it also serves as a hotel training school for youth who seek employment in this sector. Returning to the Y after my walk, the trainee who had served breakfast that morning reported that someone from Old Moshi was departing shortly and had offered to give me a ride. With my supply of shillings stretched thin, I welcomed the offer of free transportation and ran to my room to grab my bag.

Figure 3 A secondary school in Moshi with Mount Kilimanjaro in the background, 2007.

"Ah, you must be the new teacher going to Njema Secondary School," Mr. Tarimo exclaimed as we met in the parking lot. He lifted the backpack from my shoulders and laid it carefully on the floorboard of his well-worn Land Rover. He motioned for me to take the passenger's seat beside him, so I climbed up and settled in for the ride. No worse for wear, the vehicle's mighty engine roared when Mr. Tarimo turned the key. The metal doors rattled as we bounded across the gravel lot and onto the two-lane highway toward Old Moshi.

As Mr. Tarimo drove, I looked out the window at the well-dressed men and women walking alongside the road carrying their Swahili Bibles and hymnals on their way to church. Some of the teenaged girls had babies snuggled in a bright cloth called a *kanga* tied on their backs while they held the hands of their younger brothers to keep them from sullying their Sunday clothes in the nearby streams. I wondered about the history of Christianity in this part of Tanzania and why it had become so entrenched when this had not been the case along the Indian Ocean coast, where the vast majority are Muslim (Mushi 2009). I knew from doing a bit of reading at the University of Dar es Salaam library that Christian missionaries had been particularly active in Kilimanjaro and that youth from the region were far more likely to attend secondary school than in many parts of the country; however, I didn't understand why this would still be the case nearly a century later and three decades after socialist policies aimed at educational equality across Tanzania had gone into effect (Mushi 2009). I eagerly anticipated learning more about these legacies by teaching at a Lutheran school in the heart of *Uchagga*, the land of the Chagga.

After some 15 minutes, Mr. Tarimo pulled off the tarmac road and onto one of the dirt paths that wend through Kiboriloni, the junction of urban Moshi and rural Old Moshi. In the 1990s, Kiboriloni was a sprawling market with all manner of goods on offer. Two days a week, it was flooded with used clothing from abroad known as *mitumba*, making it one of the largest such venues for miles around. Over time, I would become familiar with "sock street," as I liked to call it, where, in 1996, our fifteen-year-old neighbor, Amina, would join other women and girls in neatly arranging their slightly faded wares for sale on blankets laid out on the ground. Nearby was "t-shirt alley," the terminus for tees from the United States that proudly announced Rose Bowl victors from several years before or the dates of concerts by waning rock-and-roll legends. I would learn that these American cast-offs, intended as donations to "poor Africans," instead became much-needed capital for many small-time female entrepreneurs whose profits of a few dollars a day put food on the table and kept their children in school.

Heading up the mountain from Kiboriloni on this particular day, Mr. Tarimo called out to neighbors on their way to church—Catholic, Lutheran, or Assemblies of God—explaining to me as he drove how each person was related to a larger family or clan.

"There are the Moshis, the Meros, and, of course, the Makindaras, the family of the chief."

"The chief?" I repeated, intrigued by this information as I knew President Nyerere had abolished the chiefdom system a few years after independence. Mr. Tarimo laughed, clarifying that there were, in fact, no more chiefs but that did not diminish their legacy.

"You'll see," he smiled, "Old Moshi has a *long* history." With that, Mr. Tarimo turned to shout at a relative who was resting in front of a row of small shops. As they exchanged greetings in Chagga, a language I did not understand, I had a moment to collect my thoughts before seeing Tim for the first time in six weeks.

*****

I had left Tanzania with no certainty that I would ever return to the country or to my marriage, disenchanted after a series of setbacks: the attack by my friend's Dobermans in Zimbabwe, unremitting cuts to electricity and water in Dar, and finding myself unfit for the role of trailing spouse without a professional identity of my own. From Tim's infrequent but cheerful aerograms to my parents' home in Indiana (cell phones would not allow for instant communication for another decade), I knew only that he had ceased his doctoral research and was enjoying teaching mathematics at Njema. I realized that joining him would mean living in a rural area without certain amenities and sharing our home with strangers yet again, this time with Nathan and David, two young Brits spending their gap year teaching in Tanzania. However, I was intrigued by the possibility of residing near a primary and a secondary school for the insights into education they might offer and for the opportunity to teach at a secondary school myself.

While sitting on my parents' well-worn couch, I had contemplated the uncertainty that would still surround me if I were to return to Tanzania. I was learning little from Tim's descriptive letters of his deeper feelings about our relationship, thinking at times that he might even be happier without me from their chipper tone. I searched his letters for other clues but to no avail. I knew even less about the teaching position I had been offered at Njema, and I wondered whether I was sufficiently prepared for the challenge. I grappled for weeks with the indeterminacy of the situation before settling on a course of action.

The time for reflection in the United States enabled me to see how I had been tripped up by unrealistic expectations regarding marriage, living in a new land, and my ability to adjust quickly to both. I began to understand that Tim and I approached challenging, unfamiliar situations quite differently due to gender and temperament, and it was okay if I never became quite as daring. Yet I also realized that I would have to accept greater uncertainty if I were to find a middle ground with my spouse and enjoy teaching and conducting research in Tanzania as I had long hoped to do. My attachment to the fantasy of ideal wife and intrepid Africanist had proven to be cruel and disappointing; if I continued to cling to it, both my marriage and career were doomed (Berlant 2011).

With my expectations significantly recalibrated, Mr. Tarimo and I finally pulled up in front of my new home in Old Moshi, where I found a startled husband. Tim had gone to the airport the day before, when he expected my arrival; he had not found me among the disembarking passengers. Concerned, but not overwrought, he had returned home to await a letter with updated information on my plans. No cell phones meant no expedient way to communicate about flight delays and cancellations, so guests—and spouses—had a habit of showing up unannounced at one's doorstep. As our Chagga neighbors would say countless times in the months and years ahead, God's plan (*mpango wa Mungu*) inevitably overrides our own.

*****

One of my first plans was to learn as much as I could about Chagga history, especially the history of Old Moshi, after Mr. Tarimo had piqued my interest. As the new teacher in the community, it did not take long before I met one of its most renowned members, Mr. Ramos Makindara, the son of the last chief. Mr. Makindara lived with his second wife and younger children next to Njema Secondary School, and he taught me a great deal over the years about the political history of the area. Through our conversations, I learned that there had been a vibrant precolonial economy in Kilimanjaro that centered on trade between Chagga on the mountain and the Arusha and Maasai cattle herders on the plains. There was also considerable trade related to the provisioning of long-distance caravans carrying ivory and slaves from the African interior to the Indian Ocean coast. This trade intensified in the mid-nineteenth century, and small chiefdoms were consolidated under the rule of politically strategic chiefs who profited not only from the trade but also from exchanges with European explorers and missionaries who had begun arriving in Kilimanjaro by the 1880s (Bender 2013; Moore and Puritt 1977).

It was Mr. Makindara's politically astute great-grandfather, Chief Rindi (also known as Mandara; ~1845–1891), who was widely credited with consolidating the Old Moshi chiefdom. He also formed strategic alliances with the Arusha and the Swahili, who typically led the caravans, and with Europeans from Germany and the UK (Stahl 1964). Living between two more powerful Chagga chiefs, Rindi could little afford to ignore these relationships, particularly with missionaries and explorers. He surmised that there might be advantages for his people if he allied himself with these newcomers, so, in 1885, Chief Rindi granted land to British missionaries from the Church Missionary Society to start the first school in the area. He also negotiated with the Germans to establish their *boma* (headquarters) for all of northern Tanzania on his land, leading to an influx of German (Leipzig) Lutheran missionaries, eventually including the prolific Bruno Gutmann, who established schools, a clinic, and large church north of the *boma* in the community of Kidia (Fieldler 1996; Vavrus 2003). As Kathleen Stahl (1964) concluded in her detailed study of precolonial Chagga history:

> Thus [Old] Moshi became in a sense the capital of Kilimanjaro. And though its area and population remained small, the Moshi folk got a head-start over those of other Chagga chiefdoms in receiving the newly introduced benefits which, from the Chagga point of view, could all be turned to practical, and sometimes political, advantage: the Moshi folk provided the first group to be taken to visit Germany, their children were put in schools, their bright young men picked up the German language and some gained posts as clerks in the German Boma.
>
> (257)

After Rindi died in 1891, his son, Meli, became the chief at a time when German power was intensifying and the Old Moshi rivalry with the chiefdom of Marangu grew more intense. Mr. Makindara was the first person to tell me the story of the public hanging of Chief Meli by the Germans in 1900. Meli, along with the chief of neighboring Kibosho and seventeen others, were killed due to the political machinations of their rival, Chief Marealle of Marangu (Iliffe 1969; Rogers 1972; Stahl 1964). Moreover, it is widely believed in Old Moshi that the Germans took Meli's skull to Germany to display in a museum (Ihucha 2005). On a trip to Old Moshi in 2017, I visited the recently built monument to Chief Meli near the village offices that marks the site where he was hanged. The spot also houses a column made of stone upon which a pot is resting until Meli's skull is returned and placed on top (not visible in Figure 4).

Figure 4 Chief Meli historical marker, Old Moshi, 2017.

Mr. Makindara had a particularly good memory of the history of Njema Secondary School because he had grown up in its shadow, attended it as a young man, and served as one of its former headmasters. The school, with its distinctive German architecture and panoptic view of the campus from the central tower, imposed itself on the rural landscape, making an impression as arresting in the early 1990s as it must have a century earlier (see Figure 5). After German rule ended in the aftermath of the First World War, the British converted the *boma* to a government "central school" for boys from Standard 5 to 10, one of only six in the country in the 1920s that offered schooling beyond Standard 4 (Lawuo 1984). Later, the school was converted to a government boarding school for girls and remained so until independence in 1961. It eventually became a private school when the postcolonial government changed its educational priorities and allowed for the slow expansion of private secondary schooling.

The school's transition reflects a much larger set of political changes that began to unfold during the first six years after independence. Almost immediately, President Nyerere's administration started to dismantle the highly restricted school system that had left three quarters of the African adult population illiterate (Nyerere 1985). The ruling party, the CCM, abolished

Figure 5 Njema Secondary School, 1996.

segregation by race or religion, eliminated the more expensive secondary school fees (and eventually primary school fees in 1971), and implemented a regional quota system to redress inequalities in access due to the uneven distribution of government and mission schools across the country during German and British rule (Malekela 1983; Mushi 2009). This led to the closing of schools like Njema in regions where a disproportionate number of children had access to schooling in order to set up schools in underserved areas (Vavrus 2003).

Kilimanjaro, with its long history of public and private (mainly Catholic and Lutheran) schooling, vividly illustrated these regional disparities. In 1951, it was estimated that 62 percent of children in Kilimanjaro were enrolled in primary school compared to 30 percent in the rest of the country. Even more striking were the differences at the secondary level: Twenty-five percent of the country's private secondary schools were based in Kilimanjaro, and approximately 80 percent of the students came from the region even though less than 5 percent of the national population live in this region (Samoff 1979; Vavrus 2003). When Njema reopened in the early 1970s as a private school under the direction of the YMCA, Mr. Makindara was its headmaster. In 1988, the school was transferred to the Evangelical Lutheran Church of Tanzania (ELCT), and it remained under its direction until the school closed abruptly in 2015 (focus group discussion, April 10, 2017; see the Epilogue for details).

The country's ethno-geographical inequalities, heightened by nearly eighty years of colonial and mission schooling, were one of the reasons for the establishment in 1967 of a new policy, Education for Self-Reliance (ESR). The policy was aimed at restructuring the education system to align with *ujamaa*, which was a defining feature of President Nyerere's twenty-five years in office as it described a form of socialism for a predominantly rural African country. *Ujamaa* and ESR ushered in a number of complementary economic and educational changes across Tanzania. For one, there was a dramatic increase in the size of the civil service, which included teachers and school administrators, such that by the mid-1970s, nearly two-thirds of the wage-earning positions in the country were controlled by the government (Tripp 1997). *Ujamaa* also sought to promote national development through the establishment—often by force— of villages like Chekereni where Tim had conducted his research (see Chapter 1). The aim was to concentrate scarce resources, such as tractors, in villages to build socialism and boost agricultural production (Ibhawoh and Dibua 2003).

In the education sector, socialism meant prioritizing adult literacy and primary schooling so that every Tanzanian would have some schooling, as opposed to expanding secondary or tertiary education for a more narrow segment of the population (Nyerere 1967). There was also an effort to promote self-sufficiency through school farming programs and to change the curriculum consistent with African socialism by replacing British/European geography, history, and literature with relevant African content (Nyerere 1973, 1974). In addition, Nyerere made repeated calls over the years for concomitant changes in teaching methods to make them more inquiry-based and for the examination system to become less restrictive (1967, 1974, 1985). As he wrote in the ESR policy of 1967:

> It would ... be a gross misinterpretation of our need to suggest that the educational system should be designed to produce robots, which work hard but never question what the leaders ... are doing and saying ... The education provided must therefore encourage the development in each citizen of three things: an enquiring mind; an ability to learn from what others do, and reject or adapt it to his own needs; and a basic confidence in his own position as a free and equal member of society. (Nyerere 1967, cited in Lema, Mbilinyi, and Rajani 2004: 73)

Instituting fundamental change in an educational system takes time, even under the best of circumstances, and the serious economic and political problems the country faced in the 1970s and 1980s made the changes Nyerere proposed for the education sector even less likely to materialize. For one, Idi Amin, the dictatorial president in neighboring Uganda, invaded western Tanzania and instigated a costly war in 1978 that eventually led to Amin's ouster. This occurred against a backdrop of sharp increases in oil prices on world markets beginning in 1973 and the subsequent global economic recession of the late 1970s and early 1980s (Vavrus 2005). By this point, Tanzania's nascent efforts at making schooling more practical through laboratory work and vocational training—both relatively costly endeavors—had begun to disappear (Vumilia 2010). Thus, teachers reverted to less expensive "talk-and-chalk" options, which meant lecturing, choral reading from the handful of textbooks in a classroom, and drawing microscopes and other tools on the blackboard in the absence of any tangible laboratory equipment.

Although Nyerere acknowledged the severe economic problems facing the country, it was not until the inauguration of the country's second president, Ali Hassan Mwinyi, in 1985 that Tanzania conceded to sweeping "structural adjustment" agreements with the International Monetary Fund (IMF) and the World Bank that led to cuts in the civil service, devaluation of the currency, the privatization of many state-owned companies, and financial and curricular changes in schooling (Bagachwa and Cromwell 1995; Vavrus 2005; see Chapter 4 for more details). These changes were underway during my first summer in Tanzania in 1990, when faculty at the University of Dar es Salaam eagerly agreed to serve as instructors for our Fulbright program as a way to supplement their stagnant salaries. Even though the country's macroeconomic indicators slowly began to improve during the 1990s, the nation's public and private schools were still struggling mightily when I arrived in Old Moshi three years later. The disruptive effects of these economic conditions on daily life could be felt throughout the community and particularly on the Njema campus, as I would soon discover.

*****

Journal Entry: March 14, 1993, Old Moshi

This morning at 6:45 a.m. Tim and I set off for Kidia, a small village about 45 minutes up the mountain from here. There's another secondary school there and the remains of a very beautiful old Lutheran church built on land that was once home to a well-known German missionary, Bruno Gutmann. The church still has one or two of the original stained glass windows and Biblical verses on the walls written in old German script. The views of the steep mountain slopes to the west and the expansive plains below are amazing, but it's an exhausting hike that many students and a few teachers at Njema do every day …

I had little time to rest because we had to head back home in time for me to change clothes and go to the Lutheran church near our house with Mama Nelson [our neighbor]. I enjoy the church services because I can observe, from a participant's vantage point, the significance of faith in people's lives. I think that with so much economic uncertainty in everyday life, one needs to have faith in God. At least I more clearly understand the desire for God's blessings here than I do elsewhere.

*****

It did not take long for me to recognize the impact of national economic austerity on the lives of teachers and students at Njema and the appeal of the daily prayers for divine intervention to improve the situation. One of the first clues came in the form of a humble dining utensil, the spoon. The teachers at Njema took their lunch in a small room adjacent to the kitchen where the cook prepared the midday meal for the day students and breakfast, lunch, and dinner for the 300 or so male students who lived in the dormitories (the girls' dormitory opened in 1997). This staff canteen was often filled with smoke from the wood or charcoal the cook used to prepare beans and *ugali* (stiff porridge like polenta) or, occasionally, rice for the teachers. Thus, teachers frequently sat outside around a small wooden table with a few stools, eating our one-dish meal out of well-worn plastic bowls.

On my first day at Njema, Mr. Mweka, who would become a close friend and research coordinator in the years to come, walked me to this outdoor dining area and introduced me to the other teachers. There were not enough seats for everyone, so several male teachers who were nearing the end of their meal immediately stood up and insisted that Mr. Mweka and I take their spots. Balancing my bowl on my lap and my bottom on a wobbly stool, I looked around for a spoon with which to eat my lunch. Mr. Mweka must have anticipated my question about the cutlery because he quickly said something to a female teacher in Chagga, code switching so that I would not understand. He then turned to me and gave me an abbreviated explanation.

"Mrs. Timothy," as I became known in Old Moshi in recognition of my status as Tim's wife, "we only have four spoons, so we share them during our meal. Mrs. Ringo has gone to wash two of them for us."

A few minutes later, Mrs. Ringo returned, spoons still dripping with water from the nearby tap. I suspected the untreated water would wreak havoc on my gut as it had frequently in Dar, but I did not want to appear ungrateful for this gesture of kindness. Thus, I thanked Mrs. Ringo and sank the dripping spoon into my bowl of beans and rice.

The next day, the same thing happened: A teacher nearing the end of her meal took her spoon to the spigot, rinsed it off, and offered it to me. It was a humbling experience to be graciously given someone else's eating utensil, and I tried for days to reciprocate. I sought to arrive before the other teachers so that I could be the one to wash a spoon and hand it to someone else, but it did not work out that way. There were always teachers in the canteen before me, and there was no way they were going to let their guest wash one of the communal spoons, as I still had special status as the new *mzungu* on campus. Whether my status as a foreigner or as a white woman mattered most in this scenario, I would never know; however, the use of the term *mgeni* (guest) to describe me in these first days at the school, and my subsequent observations of the similar way visiting Tanzanian teachers were treated, led me to believe that it was my status as a guest more than my gender or race that led to this initial special treatment.

By the end of the week, I had a bout of diarrhea and blamed it on the untreated water and the absence of soap at the school. I did not want to stop eating lunch with my colleagues because I was getting to know them this way. Nor did I want to appear ungrateful or play into stereotypes about *wazungu* being stingy by bringing my own spoon. What to do?

Relying on the logic of hospitality that my US dollars afforded me, I looked into buying a set of new spoons for the teaching staff when I went to the Kiboriloni market that weekend. For less than $20, I discovered that I could buy a complete set of twenty-five stainless steel utensils, enough for each teacher to have one. I decided to offer the spoons as a gift from the new teacher to her colleagues, an act I thought would save face for my less affluent hosts and stave off my gastric woes. The next week, I proposed the idea to Mr. Mweka, a wise, diplomatic soul.

"Madam," he began slowly, "I thank you for your generous offer. However, our school has far greater needs than a set of new spoons. If you would like to make a donation, let us go speak to the headmaster because he has a list of projects that require more funds than we generate through students' school fees, our only source of income."

Mr. Mweka began explaining to me how the school, which was managed by the ELCT, did not, in fact, receive any funding from the Lutheran church.

Instead, the school tried to stay afloat solely through student fees, which were, at the time, approximately US$105 for day students and $140 for boarding students per year. At the time, the gross domestic product (GDP) per capita in Tanzania was just under $100 in 1993 (World Bank 2017). The school occasionally got grants from international development organizations, such as funds from the Canadian government to start a dairy project or assistance in the form of volunteer teachers through the Peace Corps or the Evangelical Lutheran Church of America. For the most part, though, the school depended on school fees, which often arrived late, in installments of $20 or less throughout the year, or not at all given the state of the economy in the early 1990s. The result was that students were frequently sent home during the school year to collect fees, or they were expelled altogether after weeks or even months of attending classes and taking meals without paying for them. Mr. Mweka was particularly clear about the urgent need for funds to repair the school infrastructure, especially the dilapidated student dormitories and the canteen itself. And though he did not say it outright, Mr. Mweka hinted that the current headmaster was not a particularly good financial steward, and his weak management was making a very difficult economic situation even worse.

*****

With this detailed account of the fiscal state at the school, I realized shamefully that my gift of spoons would have been like offering Band-Aids to a person at risk of losing a limb. It was utterly insignificant in the face of the school's gaping budget deficit and its urgent need for major structural repairs. Moreover, I recognized years later that my gift-giving was laden with relations of power not unlike those of international development organizations as I sought to use my financial influence to address a health crisis before determining whether "the beneficiaries" viewed the spoon shortage as a problem at all. This act was imbued with a sort of "violence of hospitality," though I did not understand it as such at the time (Shirazi 2017: 358). As a newcomer to the school, I saw a crisis in the cutlery shortage contributing to the spread of water-borne disease; to my colleagues, the more fundamental uncertainty in their lives revolved around getting paid each month given the precarity of school fees and whether they would be able to buy food, soap, and other necessities for their own families.

*****

The spoon shortage set me on a long course of questioning the disjuncture between outsiders' views of a situation as calamitous and insiders' assessments of it as simply an intensification of an ordinary state of difficult affairs, as "something [already] in the works" (Berlant 2011: 10). It led me to ask my colleagues a more basic question: What were their priorities for improvements at the school and how might I contribute to their ongoing efforts? And so it was that I became the head of the Library Club, taking up the charge of resurrecting the defunct school library and making it operational again.

The library was another causality of structural adjustment, a period that had left the school with little money to buy books, much less hire a librarian. Moreover, teachers had little time to take on the task of managing the library because they were already busy with heavy teaching loads, numerous administrative duties, and additional income-generating activities like growing maize for the market or selling food to the Njema students who had a bit of pocket money for the purchase of sodas and snacks. Nevertheless, teachers and students wanted to use the library, and a foreign teacher like me without a farm to manage or sodas to sell seemed like the right person to initiate the library rehabilitation effort.

I eagerly embraced the project, assuming it would benefit students by providing more reading resources than I had found in the English department office, where a very limited collection of class readers was stored. Moreover, I wanted to contribute in a more meaningful way to the school after the spoon incident, and Mr. Mweka told me that he would unlock the library and help me get started whenever I said the word. Tim, who had seen the stacks himself, warned me that there was considerable work to be done, but I optimistically assumed that some time sweeping out cobwebs and restocking the shelves would do it. So, early one Friday morning, I arrived with mop, bucket, clean rags, and a new log book ready to go, and Mr. Mweka turned the key to the library door. No sooner had I stepped across the entryway than I realized how significantly I had underestimated the work that lay ahead.

It was neither the water-stained ceiling boards nor the walls pockmarked with missing plaster chunks that stood out to me; these were features of most of the school's classrooms as well. Rather, I was greatly surprised by the extent of the collection locked away in this one-room library when teachers and students lamented having few reading resources. The pale blue walls were lined with wooden bookshelves straining under the weight of hundreds of textbooks on topics ranging from astrology to zoology, and my first glance around the room made me realize that simply cataloguing all of the books was a task I could not do alone.

As I began to get a closer look by pulling books off the shelves, I could see that creating a catalogue was only one of the many herculean dimensions to this assignment. Every book I touched was covered by a thick coating of dust the color of the deep red dirt surrounding the school, and they would need to be delicately dusted so as not to cause any further damage to their fragile spines. In addition, someone would need to do a thorough culling of the collection because there were books, and even an entire encyclopedia set, in German even though no one at the school knew the language. Like the cast-off T-shirts from the United States that were transformed into *mitumba* at the Kiboriloni market, these outdated books had found their way to Africa bearing the benevolent "donated by" imprimatur of a school in Hamburg.

And then there were the paperback novels, a thrilling sight knowing how few there were in the English department office but one that quickly proved illusory. On the literature shelf lay multiple copies of *Mine Boy* (Abrahams 1963) and *Poems from East Africa* (Cook and Rudabiri 1971), books that teachers and students desperately needed because they were listed on the national syllabus as texts for the Form 4 examination. Yet as soon as I pulled one from the shelf, its pages crumbled; voracious silverfish had burrowed through the pages, gorging themselves on *Song of Lawino* and *Song of Ocol* (p'Bitek 1967).

Mr. Mweka, who had been sizing up the situation for himself, held up a weathered atlas and called out to me across the room.

"Madam, I believe we can identify some responsible students who could assist in the renovation of the library."

Wiping the dust off two chairs at a nearby table, he gestured for me to sit down. It was there that we hatched the idea of the Library Club, where students who wanted to share in the responsibility of the library could work with me after school on cleaning, cataloguing, and establishing a lending system that would not be too onerous for teachers to supervise. And within a few days, six enthusiastic Form 2 students had signed on. They arrived promptly at the end of the school day and worked until it was time to prepare themselves for dinner. They discarded books that could not be salvaged and worked together on a plan to reorganize the shelves. I was struck by the students' dedication to a task that left their clothes covered in dust and their hands marked by tiny paper cuts. The Library Club students worked with me until I returned to the United States several months later, and I had begun to think of them as typical of the orderly, compliant youth I had found in my English classes as well. However, my assumptions were undermined a few weeks after the initiation of the Library Club when the Njema students took the entire nation by surprise.

*****

Daily News, March 19, 1993

The Northern Diocese of the Evangelical Lutheran Church of Tanzania (ELCT) today defused an imminent crisis at a secondary school it manages in Moshi Rural [District]. Over 300 students at the school had staged a peaceful demonstration to the Diocesan offices to present their demands. The students from Njema Secondary School were protesting against [a] deteriorating food situation, accommodation problems and embezzlement. They walked over ten kilometres from the school to the Northern Diocese. After a crisis meeting held between Diocesan leadership and students, the diocese declared that the students' demands were genuine and agreed to rectify the situation in phases. The Diocesan Education Secretary ... said the diocese as managers of the school would take stern action against school administration officials proved to have contravened regulations leading to the crisis. The students claimed that food was poor and often served in broke [sic] utensils. Accommodation too has continued to be a problem despite the fact that funds have been raised to solve it. It was confirmed that students shared beds and some sleep on the floor.

Tim and I were sipping our final cups of tea before heading to Njema when we were startled by loud chanting and the pounding of hundreds of feet along the path a few hundred yards from our house. The chanting was punctuated with piercing shouts and the beating of some kind of metal drum. I quickly finished getting ready for school because I had an early morning English class and wanted some extra time to investigate the commotion outside.

When I reached the path, I was surprised to find several Njema students in their school uniforms running down the road and away from campus. I saw Eric, one of my Form 4 students, and asked him where everyone was going. He barely paused to give me the shocking news: The Njema students were on strike. Eric rushed off to join his classmates who had left the morning assembly in protest to march to the office of the Education Secretary and present their complaints.

Since I had arrived at the school, Tim and I had been hearing rumors that students had asked to meet with the headmaster and discuss problems at the school but that he had not responded. These were not minor issues like too few social events but rather profoundly problematic matters that affected students' health and academic performance. The students had posted a list of eight major grievances before beginning their march to Moshi Town:

1. The food often had bugs in it and was prepared in unsanitary conditions by a dirty cook using worn-out pots.
2. The hoes used to work on the school farm were not suitable.

3. The toilets were overflowing.
4. There were not enough beds with some young men sleeping three to a single bed or on the floor.
5. The electricity was spotty, making it difficult to study at night.
6. There were not enough chairs in the classrooms.
7. There were missing teachers in some subjects and others who were poorly qualified.
8. The money that students paid each month for building maintenance was not being used to improve the poor quality of the dormitories.

Without resolutions to these problems, students feared they would not succeed in school, thereby failing the national examinations and returning home with little to show for their years at Njema. When the headmaster could not be found that morning to discuss the bugs in their breakfast, the students lost their patience and declared a strike. Thus, they grabbed one of the corroded cooking pots and a pair of the cook's filthy trousers from the school kitchen, and, picking up a bed frame with missing wooden slats from one of the dormitories, they worked their way down the mountain, past Kiboriloni, and onto the shoulder of the national highway toward Moshi.

The sight of 300 young men and women dressed in their school uniforms, banging on a huge cooking pot and holding a broken-down bed above their heads garnered great interest among travelers along the route. Passengers on the long-distance buses that ply the highway were craning to see this unusual sight of students marching *en masse*, waving a dirty pair of pants at passersby and singing songs of protest. When the students arrived at the diocesan offices, five representatives among the older Form 4 and 5 students were selected by their classmates to meet with the Education Secretary and the Lutheran Bishop, who had been called in to address this serious situation. The other students sat quietly on the grass surrounding the office complex and spoke to reporters from the national news agency, who had appeared to ask questions of the students and shoot a few photos for the *Daily News*, a widely read national paper that carried the story on page three the following day.

The meeting lasted about an hour and a half and resulted in the Lutheran church leaders agreeing to address the students' demands in stages but to resolve the food problems right away. The Lutheran leadership wanted to maintain its reputation because the boarding students at Njema came from across the country. The sight of reporters gathering to publicize this story must have struck fear in the Bishop because it was not common for church or school officials to fold so quickly to subordinates' demands.

With this satisfactory outcome, the students organized themselves into groups, with the younger students in Forms 2 and 3 piling first into the diocese's huge flatbed trucks to be driven back to Njema. Upon arrival at the school, they were given lunch and spent the rest of the day hanging out near the dormitories without going to class. Later in the afternoon, the older students returned in the trucks, singing protest songs and looking very pleased with themselves. Shortly thereafter, the chairman of the Njema school board and the assistant headmaster arrived on campus and pulled out a large, shiny new cooking pot from the back of the chairman's tiny Volkswagen Bug. And within a few more days, the cook had a new uniform, and the provision of food increased. The arrival of the beds continued to be postponed, and their delay kept things tense on campus throughout the rest of the term. Nevertheless, the students had pulled off a surprising feat given the school's paltry resources and the threat of corporal punishment or expulsion for the ringleaders. They had effected change in a wholly unexpected manner, using the resources available to them to act.

*****

Action is the means by which a problematic situation is resolved.
—John Dewey 1929: 195

This chapter and the previous one sought to bring uncertainty to the fore by recounting the precariousness of my first year of marriage and of my initial engagement in Tanzania. My decision to leave the country without any plan to return seems, in hindsight, unduly dramatic, but it was difficult to contemplate other options when I felt depressed and was experiencing physical and psychological pain. To paraphrase Berlant's definition of cruel optimism (2011), I had become deeply attached to the fantasy of being part of an academic couple and was optimistic that Tim and I would share a life of the mind as African studies scholars. Yet the more I clung to this fantasy, the crueler it became: I could not live under the conditions I thought a true Africanist should, and Tim's decision not to complete the research for his PhD had an immediate and long-lasting impact on my life. My decision to return to Tanzania, and Tim's decision to stay and teach even after he had ceased his fieldwork, may have reflected our mutual interest in living in the country for an extended period of time and our shared goal of overcoming our different approaches to how that might be done.

The student strike at Njema also occurred in a moment of disillusionment, in this case when students sensed the threat to their imagined futures that depended on passing the national exams. The poor living and learning conditions at the school, they feared, were putting this prospect further and further out of reach. The Form 4 students, in particular, did not need any additional sources of uncertainty considering how difficult it was to get a passing grade on the exams even under the best of circumstances. That another strike occurred at Njema in 1996, and, the same year, the burning of the school's cowshed by disgruntled students, suggest deep resentment among some youth about the material conditions in their schools and the nature of student–teacher relationships therein. Students believed that both factors—the poor quality of education and hierarchical teacher–student relations—contributed to their failure on the exam, dashing their dreams of a better life.

In this chapter and the previous one, the primary actors—Njema students and I—took action in an effort to resolve suffering and problematic situations. We did not remain spectators; instead, we utilized our social networks and economic resources to try and improve our situations. Dewey reminds us repeatedly that uncertainty is inherent in practical activity, and scholars eradicate it only when they write about human encounters in the distant language of an observer, watching from high above in the stands without ever stepping onto the playing field. Yet if we expunge uncertainty from the stories of our scholarship and narrate only the tales our data tell, we fail to account for the dilemmas and difficult decision-making inherent in the process of research. Moreover, as Part II reveals, these difficulties are embodied in particular ways for female students and scholars, and bear upon the personal and professional actions available for us to take.

Part Two

Precarious Parenthood

3

A Difficult Delivery

In the spring of 1993, there was never a need to set an alarm to make sure Tim and I arose in time to get to Njema Secondary School for the start of the school day. The peaceful sounds of the night hours, with only an occasional dog barking or crickets chirping, ended abruptly each morning when the roosters began to crow in the hour before dawn. This triggered a series of events, beginning with the clattering of metal pots and lids in the kitchen of our neighbor next door, the warm, matronly Mama Nelson and her two grandchildren, Edith and Nixon. Whether our windows were open or closed, the thin glass panes did little to muffle the sounds that traveled between our two houses. While Mama Nelson prepared breakfast in the kitchen, Edith and Nixon would take their hand-held brooms and sweep away the leaves that had fallen into their yard during the night. The scraping of stiff bristles against the brittle leaves made considerable noise, especially when these two eager children sought to help us by tidying our yard and sweeping in front of our bedroom window.

If we were not awake at that point, the insistent honking of a car horn in the compound behind us most certainly spurred us out of bed. Our host, Mr. Masaki, had built a two-story cement home for himself, a very unusual structure in rural Tanzania where most houses are small, single-story structures often made from wattle and daub. Mr. Masaki had also built the house where we lived on the other side of the tall metal fence surrounding his compound, a home intended for one of his grown sons who had died unexpectedly and never lived in it. There was another small house to the other side of ours intended for lesser relatives, and it remained empty during our stay in 1993. However, by the time we returned in 1996 for my doctoral research, which included teaching again at Njema, the house was occupied by three people who would play important roles in our lives that year: Mama Eric, her two-year-old son Eric, and Amina, the domestic laborer or "house girl" as they are more commonly known.

Our house proved to be ideal in many respects, especially as I began to regain my confidence that I might one day manage to become an educational anthropologist in Tanzania after all. For instance, it lay only minutes away from Miti Primary School, a fixture of cultural life in the community since its establishment in 1943 (see Figure 6). I passed the school each morning on my walk to Njema and was able to observe the daily routine. The hour between 7:00 and 8:00 a.m. was a particularly good time for observation, as the Miti courtyard filled with children in their school uniforms lining up for the morning assembly that began promptly at 7:30 a.m. Seven- and eight-year-old children would come prancing up the road with notebooks in hand, while older students who knew the shortcuts through the banana groves would arrive just in time for the morning bell. As the headmistress emerged from her office, the students would stand up straight and shout as loudly as they could, "Good morning teacher!" As my Swahili improved and my ethnographic eye sharpened, I understood more of these daily pronouncements and came to anticipate certain routines. I also began to notice subtle forms of defiance on the part of the students—the squirming, punching, and quick waves in my direction indicated less conformity and acquiescence toward adult authority than I had anticipated based on my still rather static notion of "Tanzanian culture." Although I did not realize it at the

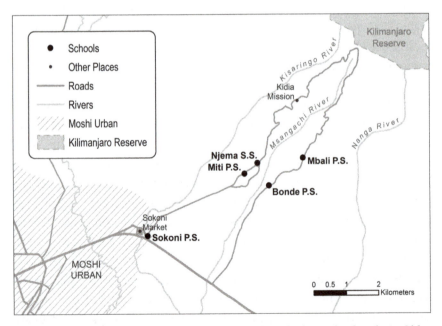

Figure 6 Primary schools in the longitudinal study and relevant landmarks in Old Moshi.

time, a line of inquiry on children and childhood was emerging. And this began with lessons from our neighbors about conception itself.

*****

When I first arrived in Old Moshi in February 1993, Mama Nelson frequently stopped by in the afternoons with avocadoes and greens from her bountiful garden and instructions on how to cook hearty meals for Tim as a new wife should. As the months wore on, this retired nurse directed our conversations toward more personal matters, fertility in particular. She indirectly offered her services to address what she suspected might be a problem given that Tim and I had been married for eight months but I had no bulge in my belly.

"Francisca," Mama Nelson would call into our living room, "come and take these avocadoes for your dinner." Wrapping a *kanga* around my waist to cover my bare legs, I would join her on the wide cement railing around the porch that made an ideal place for neighbors to sit and chat when they did not want to pay us a formal visit inside the house. In the indirect manner characteristic of many Tanzanians, Mama Nelson would tell me how women can drink special teas to help with fertility and how doctors can prescribe pills to increase male virility. She never asked me directly about our plans for having children, but she had heard something about them from her grandchildren and wanted to assist.

Once their Saturday chores were completed, Edith and Nixon liked to come over to our house and play in the living room. They especially enjoyed looking at our photo album, a common practice for Tanzanian guests in that era when televisions were rare and home computers non-existent. After a few visits, the children had mastered the names and relationships of everyone in the pictures. Once they had this down, they would bring their friends and narrate the pictures in the album: who was whom, what they did, and where they resided. "OK, now this is *Baba* Timothy (Tim's father)," Nixon told his buddy Winston one afternoon, "and he is a librarian and lives in New Orleans." Even though the names of cities and states in the United States had little meaning for these children, they helped to connect our clan to the land, an important association for Chagga families whose ancestors are usually buried on the *kihamba*, the family homestead surrounded by banana grove and coffee trees. "And this is *Bibi* (grandmother) who lives in Indiana," pointing to my white-haired mother. Bibi was, at the time, without any grandchildren, an inconceivable thought for these children who likely knew no married women of my mother's age who were not grandmothers.

Edith, seeking to demonstrate her knowledge, grabbed the album from her brother. "And do you know who is this?" circling the image of a baby in one of the pictures with her finger as she held up the album for the other children to see. Edith, the older and bolder of Mama Nelson's grandchildren, then turned to me with her question, a bit uncertain whether to pose it but asked it anyway: "When will you have a baby?" she wanted to know. Not wanting to explain family planning to a couch crammed with six- and eight-year-olds, I replied with the common response for matters that evade certainty. "*Ni mpango wa Mungu* (It's God's plan), Edith," and she nodded her head knowingly.

Edith must have passed along my remark to her grandmother because Mama Nelson's oblique references to fertility enhancement became more direct as she informed me that a woman can, indeed, help move God's plan along. Beyond Mama Nelson, word of my laissez-faire approach to conceiving a child had begun to spread to other women in the neighborhood. One Sunday afternoon, an elderly drinking buddy of Mama Nelson's, named Mama Happiness, showed up at our porch filled with *mbege* and advice to dispense. Women who have given birth are known by the name of their first-born child, so her moniker identified her oldest child, Happiness (Happy), and not her emotional state. However, she was filled with tipsy merriment on this particular day.

"Francisca, come out here!" I cast Tim a desperate look because we both knew how Mama Happiness could talk and talk, but he only smiled and tossed me my *kanga*.

"Welcome, Mama Happiness. How are you? How is Happy? Would you like to sit down?" I offered, gesturing to the railing on the porch to give her some stability. Mama Happiness had the strong, slender build of many Chagga women, a lean look from years of hauling heavy banana stocks and huge bales of grass on their heads up and down the mountain. She was not as well off as Mama Nelson as one could tell by her tattered T-shirt, faded *kanga*, and well-worn flip-flops, but she also had a connection, albeit distant, to Mr. Masaki and with it the right to gather grass for her cow from his land.

Mama Happiness leaned against the railing but did not take a seat. "Now, Franska," she slurred, "tell me again when you got married." I had only begun to speak, explaining once again that Tim and I had gotten married in September, when she abruptly cut me off. "September? My God, it's already April! My child, did your grandmothers and aunties not teach you how to get pregnant?"

"No, yes, I do know about pregnancy, Mama Happiness," and I quickly tried to get the phrase "family planning" into the conversation but failed to speak fast enough.

"Francisca, do you *know* how to get your husband into bed?" At this point, Mama Happiness stood up, tucked in her T-shirt in an effort to bolster her sagging breasts, and curled her index finger seductively as if gesturing for me to move closer. As I slowly rose to approach her, Mama Happiness put her hands on her hips and strutted over to where I was now standing. She positioned herself directly in front of me and then began to thrust her hips forward, shouting "*njoo, njoo*" (come here, come here) before she assertively grabbed my crotch. I nearly fell off the railing; I was not expecting to be sexually assaulted by this grandmother, even for pedagogical purposes. But Mama Happiness wanted to make her point, so she poked my crotch several more times for emphasis and told me that a woman should not refuse her husband.

"Thank you Mama Happiness," I cried as I tried to recover from this most illuminating lesson, "I think I've got it now." Looking very pleased with herself, Mama Happiness prepared to leave. "Francisca, I expect an excellent gift for this advice I have shared with you today," and off she strolled toward her home.

Tim, who had heard the entire exchange from inside the house, waited until Mama Happiness had disappeared before he joined me on the porch. "Well," he observed with a tickled look on his face, "now we know what we have been doing wrong and how to fix it." Two years later, back in the United States, we had proof that we had figured it out.

*****

"Deep breaths, deep breaths," Tim calmly repeated as I squeezed his shoulder during another contraction. For the past twenty-four hours, we had been slowly walking the rooms of our tiny house, which lay a few miles from the University of Wisconsin campus where I had resumed my doctoral studies after returning to the United States in the summer of 1993. The midwives at our chosen hospital in Madison assured us that my contractions were still too far apart to indicate imminent labor and that I should stay home and walk as much as possible to get our baby moving. I had been having strong Braxton Hicks contractions for the past thirty-six hours, staying up late on the Tuesday evening when they started to write in my journal and thinking we would soon be heading to the birthing center. Yet it wasn't until the wee hours of Thursday morning that my water broke, and it was now Friday afternoon. Close friends and family were on call, ready to descend from all corners of the Midwest. For now, though, Tim and I planned to stay at home as long as possible, believing that it would increase the likelihood of a "natural birth" with no medication and only the gentle, guiding hands of a midwife helping to bring our baby into the world.

*****

Through science we have secured a degree of power of prediction and of control; through tools, machinery and an accompanying technique we have made the world more comfortable to our needs, a more secure abode. We have heaped up riches and means of comfort between ourselves and the risks of the world. [...] But when all is said and done, the fundamentally hazardous character of the world is not seriously modified, much less eliminated.

—John Dewey 1925: 44

Childbirth is filled with uncertainty, but Tim and I had convinced ourselves that it was within our control to plan and carry out as desired because we had educated ourselves extensively about the process. We had attended a series of childbirth classes with other eager parents; we read everything the midwives sent home with us and then some; and I knew *What to Expect When You're Expecting* (Murkoff and Mazel 1991), the Bible for expectant American parents, so well that I could quote specific lines on labor from it. Our sense of control was only heightened by the fact that I had gotten pregnant right on schedule— August 1994—an opportune time for the plan I had laid out for my doctoral program and fieldwork in Tanzania.

It had taken me some time to get to this point of feeling sufficiently confident as a doctoral student to contemplate adding a baby to our lives. When I started my doctoral program, I had been out of school for two years and initially felt intimidated by the other students. It was a very different kind of graduate experience from my master's program—far more theoretical and intellectually combative as the top-ranked department in the United States—and I frequently felt like I was not as bright as the more advanced, extremely articulate students. To bolster my spirits during the first semester, when I gave serious thought to dropping out, Tim rewrote Dr. Seuss's famous poem, *Oh the Places You'll Go* (Seuss 1990) to inspire me to keep going and stay focused on long-term goals rather than the uncertainties of the present. I managed to do so, finishing the first year with solid grades and a growing sense of belonging in this intellectual community.

Such confidence was critical during the second year, which began shortly after discovering I was pregnant. It was a demanding year of coursework made even more challenging by the violent morning sickness I began to experience toward the end of September. There were days when the mere smell of toast would set off vomiting, making it extremely difficult to write funding proposals, concentrate on Marx and Mead, and continue teaching the ESL class at the university for which I was responsible. I did not know anyone who had been pregnant as a student in my department, and I wondered at some level whether my professors would think less of me as a budding scholar if I were bursting with baby.

I recall feeling a sense of shame when, one morning, I had to call the professor of my Friday morning seminar. He was a luminary in the field of education, and I had to explain that I would not be in class because the morning sickness was severe that day. In the era before email, there was no impersonal option for communication: A student had to tell a professor on the phone or in person that she was missing class and the reason for it. To my great relief, the professor was a parent himself and a sympathetic soul who told me to rest until I felt ready to return to class.

Nevertheless, slowing down significantly did not seem like an option due to the deadlines for the Fulbright fellowship that would allow us to return to Tanzania. If I received funding for my proposed fieldwork, the baby would be about nine months old by January 1996, the beginning of the Tanzanian school year. With almost laser-like precision, Tim and I had planned and effected the pregnancy, and I was determined to take the necessary academic steps to make a return to Tanzania possible.

*****

Our magical safeguard against the uncertain character of the world is to deny the existence of chance, to mumble universal and necessary law, the ubiquity of cause and effect, the uniformity of nature, universal progress, and the inherent rationality of the universe.

—John Dewey 1925: 44

"I have to sit down," I cried to Tim after another powerful contraction. "Are you sure they're not yet coming 10 minutes apart?" The midwives had told us to stay at home until the contractions reached this critical interval, and I swore they were coming every minute or so by how long the pain seemed to last.

As I relaxed and tried to picture my cervix relaxing and expanding, the phone rang, shaking me from this brief Lamaze moment. Tim let the answering machine pick it up so he could stay by my side. "Fran, it's William," we heard from across the room. William, my dear doctoral advisor, and father of four grown children, had been elated by my pregnancy and delighted by our plan to take the baby to Tanzania. He and his wife had piled their children into a Land Rover a few decades earlier and had driven across Africa, and he was then working with the post-apartheid government of Namibia to radically reshape the country's teacher education program.

"You may be at the hospital already, but I wanted to let you know that you passed your qualifying exam. Congratulations! Please give me a call, and we can find a time to discuss the dissertation committee's comments. Ok, bye."

At that very moment, the strongest contraction yet gripped my groin, the pain serving as a reminder that my focus today needed to be on this baby and not on my books. Before I could give this moment of both elation and agony any further thought, my dear sister Mary and beloved friend Stacie walked through the door. Stacie, who was by now well into medical school, immediately had me up on my feet again and out the door for a walk around the block while Tim rested for the long weekend ahead.

By Friday evening, the contractions had finally reached the magical ten-minute mark, and we made our way to the hospital. The midwife who met us was one of my favorites on the team, and I was pleased that she would be with us for this momentous event. However, this was not to be, as my labor progressed very slowly. A second midwife arrived on Saturday morning to relieve the first, and she found I had only dilated to four centimeters—six long, slow centimeters still to go before any real action would take place. It was back to walking the hallways and sucking on popsicles for sustenance.

The uncertainty as to when the baby might be born and my intensifying fatigue led me to rethink our entire birth plan. One can study the philosophical and physiological dimensions of natural childbirth for years, but like other "spectator theories of knowledge" against which Dewey railed (1929: 6), the pain of "practical action" may fundamentally change a woman's theoretical preferences.

"What about an epidural? Is it too late? Please don't say it is too late!" I pleaded with the second midwife.

"No, no, it's not too late," she calmly replied as she left the room to speak to a doctor about this alteration of our definitive "natural" birth plan. Tim and I realized that our birthing scheme needed to change if I was to get any rest after two sleepless nights. Yet little did we realize that this medical intervention would completely alter the dynamics in the birthing room. It meant that I would be hooked up to a machine that monitored my heart rate and the baby's, and that a doctor would be frequently stopping by to discuss my progress with the third midwife now tending to us as Saturday afternoon rolled into Saturday evening. The good news was that I was now dilated to six centimeters, and the birthing team did everything they could to keep up my spirits and mitigate the pain that was beginning to resurface even after the epidural.

However, as midnight approached, the doctor's tone changed quickly after he noticed the baby's heart rate dropping, indicating fetal distress. Within a matter of minutes, I was whisked to the surgery room for immediate action while Tim donned a surgical spacesuit. He held my hand as the medical team made the bold incision to bring our baby into the world and watched with awe as the process unfolded. And then, from the far end of the operating table, I heard our baby's first cry. Finally, in the early hours of Sunday morning, we held Gus, a healthy baby boy, and wondered at the miracle—both biological and medical— we had witnessed over the past few days.

*****

During the slow weeks of recovery after the surgery, I realized how far off Tim and I had been in our expectations about natural childbirth. Educating ourselves about pregnancy and creating a birth plan were our efforts, feeble in the end, to try and "deny the existence of chance" by imbuing labor with a rationality it does not deserve (Dewey 1925: 44). An epidural, much less major abdominal surgery, had barely crossed my mind in the months preceding the birth, and I assumed I had a nearly foolproof plan for executing the birthing experience I sought. I had eaten the right foods; I had exercised at least three days a week; and I committed to working only with midwives because I was not about to allow a doctor to dictate the terms of my baby's birth. Yet no amount of kale or Kegel exercises could save my life or the life of my baby when my cervix ceased expanding and Gus's heart rate began to fall.

As I learned more about the medical interventions that took place that night in the hospital, I could not stop asking myself about the outcome had we been living in Old Moshi instead of Madison. I knew full well about the declining state of medical care in Tanzania following years of economic crisis in the mid-1980s. During our Swahili language program in Tanzania in 1990, for example, I had the inglorious distinction of being the only student to come down with a tropical illness warranting a trip to the hospital. Our intrepid female program director accompanied me to the regional hospital in Morogoro, the region in east-central Tanzania where we were staying. I was so weak that she had to escort me all the way to the pit latrine. Without pause, she held my flowing peasant skirt high above the hole in the ground so that I could steady my shaking body sufficiently to direct a stool sample into a tiny plastic cup without dropping it into the abyss. Her reassuring words about the competence of the medical staff helped to allay my concerns about the crumbling infrastructure across the hospital grounds. Sure enough, they came up with a quick and accurate diagnosis, and I quickly rebounded and stayed healthy for the rest of the summer. Nevertheless, this first-hand encounter with the struggling Tanzanian healthcare system raised concerns for me about the country's mortality and morbidity rates, especially in situations far more serious than an intestinal parasite.

As I worked on my fellowship applications to return to Tanzania in the months before Gus was born, I had tried to push aside this enduring memory from Morogoro. My focus was on funding, not on the practical activity of caring for a baby when healthcare is far more limited and far less certain than in Wisconsin. Now, however, things had changed: The baby was real—it was not a hypothetical child but a living, breathing infant—and I learned shortly after his birth that I had received a Fulbright-Hays Fellowship to cover our family's expenses for a year in Tanzania. How I longed to know whether taking Gus to Tanzania would be a wise decision. If uncertainty, at its core, means "the limited ability to predict even the immediate future" (Calkins 2016: 3), then I had reached such a moment.

My concerns were intensified by the questions of well-meaning but perplexed strangers and family members who had never been to a "developing" country but who knew plenty from the newspapers about health risks in Africa. "Why would you take this beautiful baby there?" the sales clerk at the department store wanted to know as she assisted me in the selection of a new suitcase, demanding an answer as though I were a reckless parent. Under normal circumstances, I would not have been daunted by a clerk's questions, but they unsettled me at a moment when the future could not be easily discerned. More importantly, my parents, who were in their seventies at the time, had grown up in an era when Africa represented the unknown, the Other; it was understandable that they struggled to accept that their beloved first grandchild, named in honor of my father, would be leaving them for a year. In an era long before Zoom, Facebook, or even reliable telephone service between the two continents, they knew it would be a long separation and one filled with far more worries than if we were leaving for Moscow or Madrid, cities in Europe they knew well.

Not only did the concerns of others weigh on me, but Gus's own vulnerability as a baby made the decision to leave more difficult. He was barely six months old when he began an extensive round of vaccinations in advance of the trip. I would lay his cherubic body on the pediatrician's examination table and then watch in horror as his innocent, smiling face turned to one of pain each time the nurse stuck his soft, chubby thighs with her needle. He would predictably have a fever and a bout of irritability for the next few days, making me wonder whether the pain I was inflicting on Gus was selfish: At his age, he certainly didn't care whether I conducted fieldwork and completed a PhD. Some nights when I couldn't fall back asleep after nursing Gus, I would contemplate the list of possible dangers made even more ominous by the witching hour: HIV, malaria, typhoid, spider bites, traffic accidents, to name but a few. What if he *did* die in Tanzania, sacrificed so that I could write a dissertation?

By morning, however, these visions of calamity would dissipate. I would awake confident in the fact that the vast majority of children in Tanzania *do* live well past age one, and especially in the healthy climate on Mount Kilimanjaro, and that I had, indeed, received appropriate medical care in Morogoro when I needed it. I also began to feel that the uncertainty about what lay ahead served to propel my planning. This type of "anticipatory knowledge production" aided me in sorting, shopping, packing, and planning in an effort to "govern the future and to make it more calculable" (Calkins 2016: Chapter 1, Location 1153).

With Tim steadfast in our decision and grandparents on both sides eventually blessing the trip, we left Madison in January 1996 for our second stretch in Old Moshi. We would be returning to the same house and the same school, but now we would be seen, first and foremost, as parents. My understanding of how this would affect my research on education and women's lives was only beginning to unfold.

4

Preventable Deaths

Mama Happiness and Mama Nelson were two of the many neighbors who warmly welcomed us back to Old Moshi after a three-year hiatus. No longer Mr. and Mrs. Timothy, or Francisca, our new monikers as Mama and Baba Gus reflected our status as full-fledged adults with a child. Both Mama Happiness and Mama Nelson believed it was their fertility advice that had produced Gus, and perhaps it was. In any case, we presented them with scarves from the United States as tokens of appreciation, and they were tickled by this acknowledgment of their expertise. Therewith, they claimed Gus as their grandchild and would take him out of my arms whenever they passed by our house, carrying him down the path while talking to him in Swahili, Chagga, or a combination of the two. Older men they would encounter would invariably call out, "*Habari gani Augustino?*" asking him how he was doing and bestowing upon him the name of the popular political opposition party member from Kilimanjaro, Augustine Mrema, who had gained prominence in the country's first multiparty election the previous year. Eventually, Augustino—Gus—would be returned to us, often with another child or two trailing behind who would sit on our porch and play with him and his toys.

Returning to Old Moshi with Gus gave me privileged entree into conversations about sexuality and family planning, which, along with schooling, formed the arc of the research I would conduct during the next twelve months. I would blend teaching and research at Njema Secondary School using a technique known as "participant observation," and Tim would teach math and economics at Njema. We also had a recent secondary school graduate, Hannah, living with us for the year. Hannah had helped an American friend of ours with her research a few years earlier, and she was eagerly looking for steady employment when I contacted her before we left Wisconsin. Thus, Hannah helped to care for Gus when Tim and I were teaching, and she served as a research assistant who helped me during focus group discussions, with the transcription of interviews, and by way of her firsthand knowledge of attending secondary school. Hannah provided valuable insights throughout the year as I sought to explore how girls' experiences in secondary school might help to explain why they have fewer children than women with less formal education.

Tanzania is not alone in this respect: In almost all countries, one finds that the more years a woman spends in school, the fewer children she is likely to bear due to a variety of factors, from delayed marriage to changes in a woman's ideal number of children (Ainsworth, Beegle, and Nyatete 1995; Diamond, Newby, and Varle 1999; Lloyd, Kaufman, and Hewett 2000).[1] The demographic data for Tanzania made this pattern very clear as women in Kilimanjaro had some of the highest rates of school completion in the country and one of the lowest fertility rates (National Bureau of Statistics and Office of Chief Government Statistician 2015; Vavrus and Larsen 2003). The question driving my research was how, exactly, this came to be.

My previous experience as a teacher at Njema, discussed in Chapter 2, had provided few clues to understanding this inverse correlation between the number of years a woman spends in school and her eventual number of children. During the period I taught at the school in 1993, there had been no sex education for students. In fact, finding condoms in the dormitories was grounds for punishment or suspension, and ministers at the local church frequently railed against birth control and condoms in their sermons. Might I figure out what was going on through a year as a teacher-researcher, a participant-observer, in this year-long ethnographic project?

I planned to teach part-time at Njema as a way of participating in everyday life at the school: observing the classes of other teachers, interviewing male and female teachers and students about the schooling–fertility relationship, interviewing out-of-school girls of the same age, and carrying out a survey at both Njema and a nearby secondary school based on what I was learning from the observations and interviews (see Appendix A for more details). Given my lesson in seduction from Mama Happiness as described in the previous chapter, I knew a thing or two about the nonformal sex education girls in the community were receiving. However, her *njoo, njoo* method would have led to escalated baby making for girls with or without a high school diploma. My goal was to understand how competing cultural logics surrounding the timing and number of births manifested themselves in schools and in the community, and how young women and men made sense of them.

The preference for fewer children in Kilimanjaro, I would learn, was widely held and greatly affected by the difficult economic and social conditions people believed were compounded when they had more than two or three children. "*Watatu wanatosha kabisa!*" (three children are absolutely enough) students and school leavers would exclaim during our interviews to convey their determination to have far fewer children than their parents typically had. And demographic data showed they had largely achieved this goal. Today, Tanzanian women who have never been to school—a striking 15 percent of women aged fifteen to forty-nine—have, on average, seven children, while women who have finished secondary school are more likely to have three or four (Ministry of Health 2016).

Yet in 1996, young women who had not gone to secondary school, and some who had not completed primary school, voiced the same desires for smaller families when we discussed these matters. The latter group, however, would likely have a harder time accomplishing this goal owing to the precarious domestic situations in which some already found themselves with abusive or negligent husbands and boyfriends. And data would predict they would also be more likely to experience the death of an infant or child, leading to multiple births but not necessarily to higher rates of child survival. Data from Tanzania's 1991/1992 census revealed that a woman gave birth to, on average, 7 children by the time she was forty-nine years old, and 141 children of every 1,000 live births would not live to their fifth birthday (Bureau of Statistics 1993). In the four years leading up to the most recent demographic data from 2015/2016, under-five mortality fell by half to sixty-seven children of every 1,000 live births, and a woman on average gave birth to six children by age forty-nine (Ministry of Health 2016).

Even though my research looked at childbirth and desired number of children, I could not separate it from the subject of maternal and child death. I don't know whether there had been no such deaths in Old Moshi in 1993, or whether I was not as attuned to them as I was by 1996. As a new mother myself with my baby's health prominently on my mind, I listened attentively when talk of difficult deliveries or ailing infants arose. I also became far more aware of the deaths of children and youth, and to the circumstances that led to these tragic outcomes as a result of the economic and medical conditions in the country.

This was not a perverse form of anthropological voyeurism; rather, the pain of parents' experiences, and especially the suffering in mothers' lives, felt acute because of the "co-temporality" parents in Old Moshi and I shared at that time when I was myself the mother of an infant (Fabian 2014: 205). These moments helped me to understand more fully the potential for coevalness, as Fabian described it, and for "radical empathy," an epistemological stance that "relies on developing a relatedness that increases compassion" and intertwines "theorizing, practice and empathy" (Nencel 2014: 81–2; see also Nagar 2019). Although I did not experience such suffering and loss myself, the state of being a new mother heightened my sense of potential risk for my child as well as my ability to empathize with others who faced such situations.

*****

"Good afternoon, Mama Mary!" I shouted between the metal bars of the *duka* (small sundries shop) down the road from our house where I had come to buy some eggs and sodas. Gus, comfortable on my back in the backpack in which we frequently carried him, began swinging his legs excitedly and calling out "Mama" as he echoed my call.

"Ah, Mama Gus!" she exclaimed, wiping her hands on her *kanga* before stepping out of her shop and handing Gus a cookie to gnaw on while we chatted. Mama Mary always had a lot to tell me about the goings-on in the neighborhood, especially about women's lives as she knew this was the broad topic of my research. Her shop, located amid a small cluster of well-worn buildings that included both an *mbege* bar and the headquarters of the ruling party, provided an opportune spot from which she could watch people and vehicles traversing the main road through Old Moshi.

"Sit down," she gestured to the small wooden bench outside her *duka*, and I rested the aluminum frame of the baby backpack on it as I took a seat next to Mama Mary. "Ah Mama Gus, *maisha ni magumu* (life is difficult)," she sighed with great exasperation in her voice as she began to recount for me the events of the previous evening.

"You know Mama Justin, right? The woman who lives down the road with the little boy who has *maji maji* (a chronic leaking of the umbilical cord stump). You know her husband won't give her the money she needs to take the poor child to the doctor, so she just goes to the *mganga* (traditional healer) and gets some herbs for the boy, but they are certainly not working!"

Mama Mary, who had finished primary school and a six-month training program at the YMCA, had more formal education than Mama Justin, who had only completed a few years of primary school. In Mama Mary's view, Mama Justin's problem was a lack of education that led her to marry an irresponsible man because she had few other options. Mama Mary continued with the details of the night before.

"Well, Mama Justin was very pregnant with another child, as you know, but yesterday her husband still made her walk down the mountain to their *shamba* (family farm) to collect firewood and corn stalks for their cow. She didn't have enough money to pay for transportation back home, so she walked up the road with the firewood and stalks on her head. Not only that, she then had to prepare dinner, wash her son, clean the house and the cow shed, all the while her no-good husband was right here (pointing to the *mbege* bar) drinking!" Mama Mary shook her head and paused only long enough to check on Gus in the backpack and hand him another cookie.

"Later in the evening, Mama Justin started having labor pains, and her husband was nowhere to be found. So Mama Goodluck and I had to find a vehicle to take her to the hospital, and we didn't even have time to help her change clothes because a truck was coming at that very moment. Mama Goodluck went with her, in this filthy state, without even a bath after her hard day's work. And we couldn't find any clean *kangas* to wrap around her, so I grabbed some from the shop to cover her dirty clothes. *Haki ya Mungu* (For the love of God)!"

Mama Mary continued to shake her head in disgust at this pitiful situation, and we contemplated what could be done to help women like Mama Justin, and her son with *maji maji*, when husbands and fathers do not act responsibly.

"Look at me, Mama Gus. I didn't go to secondary school, but I saved enough money as a seamstress so I could rent this little shop, and I continue to save so that I can take care of my children if my husband turns into a drunk like this one," she pointed to a man staggering by as we spoke. "And you," she declared, poking her finger into my chest, "you are a teacher who can take care of herself, and now you must be careful to save money for Augustino in case there are ever any problems between you and Baba Gus. You have to make your life certain by saving, Mama Gus, because these men, eh … "

Mama Mary's voice trailed off as though recalling moments in her life when she had been deceived by men, and I took this as our cue to depart. With the eggs and a few bottles of soda in my bag, I thanked her for Gus's cookies and asked her to give Mama Justin my best wishes when she returned home from the hospital. After two cookies, Gus was high on sugar and proceeded to tug at my hair as we walked back home, but I hardly felt it as I was consumed by thoughts of Mama Justin.

I vividly recalled how, during my own labor, it had been very painful to drive from our house in Madison to the hospital only a few miles away, and on a smooth, paved road. Each tiny bump in the asphalt felt like a knife in my groin, stabbing the taut tendons between my hips. And here was Mama Justin, who was probably in a more acute stage of labor, being bounced along the deeply rutted dirt road through Old Moshi in a crowded pick-up truck with only a distant neighbor to help her through her pain. And what to make of her son, who could have been no more than two years old, oozing fluid from his umbilical stump for the lack of a few dollars to have it treated? I could identify with Mama Justin's labor pains in a manner that a male researcher could not, but I could also sense the gulf between us formed by financial and racial privilege that would mean that I would likely never experience the precarity she confronted. If need be, we could hire a car to take me, or Gus or Tim, to the hospital; I could buy with my own money any medicine Gus might need someday; and being white in Tanzania literally opened doors to better clinics and hospitals and doctors. The same conditions simply did not apply to most of our neighbors.

*****

Stacie, my best friend from the University of Illinois, arrived in mid-March for six weeks to conduct her own doctoral research on the history of colonial medicine in Tanzania. While I conducted interviews with students, she visited church archives and hospitals across Kilimanjaro, collecting historical records on childbirth and infant mortality dating back to the German colonial era of the late 1800s. Our research interests overlapped in several areas, most notably on the question as to why birthrates go up and down during different historical periods. We were both finding that politics, economics, and the quality of the medical system were inextricably connected to mortality and fertility. Contrary to much of the colonial record, Stacie found that high infant mortality rates were not the result of Tanzanian women's "backward" cultural beliefs, or what she called "the trope of the timid tribeswoman" who rejected modern health services (Colwell 2001: 566). Rather, it was the abysmal lack of health services during the 1930s that was primarily responsible for morbidity and mortality. She carefully documented how Chagga leaders in Kilimanjaro, in particular, continuously petitioned for more health facilities and how women made use of them whenever they were provided. At the same time, colonial administrators continued to believe that substandard medical care was acceptable "for the native peoples, the collective body of 'not us'" (Colwell 2001: 566).

Yet by the mid-1990s, it was not colonialism per se but rather its vestigial effects, coupled with national economic policies of the past two decades, which had produced the healthcare crisis in the country. As a historian, Stacie had to comb through the archives to piece together and reconstruct the scene from a prior era; as a temporary resident in contemporary Kilimanjaro, she did not need to go far to understand the state of postcolonial medicine.

One morning in April, Stacie and I walked to Kiboriloni and then took a minivan to Moshi because she had a meeting with a doctor at Mawenzi Hospital, the only public hospital in the district, and I was setting up interviews with out-of-school girls at a nearby community center. We decided to meet a couple of hours later at the Lutheran Center, one of the few coffee shops in Moshi at the time and with a spectacular view of the town and the mountain on clear days. My meeting with the director of the training center was brief as he had another appointment, so I spent my remaining time browsing the shelves of the Moshi Book Shop, a small business affiliated with the large Catholic church that sits prominently at the intersection of two major roads through town. In addition to Bibles and biblical stories in Chagga, Swahili, and English, the shop sold school books and syllabi for each school subject, a necessity for teachers to help their students prepare for the national exams. With the exception of the smaller book shop at the Lutheran Center, there were no other places to buy new school texts in town, and used books had to be inspected thoroughly for missing pages and permanent stains from spending many days in open-air stalls near the busy bus station.

By the time Stacie appeared at the Lutheran Center, I was deep into a collection of "past papers"—previous national Form 4 examinations—I had purchased to help guide my lesson planning during the rest of the year. I was eager to get back to Njema to share the book with the other English teachers; however, Stacie's expression indicated that she needed a cup of tea, if not a shot of *Konyagi*, the strong national liquor known as "the spirit of the nation."

"Fran, do not get sick, and do not take Gus to Mawenzi Hospital," insisted Stacie as she slowly sipped her tea. She had worked with indigent patients at New York's Floating Hospital before she started the MD/PhD program and was no stranger to under-resourced medical facilities. Yet, Mawenzi had left her shaken.

"Before you enter the building, there is a sign that lists the prices of everything: 500 Tanzanian shillings (Tsh) for an exam (less than $1); 1,500–2,000 Tsh (about $3.50) to stay the night, with no food; and the list goes on and on." Stacie noted how inexpensive, by US standards, these prices seemed to be. Nevertheless, she observed a number of people with open sores from leprosy and others with arms in homemade slings sitting on the hospital grounds, waiting for family members to pool their resources to pay for needed medical care.

Stacie then told me about the American doctor, the head of surgery, whom she had gone to the hospital to meet. When she arrived at his office, she could hear him listing for a potential patient all of the supplies he would need to do the surgery: gloves, bandages, and clean *kangas* for bedsheets because the hospital no longer supplied them. If the patient produced these items before the operation, then the doctor would put her on the patient list for the next day; if not, no surgery.

The hospital, Stacie knew, had a long history. It opened during the German colonial era as a dispensary for German soldiers and grew into a hospital under the British in the mid-1950s. After independence, one of the aims of President Nyerere's government was to create a socialist state where all citizens would have access to free social services, including healthcare and schooling. In both areas, the country made remarkable gains. Vaccination coverage for five common vaccines grew from 8 percent in 1975 to more than 50 percent in 1980 (Lyima 2017). When a national literacy test was administered in 1975, 37 percent of adults who took the test countrywide passed, while the pass rate was 43 percent in the Kilimanjaro Region. A decade later, 57 percent of adults passed the test across the country while an even greater percentage, 63 percent, did so in the Kilimanjaro Region (Ministry of Education 1991).

However, many of the economic policies of the *ujamaa* era led to inefficient use of resources. This stemmed in part from internal problems, such as a concentration of healthcare workers in urban centers and a curative rather than comprehensive approach to healthcare delivery. But external problems played their part as well. The two most often noted by scholars of this period are the war with neighboring Uganda in the late 1970s and rising prices for oil on the world market during the same period, leading to a precipitous decline in the Tanzanian economy in the 1980s (Ibhawoh and Dibua 2003; Tripp 1997). The neoliberal policies that began to take shape by the middle of the decade included the emergence of private healthcare facilities and the imposition of "user fees" for patients at hospitals and clinics, and for students at school (Beckman 2015; Lugalla 1997; Turshen 1999; Vavrus 2005). Stacie's observations at Mawenzi revealed the human face of "cost sharing," another euphemistic term used to gloss over the toll that fees take in communities where most people cannot afford them.

Even so, this public hospital had undoubtedly saved many lives because it provided services at a much lower cost than one could find at the only other hospital in Moshi at the time, the private Kilimanjaro Christian Medical Center (KCMC). Established in the early 1970s and affiliated with the Evangelical Lutheran Church of Tanzania, KCMC was, and remains, a referral hospital with the best services in the region. The KCMC staff had taken good care of Nathan, our roommate in 1993 who was stricken with malaria, and we saw an excellent Tanzanian pediatrician throughout 1996 whenever Gus needed his well-baby check-ups. However, to most "Western" eyes accustomed to cheerful, well-lighted hospitals, the peeling paint and dim hallways of KCMC did not instill great confidence. Nor did the throngs of coughing patients waiting on wooden benches near the entryway and the gravely ill HIV/AIDS patients being whisked past on well-worn gurneys. Yet it was a good facility, and even with rates at five times the cost of the public hospital, it was still very affordable for foreigners and for the small but slowly growing group of middle-class Tanzanians who could pay for its services.

Feeling rather glum about the state of healthcare in Tanzania, we walked slowly to the bus stand to get a ride back to Kiboriloni and sat quietly at the back of the minivan hoping there would be no accident along the way. Yet our mood only worsened once we got home and saw Tim sitting somberly at the dining room table. He had us take seats and told Stacie and me that one of my Form 2 students, Albert, had died the night before from an asthma attack. Tim then began to relay the full story he had been told on campus that morning.

It seems that several students from Albert's dormitory went to see Mr. Massawe, the Teacher on Duty, around 8:00 p.m. to report that Albert was having difficulty breathing. Mr. Massawe and the school nurse monitored the situation for a while before deciding Albert needed to go to the hospital. However, the school had no vehicle of its own, so Mr. Massawe had to find a neighbor willing to loan a pick-up truck for a night-time drive down the mountain and into town. Finally, Mr. Massawe commandeered a vehicle and asked the school nurse and one of the older students, an evangelist studying at Njema, to accompany him and the ailing student.

They went directly to Mawenzi Hospital because it was the cheaper, public hospital, and they did not have a referral for KCMC. By this time it was nearly midnight, and no doctors could be quickly found at Mawenzi. So they drove on to KCMC, but by the time they arrived, Albert no longer had a pulse. He had passed away between the two hospitals. Leaving the boy's body in the morgue, Mr. Massawe and the others returned to Njema in the wee hours of the morning, and classes were cancelled for the day so the teachers and headmaster could figure out what to do. Albert's parents lived far away, in the Kagera Region of western Tanzania, which meant a great deal of expense to have the body sent home. Despite their own limited salaries, the teachers immediately took up a collection to help Albert's family pay for the cost of returning his body.

With Stacie's description of her trip to Mawenzi fresh on my mind, I could not help but wonder how Albert's fate would have been different had Mr. Massawe gone directly to KCMC, where there were always doctors on duty, rather than going first to Mawenzi to get a referral. I also contemplated whether Albert would have lived if the school nurse could have afforded to keep a nebulizer in her office at all times. And I thought about how he would have still been alive if the school had had a truck of its own for rapid use in case of such emergencies. There were so many contingencies that might have led to a different outcome for Albert, but they all required more resources than this school—most schools in Tanzania at the time—had to offer.

My mind started to wander to Gus and how I would deal with a call like the one Albert's parents had received that morning, telling them their child had died. What if the school to which I had entrusted my child became the site of his demise? It was a chilling thought. Albert's death as a teenager was certainly unexpected, but premature deaths of young children in Tanzania were still quite common in the mid-1990s: Eight percent of babies never made it to their first birthday, and nearly 14 percent of children did not live to age five (Kent 2010).[2] Although many of these deaths befell the children of parents with limited schooling, a college degree was no guarantee that one's children would survive into adulthood. The grave uncertainty of childbirth affected primary school leavers like Mama Justin as well as secondary school teachers, as I would learn only a few months later.

*****

September 24, 1996

Dear extended family (including Stacie),

Because I'm pressed for time, I thought I would write to all of you rather than in my journal about the events surrounding the death of the child of one of the teachers at Njema, Mr. Kabwe. His wife gave birth last week to their second child, two months prematurely, and now the child has died. Mr. Kabwe's wife gave birth at the public hospital (I'm sure Stacie, who has seen Mawenzi Hospital, is now anticipating what I am about to write). Mother and baby were declared fine after the birth, so they were sent home. A few days later, the baby fell ill, so Mr. Kabwe and his wife went back to Mawenzi. In order to go to KCMC, the much better private hospital, a Tanzanian must get a referral slip from the government hospital, unless you're wealthy like Mr. Masaki [our neighbor] and can go straight to the KCMC guards with your bribe. If you're white, you're also let right in, without a bribe (at least this has been our experience).

So Mr. Kabwe, wife, and sick baby were waiting and waiting at the public hospital,
and finally a doctor appeared and told them not to worry; he would take care of
things. But according to Mr. Kabwe, who told us all of this two days ago, the doctor
was just waiting for Mr. Kabwe to give him some money so that he would write the
referral slip to KCMC. Meanwhile, the doctor was doing nothing for the baby, and
she was getting worse. Finally, Mr. Kabwe went in search of a friend who worked at
the hospital, and the friend was able to get the referral slip, but still with a bribe. By
this time the baby was very ill, and shortly after they got to KCMC, the little girl died.

At each step along the way, Mr. Kabwe had to pay money that teachers, and
many, many others here, just don't have: Money to pay someone to take him and
his family to the government hospital at night because he does not have a car;
money to have the baby admitted to the hospital; money to bribe a doctor; money
to have the baby admitted to KCMC; and finally money to keep the baby in the
morgue until yesterday's burial [...] It's a sad tale.

*****

In her study of uncertainty and maternity in East Africa, Natalie Beckman (2015) documented the poor state of reproductive healthcare in Zanzibar as the result of the political and economic policies from the 1980s onward that affected life throughout mainland Tanzania and the islands. She, like me, recounted instances of maternal and child death that occurred during her fieldwork while homing in on women's many strategies to manage the precarity of this liminal period. These strategies included utilizing the best biomedical care they could afford, consulting with more experienced women, and putting their trust in God—in other words, in *mpango wa Mungu*. Yet, Beckman argued this is neither blind faith nor women relinquishing their agency. Instead, she considered faith and trust to be a pragmatic attempt to address uncertainty:

> [F]aith also implies an element of pragmatism based on the notion that one
> has to try to make the right choices and find the person or practice that is most
> trustworthy and thus likely to lead to a positive outcome. Zanzibari women, and
> their wider social network, try to establish a sense of security in the face of deep
> uncertainty by taking an active but pragmatic approach in pregnancy, according
> to their means.
>
> (2015: 68)

The childbirth and child death stories in this chapter and the previous one serve as a reminder of the uncertainty of everyday life and the role of social networks, and of faith, in seeking to combat it. Whether in the United States or in Tanzania, strong relationships with friends and family during precarious periods of life are a critical means of buffering ourselves from the harshest blows the world may throw at us. During pregnancy, in particular, we may also rely on other social strategies, such as consulting the expertise found in books, traditional healers, and the God of our faiths.

These chapters also illustrate how coevalness is fostered by "copresence," which is itself the very "condition of ethnographic research" (Fabian 2014: 204). Nancy Scheper-Hughes used the metaphor of "witnessing" in explaining how deep engagement in a community over many year is not merely a methodological decision but rather an ethical stance: "If it is to be in the nature of an ethical project, the work of anthropology requires a different set of relationships. In minimalist terms this might be described as the difference between the anthropologist as 'spectator' and the anthropologist as 'witness'" (1995: 419).

By returning to Old Moshi following Gus's precarious birth, I found myself witnessing up close the precarity of women's lives. This was certainly the case with Mama Justin even though the degree of precarity surrounding our babies' births was vastly different. Similarly, the concern I felt toward Mr. Kabwe and his wife upon the loss of their child was arguably more acute owing to the intense empathy generated by sharing the same intersubjective space as parents of young children. As I reflected on these moments years later, I have come to believe that relationships grounded in copresence are the foundation upon which relational knowledge, forged in the "practical activity" of daily life, is built (Dewey 1929: 6).

At the same time, there are distinct limitations to coevalness revealed in these chapters. For one, the uncertainty surrounding Gus's birth was mitigated because he was born at a very well-equipped hospital where maternal and infant mortality are extremely rare.[3] Access to such high-quality medical care is available to a small minority of people around the world, and certainly not to most women in rural Tanzania. And had Gus suffered from a condition like Mama Justin's older child, I would have been able to pay for his treatment whether or not my husband cared to contribute.

Finally, these two chapters remind us that schooling, in and of itself, is an unreliable prophylaxis. Albert died even though he was among the privileged 5 percent of the Tanzanian population at the time that had the opportunity to attend secondary school. Moreover, he was residing at a boarding school relatively close to two hospitals at the time of his death. Yet it still took too long to get the basic treatment he needed to ease his asthma, a disease that can typically be managed with proper medication, if one can afford it (Rosenthal 2013).[4] Mr. Kabwe was even more unusual as the holder of a bachelor's degree, but he still could not get timely treatment for his daughter at the private hospital where her life would likely have been saved. There are serious limitations on how certain education alone can make our lives, and the lives of our families, when critical health resources are restricted by geography, economics, and race. As we will see again in Part IV, education is thought by some experts to be a "vaccine" against illness, especially HIV/AIDS, but there are structural forces that severely restrict its efficacy (Vandemoortele and Delamonica 2000).

Part Three

Fallible Expertise

Questioning Dr. Spock

Can infants contribute to social theory?

—Alma Gottlieb 2000: 127

The sun had barely begun to rise when Mama Eric appeared at our doorstep, a highly unusual time for a visitor, especially for a teacher like her who should have been on her way to school.

"*Hodi* (Hello)," Mama Eric called out with an unusually stern tone in her voice.

Tim had already left the house for his morning run, and I was still in bed after a night of little sleep. I could hear Hannah unlocking the gate, and, a few minutes later, she quietly knocked on our door and poked her head in. "It's Mama Eric," she whispered so as not to disturb Gus, who was still sleeping in the portable playpen that served as his bed. "She wants to talk to you, now."

Wrapping a versatile *kanga* around my pajamas and running my fingers through my hair in lieu of a comb, I walked out to the living room to see what was troubling our neighbor.

"I came to see you before school because I'm worried about Gus. I heard him crying so much last night!"

"I'm so sorry, Mama Eric," I replied apologetically. "I thought with the windows closed and the curtains drawn that we would not have disturbed you. I'll try to keep him quieter tonight."

From the puzzled expression on Mama Eric's face, it appeared that my explanation did not address her concern. "It's not the noise, Mama Gus, it's the reason for his crying. What did you do to him?"

Now I was the one who was confused. Swahili speakers rarely ask such direct questions when there is an implicit accusation to them. An indirect question in the passive voice—*what had been done to Gus by someone*—would have been the more appropriate form, but Mama Eric was not messing around with niceties this morning. In no uncertain terms, she was accusing me of hurting my son.

The precarity of parenting does not end after childbirth, and my limited experience with infants left me feeling uncertain about the many decisions we needed to make regarding Gus's care. Mama Eric had only one child as well, but she had grown up in a large family where the older girls cared for their younger siblings starting not long after birth. I, on the other hand, had no experience caring for children below the age of two, not even my younger brother due to the proximity in our ages. In our neighborhood, the mothers had made a collective decision to hire only teenage girls to babysit infants. By the time I reached high school, I had lost all interest in childcare, opting instead to work as a dishwasher in a sweltering kitchen rather than wiping babies' behinds.

Tim and I were now far from our parents and their sage advice on infants and young children. Nevertheless, we had other experts to consult by way of the authoritative pediatric texts we had brought with us. It had scarcely crossed my mind that none of these professionals had any experience in Africa or that their biomedical advice might be inflected by their cultural assumptions about infancy.

So, after Gus's first birthday, we followed the recommendations of Dr. Benjamin Spock by putting Gus to sleep in his own bed and encouraging him to sleep throughout the night. As the good doctor explained:

> Newborns sleep wherever they are. But by about three or four months, it's a good idea for them to get used to falling asleep in their own beds, without company … A baby who gets used to being held and rocked to sleep tends to need the same attention for months or even years; when she awakens in the night, she expects the same treatment.
>
> (Spock and Needlman 2011: 60–1)

Sure enough, Gus learned to fall sleep in his playpen, but it was a different story altogether in getting him to fall back asleep on his own. He quickly learned a keyword in Swahili—*nyonyo*—which he used to indicate both breast (correct usage) and breastfeeding, and he would howl in the middle of the night unless *nyonyo* was forthcoming. Assured by the experts that a one-year-old eating solid food no longer needed to nurse on demand, I had decided it was time to try the "cry-it-out method" so that I could finally get a full night's sleep. The *What to Expect While Expecting* gurus, Heidi Murkoff and Sharon Mazel, had sanctioned this method and assured parents that it was actually good for a child: "Crying won't hurt her nor will she be scarred for life by this process. And ultimately—if you can stand it—you're doing her a favor by helping her learn to go to sleep on her own" ("Crying It Out" 2014).

Drawing on this expertise, I explained to Mama Eric that I had not done anything harmful to Gus. Instead, I was helping him, teaching him, to sleep through the night. If he didn't learn to fall back asleep on his own, Gus would remain dependent on me rather than taking this first significant step toward self-efficacy. I assured her that the cries should only continue for another night or two until Gus learned to console himself.

Mama Eric sat down on the couch, leaned forward on the coffee table, and asked me to repeat what I had just told her. "Gus sleeps in his own bed? You want your baby to stop nursing at night?"

With a note of condescension, Mama Eric declared that "we" do not allow our babies to sleep alone at such a tender age because they will not develop properly if they do. And if the mother is unavailable, then the baby sleeps with his grandmother or strapped to the back of an older sister or house girl. Furthermore, Mama Eric asserted, babies need to nurse whenever they are hungry—day or night—and should be given the breast on demand.

Shaking her head in disbelief, Mama Eric gave me the cocked head, "*wazungu* are crazy" look that I was beginning to recognize the longer we lived in Old Moshi. It was the same expression I had encountered a few days earlier when an elderly Chagga man asked me if it were true that Americans put their elderly parents in "old-age camps," something akin to a concentration camp in his mind. When I attempted to explain that they were not camps in this sense but rather communities where the elderly are taken care of by trained nurses, he gave his head a similar tilt indicating incredulity. Older folks ought to live with their grown children, he snapped, or a grandchild or two should be sent to care for them in their homes as Chagga families typically do, or did (see Chapter 8). My elderly companion sought to understand why anyone would trust strangers, even if they were professionals, to provide proper care for one's own parents (see also Beckman 2015 for a comparable case in Zanzibar).

Mama Eric's comments carried echoes of this earlier conversation. She wanted to know how I thought infants would establish trust and familial bonds without the constant comfort of their mother's bodies. I was beginning to see that my views about trust, care, and expert knowledge differed considerably from my Tanzanian neighbors.

Mama Eric's obvious concern for Gus prevented me from taking offense at her suggestion that I was not caring properly for my child. Fortunately, I was awake just enough to begin thinking anthropologically about this encounter. I knew from one of the most extensive anthropological accounts of childrearing in Kilimanjaro, Otto Raum's *Chaga Childhood* (1940),[1] that Chagga mothers typically viewed breastfeeding on demand as essential to developing familial intimacy, or at least they did when he conducted this study. Reflecting colonial sensibilities about the superiority of European ways, Raum averred:

> They [Chagga Christians] carry their babies in their arms continually and when its limbs have grown firm place it astride on the hip, where it can always reach the breast. During the night the child is bedded on the breast, and it sometimes happens that it is suffocated by it. Apparently this prolongation of intimate contact has no detrimental effect on the character of the children as might be suspected by a psycho-analyst ... Of course, it makes impossible the early training in nutritive habits to which the European child is subjected.
>
> (106)

As Raum would have predicted, these practices did not seem to have any negative effect on the character of my neighbors, young or old. Yet I could say the same thing about the shorter period of breastfeeding and the separate sleeping spaces common among middle-class Euro-Americans, my "tribe." Thus, I wanted to know what Mama Eric thought might happen to a child if he did sleep by himself.

"Well, we just don't do it," she replied adamantly to my question. "It's not good for a child."

Hannah, who had been listening to the entire conversation while setting the table for breakfast, interjected with her own explanation. "It's like this, Mama Gus. We think it's not good for young children because they might develop bad *tabia* (character) if they do not feel close to their mothers as babies."

The conversation went back and forth as I asked questions about why they thought *wazungu*—or at least some of us—would want our babies to sleep in their own beds while Chagga parents generally do not. Mama Eric ventured that Europeans and Americans put a high value on independence and think that everyone, even children, should have their own opinions and act as they pleased. This might begin with how they sleep as babies. In contrast, Mama Eric and Hannah thought that Africans, not only Chagga, believe people are, first and foremost, part of a family, part of a community, and conforming to other people's bodies—on their backs or in their beds—might help babies learn this lesson. If we hold such different views about proper character for adults, Mama Eric wagered, then this cultivation of independence or interdependence must start in infancy.

The more I listened, the less certain I felt about the cry-it-out method. Thus, I assured Mama Eric that Tim and I would discuss Gus's sleeping and nursing situation before nightfall. She smiled with satisfaction and announced it was time for her to depart for school. We chatted about the day ahead as I accompanied her down the path in front of our house, waving goodbye as she disappeared into the banana grove.

Still in my pajamas and *kanga*, I hurried back toward the porch but was stopped by the sound of Mama Nelson calling my name from her doorway. "Francisca, come over here," she demanded as though I were a schoolgirl. "What is wrong with Augustino? Is he sick? I heard him crying last night."

Haki ya Mungu, here we go again, I thought to myself as Mama Nelson launched into her lecture. She did not hesitate to remind me that she was a retired nurse as well as a mother and grandmother, thereby claiming even greater authority for her views about nursing on demand and sleeping with one's infant. She concluded with a lyrical Swahili proverb for me to ponder: "*Kila kitu kina mama, dawa yake na salama*," a reminder that everything has a mother, and it is she who serves as its medicine and its security. If Gus were to develop *tabia nzuri*, good character, then it was my duty to keep him safe and secure by my side.

*****

Yet if cultural anthropology has taught us anything over the past century, it is that the most seemingly transparent of categories often turn out to be the most unexpectedly non-commensurable.

—Alma Gottlieb 2000: 122

Despite my uncertainty about the best sleeping arrangements for Gus, I fully assumed that broader childrearing concepts like trust, care, and character-building were relatively transparent and transferable from one place to another. Before moving to Old Moshi with a baby, I had not had occasion to think about them analytically by "making strange" or "bracketing the familiar," terms I had learned in my graduate anthropology and education courses but had not actually put into practice. And so began my exploration into the certainty of categories and concepts related to child and youth/student development that are often treated as commensurable even though they are deeply embedded in cultural, historical, and economic relations. As this chapter and the next reveal, one of the most striking of these concepts for me as parent and teacher was discipline and the corporal punishment that frequently accompanies it.

Backing up a bit, it was during this period of fieldwork with Gus that I began to question the very categories used to describe childhood, such as *infant*, *child*, and *adolescent*. These periods are typically treated as universal, but they do not, in fact, correspond to the same ages or stages in different societies; they may not even exist as categories as all. Even more culturally ambiguous, I came to realize, are corresponding concepts ascribed to these stages like "colicky baby," "terrible twos," and "rebellious teenager," for which explanations range from the biomedical to the psychological to the spiritual. Because the presumed etiology for such conditions varies, one finds the treatment varying widely as well. If, for instance, a mother believes that her infant who cries inconsolably is the reincarnated spirit of a recently deceased sibling—a common explanation among the Beng in *Côte d'Ivoire*—then treatment may entail consultation with a diviner and wearing a prescribed bracelet (Gottlieb 2004). If, instead, she thinks the crying is due to a more pedestrian problem like intestinal gas, which mothers in the United States are regularly led to believe, then the doctor is likely to recommend laying off dairy products, wheat, and cruciferous vegetables until the baby is weaned.

The coevalness produced through shared time and space with neighbors and fellow teachers in Old Moshi helped me to understand the non-commensurability of categories and practices regarded as "common sense," such as not spanking babies and not caning teenaged students. Such understanding did not occur simply by getting myself into "the field" and conducting interviews and surveys over the course of a year; rather, it was through the sharing of some of the "practical activity" of everyday life that this ethnographic knowledge was produced (Dewey 1929: 6). For this young ethnographer-parent interested in schooling, the practical activities of feeding my son, teaching my students, and trying to instill in all of them good moral character consumed most of each day. It also generated considerable intellectual energy through the friction of my common sense rubbing up against the convictions of neighbors and colleagues (Tsing 2005). The back-and-forth nature of dialogue on these matters, with Mama Eric and others, opened up space for my assumptions to be interrogated, revealing the cultural arbitrariness of childrearing beliefs and practices assumed to be sacrosanct.

*****

August 8, 1996

Dear Mom and Dad,

In other news, a funny thing happened yesterday that illustrates a lot about caning and authority here. Tim and Hannah were feeding Gus while Eric looked on. Gus kept throwing food on the floor as if it were a game, but Tim and Hannah were not too amused. Finally, Tim, in jest, said to Eric to go bring him a stick to punish Gus. [Caning] is the most common way of punishing kids here, it seems. Eric looked very sad, and he slowly went outside to look for a stick. Finally, he returned and handed Tim a very thin, limp leaf. What a creative solution to Eric's dilemma of not wanting to hurt Gus while still needing to respond to an adult's command (see Figure 7).

*****

How does one make sense of the different assumptions about childhood and children's development as a parent and researcher living in a community where expectations regarding discipline, punishment, and intergenerational relationships are quite distinct? The literature on the anthropology of childhood provides a useful starting point. It takes as its foil the beliefs and practices about infants and children in WEIRD societies, meaning those that are "Western, Educated, Industrialized, Rich, Democratic" (Lancy 2015: 2). This is decidedly not the milieu in which Eric, or his mother, was raised, and, therefore, their responses to Gus's behavior often surprised me. However, authoritative knowledge about human development, especially in the field of psychology, is based almost exclusively on the small percentage of the world's population that could be classified as WEIRD. For example, the United States constitutes a

Figure 7 Gus, Eric, and Tim playing on our front porch, 1996.

mere 5 percent of the planet's population, and the countries of the Organisation for Economic Co-operation and Development (OECD) as a whole only about 17 percent, and yet some 95 percent of the academic publications in psychology are based on research with these overwhelmingly WEIRD people (Wagner and Castillo 2014). Despite this very narrow profile, the findings from such studies are extrapolated to vastly different peoples and places, where their views on raising children are often found wanting. Anthropologists have rightly called into question these so-called universal understandings of infancy, toddlerhood, adolescence, and parenting by documenting the myriad ways children of "good character" can be raised (e.g., Gottlieb and DeLoache 2017; LeVine 2007; LeVine and LeVine 1988; Prout and James 2005; Scheper-Hughes 1992).

Alma Gottlieb's research has been particularly influential in this field and for me in particular. Her work, combining ethnography and memoir, has shaped my views on the contingent nature of childhood as well as my approach to writing about it (Gottlieb 2004; Gottlieb and Graham 1993, 2012). When I encountered her book on "the culture of infancy" among Beng parents in *Côte d'Ivoire* and Euro-American parents in the United States, it helped me to reinterpret my exchanges with Mama Eric, Mama Nelson, and other neighbors. These were not simply quaint conversations among mothers about children and child rearing. Instead, I was learning through dialogue how quotidian activities like holding and feeding a baby produce certain kinds of persons with the *tabia*, or character, valued in a particular society. Gottlieb reminds us that through "stark comparisons" between our beliefs and those of others, we can begin to see "that both systems are the result of cultural constructions" (Gottlieb 2004: xviii). And in the specific case of sleeping arrangements, Gottlieb wrote:

> Most parents in this subculture [middle-class European-Americans] are uncomfortable [sleeping with their infants] for a variety of reasons. These include a fear of crushing the baby and a sense of shame concerning the possibility that their child might see or hear their acts of sex. In some of these parents there may also be a conviction—whether fully conscious or not—that learning early to sleep solo produces strongly independent people who will later do well in a fiercely competitive world. Things could not be more different in Beng villages. There, the notion of an infant sleeping for any appreciable length of time in a separate space unconnected to another human being is very far not only from the norm but also from the ideal, while the practice of a baby sleeping attached to the back of a moving body (or sometimes curled up into the lap of a seated body) during the day … is heartily endorsed as the ideal.

(2004: 183–4)

It seemed that the fuss among my neighbors about where Gus lay his head each night had little to do with the cries he emitted and everything to do with the kind of child they thought he should be.

The more I have read in the anthropology of childhood in recent years, the more I recognize that the stages I considered normal for Gus and the childrearing practices I thought sound were largely a reflection of my WEIRD views. This became particularly clear when revisiting field notes, videotapes, and letters from this year in Old Moshi with baby on board. Though it made for slightly uncomfortable—at times even embarrassing—reading, I knew the examination of my changing understanding of these issues over time was itself part of the production of ethnographic knowledge.

*****

Field Note Entry: August 4, 1996

I think I should entitle one chapter of my dissertation "Lete fimbo!" (Bring me a stick!) and include in it a discussion of discipline. It struck me how, at the wedding we attended today, even very young children were told to obey their mothers and house girls or else they would be hit. The children were repeatedly threatened, "Nitakuchapa!" (I will hit you!). The wife of Mr. Mmari [a teacher at Njema] shouted this at their seven-month old who was crying in our car. Then, when we got home, I could hear Mama Eric shouting, yet again, at Eric to "lete fimbo" because he was crying.

*****

Most of my informal records—letters to my parents and video recordings of Gus and his playmates—document children cooperating and sharing to a greater extent than I recalled from my own childhood. Therefore, through my eyes, there did not seem to be many moments that might warrant caning, if one were to do so at all. In one long passage in my journal, I described several young neighbors playing in our living room and distributing Gus's toys so that everyone had something in his or her hand; they did not hoard the toys for themselves as I had expected. In a video clip several months later, I shifted from filming Gus on our porch to capturing a group of rowdy five- and six-year-olds who came racing through the yard, each "driving" a round plastic lid nailed to a stick. When they reached the far end of the clearing, they did not continue on their wild journey. Instead, they handed these home-made "cars" to the children standing nearby without any toys. And in a particularly memorable scene near the end of our stay, Tim filmed Eric's third birthday party as the mothers, myself included, stood around the table on the porch watching the children. They ranged in age from twenty months (Gus) to around seven years old, and they all sat remarkably quiet—or remarkable to me—as Eric ceremoniously fed each of his friends a bite of cake, placing it in their mouths with a communal fork. Each time, Eric was cheered on by the mothers as he generously offered this treat to the other children and then the adults before receiving his own small piece.

Yet squabbling inevitably occurred, and these were often moments where adults issued verbal reprimands followed by spanking or caning in many, though certainly not all, families I observed. Inevitably, the explanation for the disciplinary act had to do with improving the child's character. In one illustrative video clip, Eric was on our porch playing quietly with a truck that Amina had fashioned for him out of an empty carton of milk. His characteristically gentle demeanor changed dramatically, though, when several other children made gestures indicating they wanted the truck. Eric grabbed the truck, held it to his chest, and shouted at them to leave it alone. Rather than talking about the virtues of sharing, Hannah and Amina can be heard admonishing Eric not to withhold his toys lest he be considered *mchoyo*, a selfish person. The term has a particularly negative connotation in this community where family and clan allegiances remain strong and certain socialist sensibilities still linger.

Examples like this one seemed quite familiar to me as this was the kind of parenting practice I had experienced and observed in my WEIRD world. Thus, it was the many instances I observed of corporal punishment, or threats thereof, that captured my attention. Although spanking is not uncommon in middle-class Euro-American families in the United States, its use in public is rare, with alternatives like "time out" or loss of a privilege deemed far more socially acceptable. Corporal punishment, US experts warn, can lead to bullying, physical injuries, and psychological problems (Smith 2012). Dr. Spock himself called it "hurting children," and he warned that "it teaches children that the larger, stronger person has the power to get his ways, whether or not he is in the right" (Spock and Needlman 2011: 687). These views were incontrovertible, or so I thought, and I did not question them as parent or teacher until they were made strange in Tanzania.

One reason for my lack of cultural analysis of corporal punishment is the scant research on this topic. Lancy's (2015) meta-review of anthropological research on childhood included a few examples of different types of punishment, and he concluded with only one brief note about the use of discipline around the world: "If the child deviates from expectations, brief and sometimes harsh directives are used to correct. Other harsh correction tactics may include frightening the child or corporal punishments. Parents who don't discipline their children are pilloried" (404). The limited research on the cultural values ascribed to corporal punishment, or its repudiation, is unfortunate because punishment reflects deeply held views about how children learn and how their character can be shaped (Tao 2015). And, as I was to discover at home and at school, its implementation is also closely tied to postcolonial politics of race and material poverty, matters that Euro-American childcare experts rarely acknowledge.

*****

One morning a few months into our stay in Old Moshi, before the failed attempt to get Gus to sleep quietly in his own bed, I rushed home between classes to nurse him. To my surprise, I found him and Hannah playing a game that involved tearing up the latest *Newsweek* magazine my mother had sent and tossing the colorful pieces of paper into the air. When I arrived, Gus was sitting proudly on the floor amid bits of President Clinton's image and tattered scenes of the Taliban as they marched into Kabul. He held up a handful of his work and exclaimed "*hii, hii*" (this, this), one of his newest phrases that could be used to identify any object whose name he had not yet learned.

"*Karibu Dada*," Hannah said cheerfully greeting me as her "older sister" (*dada*). "We're doing an art project."

"Yes, I can see this is a project of some sort," I wailed, "but I had planned to take the magazine to school and use it in my Form 5 class for a lesson on politics. We have no textbooks."

In 1996, I was teaching both English and General Studies, a course that was supposed to address current affairs but did not have a well-established curriculum or any corresponding materials. Thus, *Newsweek* had become an essential element of my lesson planning, and here was the latest one lying in a crumpled mess on the floor.

Hannah apologized, and she tried to wiggle the rest of the magazine from underneath Gus's diapered bottom. He let out a yell and tried to grab the cover until Hannah distracted him by placing his favorite book, *The Very Hungry Caterpillar*, into his hands. As I picked up Gus to feed him, I asked Hannah whether her little siblings had ever done a similar "art project" at her home.

"Absolutely not! They would have been hit."

"That's what I thought. So why allow Gus to tear up this magazine and not hit him when he refused to give it back?"

"*Dada*," Hannah began as though explaining the obvious, "he's an *mzungu*. You people don't cane your children. You and Baba Gus don't even yell at him. I don't hit Gus even when he strikes Eric with his truck."

Gus hitting Eric with his toys? This was news to me, and the revelation left me feeling like a delinquent parent who had not been spending enough time with her child. Hannah assured me it had only happened a time or two and that Eric didn't seem to mind very much.

"Doesn't mind? Gus shouldn't be hitting Eric or anyone else!"

"Oh, I know that, so now when I see Gus getting frustrated and raising his arms, I move him or distract him with another toy. He's learning, and he's still very young."

"Good idea, but I'm still curious—why would you redirect Gus when he is doing something wrong but not your own brother and sister?" Holding up the remains of the *Newsweek*, I further inquired as to why she would let Gus tear it up when I had seen photographs like the ones from its pages pasted on the walls of her parents' house like wallpaper.

Hannah paused to give these questions further consideration. She then provided a lengthy explanation that clued me in to the ways that economic circumstances might affect how parents punish their children.

"When I was little, my mother didn't have time to sit on the floor and play with me the way I play with Gus. So when I did something wrong, she had to discipline me quickly because she was also feeding the cow or working in the garden or cooking dinner. Hitting a child is fast; distracting them and explaining to them what they have done wrong takes time, and we don't have that luxury the way you do."

Hannah continued to think about this matter and reminded me that my mother sent *Newsweek* every week or two. Thus, she didn't think that using one of them to entertain Gus would be a problem. When he grabbed it from the table and started tearing at the pages, she had turned it into a game and had him squealing in delight.

"But you're right," Hannah concluded. "If we were at my house, we would have carefully cut out the most colorful pictures in the magazine and pasted them to the wall. But this is Mr. Masaki's house. The walls were painted only a few months ago, so they do not need to be covered in pictures to hide the holes."

*****

Hannah's analysis of the *Newsweek* situation proved to be prescient. For one, she directed my attention to the contingent and highly contextual nature of punishment. She made clear that her siblings would have been caned had they torn up a magazine because it could have served as a badly needed source of paper with which to cover over peeling paint and nicks in the cement walls; in contrast, *Newsweek* was not necessary in the same way for our family and so had a different value in the two households.

Hannah also pointed out that punishment practices are affected by race and class. She would not strike Gus for refusing to relinquish an item she needed or for clobbering his friend even though such behavior would not have been tolerated if it had been Hannah's brothers. This moment helped me to make sense of a Tanzanian friend's refusal a decade later, in 2006, to allow Gus and his younger brother, Oscar, to study at her school when we moved back to Moshi for a year. My friend was the headmistress of the primary school in Old Moshi where we wanted to enroll the boys, but she would not allow it due to racialized practices of corporal punishment. "Mama Gus," she patiently explained to me, "your sons are not accustomed to seeing children caned, and the teachers have never struck a white child. Honestly, they would be scared to do so." Feeling ashamed by these racialized circumstances as well as the stinging awareness of their truth, we decided to enroll the boys at the International School in Moshi (see Chapter 10).

Finally, Hannah's remarks reminded me, yet again, that there is great variability and non-commensurability of concepts like care, character-building, and discipline owing to different circumstances that surround their use (Gottlieb 2000). My neighbors' convictions about infant care and toddler discipline did not match my own, but, over time, I could see that it didn't matter a great deal. In the aggregate, neither set of practices had had any "detrimental effect on the character of the children" (Raum 1940: 106), and this helped me to recognize the cultural arbitrariness of these deeply held views.

Yet the recognition of difference ought not to translate into acceptance of every parenting style or disciplinary practice one observes. There are times when the treatment of children and youth is abusive, regardless of how widespread the practice may be. The process of bracketing the familiar does not mean suspending ethical judgment and wholeheartedly embracing moral relativism. At the same time, coevalness makes a researcher more appreciative of the interplay of the cultural and material domains of life that influence views on "good" parenting and teaching. There were certainly ethical lines I refused to cross even though, as the next chapter reveals, I came awfully close to doing so.

Questioning Corporal Punishment

Few experiences can more quickly upset a person's certainty about herself as a compassionate educator than learning she is responsible for her entire class being caned for following her instructions. A few weeks into the first semester at Njema Secondary School, Mr. Osaki, the academic master who planned the school schedule, had still not finalized our teaching assignments. He pleaded with the staff to be patient and promised to inform us when changes to the timetable were made. This latter promise was not kept, and my students paid the price for it.

On this rainy morning in early February, I sat swearing under my breath in the cold, damp staff room as I labored through the completion of my "scheme of work," a massive notebook in which teachers must record their plan for the year. Each subject is supposed to be broken down into neat columns and rows that indicate the semester, the topics in the national syllabus, and the month, week, and day when each topic will be taught. If a school inspector arrived at the gates, the schemes of work were supposed to be produced to show how teachers would "cover the syllabus" by the end of the academic year. Yet I knew from teaching at Njema in 1993 that such certitude flew in the face of the unpredictability of everyday life in Tanzanian schools, where disruptions for teachers and students were commonplace. The SOW, as it was known, truly felt to me like a sinister scheme: Teachers were deceived into thinking they could possibly teach everything in the ambitious national syllabus, and students were misled into believing they should be able to grasp complex material presented to them in a single lesson, and in a foreign language, English, which they typically struggled to comprehend.

Stepping out of the staff room for a break from this tedious task, I bumped into the school secretary who had been trying to track me down. That morning, she had stopped by our house to visit Hannah, and they had accidentally locked our only set of keys inside. It was not the first time Hannah had made this mistake, and Mr. Masaki's wife, Mama Anna, the holder of the only other set of keys, had not been pleased when Hannah had called on her for assistance. Thus,

I was being summoned by Hannah to go to Mama Anna and tell her that it was I who had locked the keys in the house.

I could appreciate Hannah's reticence because Mama Anna had a tongue like a spear that quickly pierced the ego. Her recent comments about Gus's "late development" had not endeared her to me as she was convinced that a Chagga child of his age—ten months at the time—would already be walking and peeing on command. Yet Hannah knew that Mama Anna was unlikely to insult me for being absentminded as I was a white teacher with far more formal education than she had. So off I went to explain to my Form 2 English students that I would be late for class that morning but they should start the assignment in my absence.

A tardy teacher was only one of many kinds of interruptions that prevented the perfect execution of the scheme of work. My colleagues, and I, were frequently absent due to a sick child, a funeral, or a phone call in this era when the only working phone in the vicinity sat in the Njema secretary's office. Students, too, missed countless classes because they were sent home to collect school fees, were running errands for teachers, or, in the case of girls, were menstruating but without enough pads or places to wash them. Students were also frequently absent due to corporal punishment that often took place during the school day rather than before or after classes.

Following the practice of other teachers, I told the students to work on the vocabulary assignment I was writing on the board and asked the class monitor, the very earnest Ernest, to supervise, to which he readily agreed with a sincere "Yes, Madam." Anticipating that I would return before the eighty-minute period was over, I told Ernest to distribute class readers to students when they finished the vocabulary exercise. We would then discuss the next chapter in our text when I returned. I had no intention of deviating from my carefully planned SOW so early in the semester if I could avoid it, and this assignment would keep us on track.

When I arrived at Mama Anna's home, Machel, the guard, told me she had gone to Moshi, and he did not know where she had left the keys to our house. "Don't worry, Mama Augustino," Machel assured me, "she'll be back soon." These words, I knew, spelled trouble: I had learned in 1993 that the phrases "will be back soon" or "just coming" or "not much farther" signaled hopefulness and not reality. Thus, there was nothing else to do than wait with Machel on the creaky wooden bench where he spent hours each day guarding the front gate to the compound and listen to his colorful tales of his younger days as a skilled hunter.

Fortunately, Mama Anna returned home shortly thereafter. She pulled out the keys to our house from her bag, tossed them to Machel, and instructed him to assist me without any further comment. Machel knew very well that it was Hannah who had locked herself out of the house, but he said nothing in front of Mama Anna as he escorted me home. However, as we passed Mama Eric's house, out of earshot of Mama Anna, Machel called out commandingly to Hannah to say that he would be waiting for a big piece of meat, a favorite double entendre in this beef-loving area, in return for his help. Hannah shouted back that she gave little Gus and Eric all of her meat, which set Hannah, Amina (Mama Eric's house girl), and Machel howling and hurling sexual comments at each other. I, on the other hand, had to get back to school, so I bid them farewell and hustled back to Njema for the last few minutes of my class.

As I approached the campus, Tim caught me before I reached the main building. "Hey, your Form 2 students are being caned in the staff room, four strokes each. Aren't you supposed to be teaching them right now?"

"Yes, I am!" I cried. I explained to Tim the problem with the house keys and that I had left an assignment for the students to do in my absence. "I was on my way back to class right now because the period is not yet over."

"Well, I think you'd better go see Mr. Osaki. I heard that another teacher had showed up to teach during your periods, and the students refused to let him erase the assignment you had left for them on the board."

"If Mr. Osaki changed the timetable again without telling me, I'm going to be furious!"

"You're already fuming, Fran. Take a deep breath and go see what's going on."

So off I went to the academic master's office, and sure enough, Mr. Osaki had switched Mr. Kabila's periods and mine without informing me. Therein lay the problem, or so I believed. Yet, Mr. Osaki saw things rather differently. He apologized for failing to notify me of the schedule change, but he complained that my students had disobeyed Mr. Kabila, who came in to teach them after I had left to get the house keys. When Mr. Kabila arrived, my students were copying the assignment from the blackboard, but Mr. Kabila told Ernest to erase it so that he could start writing his own notes. This must have been quite a dilemma for deferential Ernest, but he didn't follow Mr. Kabila's instructions because he thought it was time for English class. The other students backed him up, so Mr. Kabila went to check with Mr. Osaki to make sure he was, indeed, supposed to teach Form 2 at this time. Yes, announced Mr. Osaki, these are your periods now. Mr. Kabila marched back to the Form 2 classroom and told the students to put away their English notebooks immediately, and they refused. Wasting little time, Mr. Kabila ordered the students to the staff room, lined them up one by one, and personally administered four blows to the boys' buttocks and, following regulations at the time, four strokes on the girls' knuckles.

"Students must learn to respect their teachers," insisted Mr. Osaki, "and it was Mr. Kabila's class to teach."

"But I was the one who told them to do the assignment on the board," I argued. "They were simply following my instructions because I had been assured these were my periods. How could they have carried out my assignment and followed Mr. Kabila's directions at the same time?"

Mr. Osaki shrugged, clearly unconvinced by my views on the matter. I walked out of his office feeling miserable that following my instructions had resulted in corporal punishment for every student in the class. Later in the day, when the Form 2s were awaiting the arrival of another teacher, I stepped into the classroom and apologized. A few students smiled; others chuckled nervously. I later learned they were surprised by this unexpected behavior because teachers rarely made such apologies. Such an act, some teachers contended, might be perceived by the youth as a diminishment of adult authority. I, on the other hand, struggled to understand the logic of corporal punishment, especially with teenagers who were, in my view, well beyond any developmental stage where spanking and swatting might contribute to *tabia nzuri*, good character. In fact, I was certain it would have the opposite effect.

Mr. Osaki must have told some of the other teachers that I was upset about this incident because a colleague came to see me that afternoon to apologize for keeping some of the Form 6 students from attending my class the previous day. "I'm very sorry, Madam, about the disruption to your scheme of work," Mr. Mshana began, "but the Form 6 boys are a very disrespectful lot. I am the Teacher on Duty (TOD) this week, and several of boys were not in their dormitories when we conducted our evening check. Their dorm mates would not tell me where they had gone, so I sent all of them to dig trenches down the road for the entire morning."

"Mr. Mshana," I inquired, "our Form 6 students are adults. Some are older than 21, 22 years of age. We have agreed as a school not to cane these older ones, but don't you think punishing them through hard labor, and during the school day when they also miss their lessons, is inappropriate?"

I suggested we try "psychology," a term I heard from a few teachers who, like me, disapproved of the widespread use of corporal punishment, to find out why the Form 6s were not in their dormitories.

Mr. Mshana was a thoughtful teacher, and I often heard him speaking to students in a calm, measured manner to determine the cause of a problem rather than immediately picking up a stick and striking them as some colleagues would do. Yet, he seemed puzzled by my suggestion: "Madam, the Form 6 boys are students. Regardless of their age, they must follow the rules of the school. If they do not, then they should be punished swiftly."

I confessed that I was struggling to understand. Some of the students were old enough to be fathers, and I had seen them given punishments like manual labor as well as caning and "frog jumps"—painful squats—all of which seemed humiliating and took them away from their classes, thereby punishing them twice.

Mr. Mshana listened attentively, but he would not concede that the school's punishment practices might be too harsh. From his perspective, the more shame the students felt, the more effective the punishment; the more lessons they missed, the greater the penalty for their misbehavior. He continued, "I have read that students are not caned in the US, and I have also seen pictures of very improperly dressed students in your country who speak harshly to their teachers. We do not want this in Tanzania, and punishment is one way to make sure students realize that it is teachers who are in charge."

*****

Corporal punishment was, without a doubt, the subject upon which my Tanzanian colleagues and I had the most striking disagreements. I may have been skeptical about the time spent developing detailed schemes of work or the wisdom of holding staff meetings during the school day and missing our classes; however, I was certain that striking students' bodies was not only pedagogically unsound but also a violation of children's rights. This pronounced difference made it clear to me that "copresence," or living in the same intersubjective space as my colleagues, did not mean we held similar views on all matters or agreed on this most fundamental disciplinary issue (Fabian 2014). Indeed, I struggled in my dissertation with Fabian's admonishment about the "denial of coevalness," or the placing of one's interlocutors "in a Time other than the present of the producer of anthropological discourse" (2002: 31). When it came to corporal punishment, it seemed to me that most Tanzanian teachers' views on this matter were old-fashioned and out of touch with international norms. I knew caning was not based on WEIRD psychological research or on the United Nations Convention on the Rights of the Child, which explicitly forbids the "degrading treatment or punishment" of children (United Nations General Assembly 1989). How could caning, frog jumps, or working in the hot sun be taken as anything but degrading, especially when the "children" in question were well past puberty?

During my first few months at Njema, the disciplinary differences between Tanzanian and US educators came up frequently in conversations with fellow teachers. This became even more pronounced once Mr. Salema, a fellow English teacher, returned in March from an exchange program in which he had spent several weeks visiting American schools. In addition to stories on television or in the newspaper about US education, my colleagues marshalled evidence from Mr. Salema's accounts to argue for strict discipline at Njema lest our students start behaving like Americans. Mr. Salema spent hours in the staff room regaling us with descriptions of wondrous educational technology in US classrooms and the abundance of food in the high school cafeterias. He clearly had great admiration for the American teachers he met and brought back a lot of useful materials for his colleagues to use. Yet, moments later, his face would grow stern as he described students who put their shoes on the chairs in front of them and covered their faces with baseball caps to avert the gaze of their teachers. He could not understand how such insolence could be tolerated and wondered aloud about how the United States had become such a powerful nation when its youth were so unruly.

As the months went on, I began to discern differences among my colleagues regarding their views on and uses of corporal punishment. No one called for an outright ban; however, the outline of two distinct camps began to form. There were those who thought corporal punishment should be used with far less frequency, and those who believed it needed to be continued, if not amplified, because it served a critical role in maintaining order, discipline, and teachers' authority. Their positions were similar to teachers I met at the ten other secondary schools I visited during the year, leading me to conclude that there was little support among the country's teachers for a prohibition on corporal punishment but a wide range of views as to how often and for what offenses it should be used.

I began to ask more explicitly about punishment during school visits after an incident that shocked teachers, parents, and students across East Africa. In July 1996, a Kenyan primary school student died as a result of caning by a teacher (Human Rights Watch 1999). The story was covered widely in the Tanzanian media, but it was only in Kenya that it led to changes in national legislation regarding who would be allowed to cane students, how many times, and for what offenses. There were already such laws in place in Tanzania specifying that only the headmaster or headmistress was authorized to administer strokes, and only a maximum of six and with a small switch. This law, however, was rarely enforced. Instead, it fell to the Discipline Master at most schools to carry out punishment. Or, as in the case of Miss Mosha later in this chapter, teachers simply continued to cane, assign frog jumps, or require students to stand in uncomfortable positions in the sun to atone for their behavior.

By the end of the first few months at Njema, I began to notice a connection between punishment and uncertainty. My colleagues would periodically express their frustration, similar to my own, when their students were absent from class with no advance warning or no explanation only to find out after the fact that another teacher had assigned the students work to do in response to some offense. Not knowing whether the majority of students would be in class each day meant that I needed to have a contingency plan in case ten, twenty, or more of my forty students were missing. As I wrote my lesson plans each week, I also made notes about what the alternative lessons would be if there were not enough students in the classroom to move on to a new topic, thereby messing with my carefully planned scheme of work. "Anticipatory knowledge production," as Calkins (2016) has termed this element of uncertainty, seemed like an apt description as I began "to organize and govern the future and to make it more calculable" (Chapter 1, Location 1153). I learned, over time, to anticipate frequent disruptions by keeping different sets of materials at the ready; students, however, faced even greater precarity.

At the different schools I visited, students frequently talked about the unpredictability of the punishment they received. Regarding tardiness, for example, they reported that some TODs caned students on the spot if they arrived late to campus, but then they would quickly send them along to their classes. Other TODs at the same school would force students to carry stones from one spot to another for an hour or two before allowing them to return to the classroom, and still other TODs looked the other way altogether, especially during the rainy season when they knew how challenging it was for students who lived far away to navigate slippery, muddy roads. The students' sense of uncertainty regarding corporal punishment was palpable, even though they generally endorsed its limited use as a way to promote discipline in schools.

Twenty years later, I wondered whether the disruptions to teachers' and students' lives due to punishment were as frequent as I recalled. Therefore, I went back to my field-note binder from 1996 and marked with Post-It notes all of the pages where I described instances of caning, frog jumping, digging trenches, or work on the school farm owing to a violation of the school's regulations. By the time I finished, the binder had a flurry of yellow and pink tabs flying from the top. There were far too many instances to recount, but the following represent typical examples:

February 7, 1996: During the staff meeting, Mr. Suma announced that the Form 6 students were upset about the punishment seven of them received yesterday. An unexpected pre-lunch assembly had been called yesterday, and some students did not know about it. Mr. Suma explained that the Form 6 students had already left class for lunch, so someone was sent to tell them to come back to the main campus for this assembly. Seven of them walked back very slowly, so they were called out to be punished in front of the other students. Mr. Suma told them to kneel, but they refused. The punishment for disobeying a teacher is six strokes, which they were given later in the day. Mr. Suma said that he is concerned this disobedience was observed "by the younger guys" and set a bad example. According to Mr. Suma, the students feel like the staff is divided between the teachers who teach and "love" them, and the rest of the staff who treat them like children and punish them excessively.

March 11, 1996: *There were a lot of absences in my classes today (Monday), especially among the girls. I thought at first it was due to the rain, but then I realized that the girls who were absent were those I had seen being punished on Friday for missing days of work during the school holiday in December.[1] On my way home later in the morning, I saw several girls wearing their regular, non-school clothes with their heads covered, hoeing the ground along the road to the school. Further down the road, I saw the rest of the girls working on the school farm. They greeted me and told me they would be working on the farm all week as punishment and would not be in class at all.*

November 18, 1996: *During tea break (~10:30–11:00 a.m.), Mr. Mabala and Mr. Suma announced they wanted to do a dormitory search for a missing mattress, so all of the students were assembled after tea and told to turn in the keys to their dorms to Mr. Mabala. Along with this, Mr. Suma called a Form 1 boy to the front of the assembly and announced that he had sold his mattress for 5,000 shillings and bought another student's bedding for 3,000 shillings. He was given six strokes in front of everyone. Then the day students were told to go to their classrooms and wait while the boarding students went to sit on the football pitch [field] as their dorms were inspected. [...] The inspections went on until 1:15 p.m., with a small group of five teachers going inside the dorms to see whose mattresses were whose. Each of these teachers carried at least one stick. There was caning in every dorm I observed (about six dorms), especially because the dorms were dirty. Students told me that they have no buckets, brushes, or soap, and there is only one shower that is operable in each dormitory block, so keeping body and bweni [dormitory] clean is quite a task.*

In each of these cases, and the many others not mentioned here, punishment meant disruption of the scheme of work and many hours of missed instruction. The frequent absences of students from class due to punishment, unplanned school assemblies, unannounced dormitory inspections, and other events left little time to cover the syllabus and, at a minimum, to touch upon each topic in the ambitious national curriculum. Slowly, very slowly, my students and I moved ahead with the national English and General Studies curricula because I wanted to make sure they grasped the material before we moved on. However, this approach meant we fell further and further behind in my scheme of work with each passing month.

*****

The frequent use of corporal punishment by some school administrators and teachers produced considerable uncertainty for their colleagues whose classes and SOWs were disrupted as a consequence. Moreover, students told me repeatedly that it left them in a distracted, fearful state when teachers used corporal punishment as one of their primary pedagogical tools. Miss Mosha's English class was a case in point.

By the end of my second month at Njema, I felt sufficiently comfortable with my colleagues to begin asking whether I could observe their classes as part of my doctoral research. Thinking it wise to start with the teachers I knew best, I approached Miss Mosha because she was one of my colleagues in the English department. A tall, confident woman in her early thirties, Miss Mosha was an outspoken teacher who did not hesitate to raise her voice in staff meetings, or in her interactions with students. She had a wicked sense of humor, particularly dark humor about the conditions of women's lives in Tanzania that we often discussed in the English department office or at her house on campus when she would have me over for tea. It was unusual for a woman of her age not to be married, and though she did wed later that year, I sensed she had been in no hurry to find a mate and relinquish any of her independence.

Miss Mosha's intensity extended to her interactions with students, with several female students telling me how they revered her as a strong, single woman. Yet many others found her unduly punitive, and I often felt conflicted about whether to intervene. On one particular morning, I approached the English office to collect my class readers and heard Miss Mosha shouting, "Forty percent? Why did you only get forty percent on this test?" This was followed immediately by a sharp whack and muffled murmuring. When I stepped into the office, I could see that Miss Mosha had lined up her students between her desk and the office door, demanding an answer from each one about his or her test score. Knowing that I disapproved of caning, Miss Mosha stopped long enough to greet me warmly and allow me to collect the readers. As soon as I was out the door, she returned to her inquisition.

Given our relationship, I was not surprised that Miss Mosha readily agreed to have me observe her Form 3 English class; however, I was not fully prepared for the extent of her use of corporal punishment throughout the lesson. Teachers at Njema and elsewhere often spoke critically to students and taunted them with questions like "Are you stupid?" or "Are you lazy?" In an effort to motivate students, some teachers would accuse the boys in their classes of being "slow learners" or of "falling behind the girls," an interactional pattern noted as well by other researchers in Tanzania (Thomas and Rugambwa 2011). However, no teacher I observed used verbal and corporal punishment as frequently as Miss Mosha.

Beginning the classroom observation phase of my research, I followed Miss Mosha to her third-period class of thirty-one boys and five girls and took a seat at the back of the room. As we arrived, Miss Mosha called for one of the boys to erase the board even though a girl was still trying to write down the notes left by the previous teacher. Another boy walked into the room right behind us, and she shouted "Hurry up!" at him.

As soon as one side of the board had been erased, Miss Mosha began writing with her stick of chalk: *ENGLISH/Continuous Aspect (Progressive aspect)*. She then turned to the students, walked up and down the rows of desks, and asked for examples of modal auxiliary verbs. In my observation notes, I simply referred to the male students as "B" (boys) with different numbers and the female students "G" (girls) with a number assigned to each one.

The first student at whom Miss Mosha looked, B1, did not respond, so she reached over and yanked his left ear while continuing to ask the class for examples. Miss Mosha then returned to the board and wrote: *He, She, It Examples*. She asked for an example sentence, and B27 offered, "He is playing football," to which Miss Moshi shouted, "What?" B27 repeated his sentence, and Miss Mosha commented, "Speak English. Let's move to 'we, you, they.'" B24 gave the example, "They are eating food," and Miss Moshi queried the class, "This is what?" and pointed to G3. The first female student to speak during the lesson responded, "Third person plural" to which Miss Mosha replied with the first, and one of her only, positive affirmations, "Good. Any problems so far?" The students wisely responded in unison, "No."

This pattern of writing a verb tense category on the board, such as present continuous or past continuous, asking for examples, and assessing the students' accuracy continued for nearly thirty minutes. Miss Mosha pulled ears, accused students of having forgotten basic English, and, a few times, noted a correct answer with "good" or "yes." She also gave the class a brief writing assignment based on the present and past continuous forms. After a few minutes, she began looking over students' shoulders to see whether or not they were responding correctly in their notebooks. As she approached B14, I could see him bend over his notebook as though trying to cover it from her gaze. Miss Mosha leaned over even further to see it and then slapped him hard on his back. She turned to B25, who was sitting next to B14, and tried to pull his ear after noticing a mistake in his assignment. However, he was faster and quickly put his hand over his ear. Not deterred, Miss Mosha pulled B14's hand away from the left side of his face and gave his ear a vigorous yank. Behind him sat B16, at whom Miss Mosha shouted, "You can say, 'They was'?" as she pulled his ear. Then she moved over to B21 and demanded, in Swahili, "Why have you forgotten 'They will be eating'? Who taught you … ?" Whack.

With the period rapidly coming to a close, Miss Mosha moved quickly to G5 and then to G1, who had made a mistake. Miss Mosha softened her tone a bit to ask, "They was?" and demanded a correct response. Notably, she did not pull the ear of the female student who made this mistake, but nor did she continue checking the other girls' notebooks. She returned to the boys' rows until the bell rang to indicate the end of the period. The students quickly collected their pencils, put them in their metal pen set cases, and walked out the door clutching their notebooks in their arms. Miss Mosha called to me at the back of the room to hurry to the staff room for tea before our male colleagues drank it up.

*****

The first few observations in classes where teachers used corporal punishment had me feeling quite indignant because it seemed unnecessary as a disciplinary tactic with these young adults. I had found Tanzanian students to be generally well behaved, especially in comparison to US high school students, as Mr. Salema had noted. Moreover, teacher education programs in Tanzania and in the United States taught many alternatives to it. Why, then, was it so widely used?

I continued to ponder this question throughout the year, but I could also sense my certainty about teacher–student relations slowly beginning to change as I grew more accustomed to the formal, hierarchical interactions around me. I, too, began to expect students to rise when I entered the classroom as they did with their Tanzanian teachers, even though I had found this uncomfortably colonial when I taught at Njema in 1993. Moreover, I used far more "teacher-centered" instruction as the school year progressed, with a piece of chalk for writing notes on the board never far from my hand and lecture notes always at the ready.

Yet none of these changes troubled me as much as the day I toyed with caning one of my Form 5 students, all of whom were in their upper teens or early twenties. I had struggled with Marco most of the year, and his other teachers also considered him *mkorofi*, a troublemaker. Initially, I assumed I would find the right "learner-centered" approach to working with him as I had always been able to do with American students, but this certainty gave way as the year progressed. The first major incident occurred in May, when I was "invigilating" (monitoring) a midterm exam for Form 5 students. Marco and his classmate, Richard, had whispered back and forth during an earlier exam I had invigilated that week, stopping only when I leaned on the wall between their two desks for the rest of the hour. They kept turning to look at me, as though they were checking to see if it was okay to whisper again to each other. This time, I decided to act preemptively by moving my desk so I could watch Marco and Richard without an obstructed view. Neither of them looked happy about this arrangement, particularly Marco, who scowled at me whenever our eyes met.

Forty minutes or so into the three-hour exam, Marco had had enough. He defiantly stood up at his desk and walked to the door of the classroom. When I asked him where he was going, Marco turned to look me straight in the face. "*Choo*," he said with a sly smile and a glance back at his chuckling classmates, and then he walked out the door. *Choo*, it should be noted, means both "toilet" and "shit." Rather than using the more polite phrase, *kujisaidia*, meaning "to help myself," Marco evidently wanted to make a bold statement by using a crasser term. To add insult to his delivery, he did not ask to use the toilet as a student would normally do; instead, he tossed out the word *choo* as if he were telling me to "take a shit." This incident only added to my dislike of Marco, and his frequent absences during the second half of the term due to punishments by other teachers did not bother me in the least.

One day near the end of the term, I had run out of spots to which to move Marco as a way of redirecting him and had no more activities to offer of the sort that sometimes kept him engaged. When I heard him laughing as I wrote something on the board, I eyed the stick in the corner of the room and gave it a long, serious stare. Never before in my nearly twelve years of teaching had I ever considered hitting a student. It was anathema to my ethical-moral code, my beliefs about children's rights, and my professional views about learner-centered education. And yet there I was, stumped by this student, and there it was, a stick that one of the other teachers had left behind.

I don't know whether it was my sudden stillness at the board or my obvious contemplation of the switch in the corner that alarmed the other students. I could hear a couple of them telling Marco, in no uncertain terms, to shut up. I slowly turned back to the class and, as calmly as I could, I asked them to complete the writing assignment on the board. They were remarkably quiet the rest of the class, and I had no more conflicts with Marco during the remaining few days in the school year.

*****

I have returned to this moment with Marco many times over the years because it led me to ponder both the certainty of my convictions regarding corporal punishment and the ways that the material conditions of schooling might correspond to disciplinary practices. I naively assumed at the beginning of the year that my pedagogical beliefs and ways of acting in the classroom were a deeply ingrained part of my *habitus*, a central element in Bourdieu's sociological framework that refers to the enduring dispositions, emotions, and attitudes a person embodies owing to her social class, race, gender, and upbringing (Bourdieu 1977; Bourdieu and Wacquant 1992). It did not occur to me that such dispositions, "durable, but not eternal" (Bourdieu and Wacquant 1992: 133), could be influenced in a matter of months by the new social field in which I was located. My socialization as a teacher, particularly a *mzungu* with a master's degree in education, led me to believe that I could maintain order in the classroom, any classroom, without resorting to corporal punishment. For the most part, it worked; yet Marco and a few other students in his class set me off course, leading to feelings of insecurity about my teaching skills.

I began to give more thought to how discipline in schools, and specifically the use of corporal punishment to achieve it, might reflect a broader social landscape as I reflected on a lengthy interview with a veteran teacher, Mr. Lyimo. A sagacious senior member of the Njema staff, Mr. Lyimo and I had taught together in 1993, and he had often expressed his disdain for corporal punishment then as he did again in 1996. Even though I had not intended to focus on this topic during our discussion, we spent considerable time talking about caning and discipline more broadly as the interview unfolded.

Mr. Lyimo, like many relatively prosperous Chagga who lived through the late colonial and socialist eras, felt that his standard of living had declined under President Nyerere. This was felt acutely by the mid-1980s, when there were severe shortages of everything from gasoline to soap. He also believed that discipline—in government and in education—had decreased precipitously owing to some of these same economic policies and to the ones currently in effect in the country. To my surprise, he seemed to long for the kind of teacher education he had received from the "colonial man," the British whom he described with great animosity earlier in the interview. It was colonial education policy that set up roadblocks to student advancement for the vast majority of Tanzanians, he explained; nevertheless, as one who had gotten past these barriers, he also praised his British lecturers in Tanzania and the UK, where he got a bachelor's degree, for introducing him to child-centered pedagogy:

> *Another [reason for corporal punishment] is the economy of the country today. The economy of the country, I think, plays a very big role in helping the administration of the schools and other developments, other academic institutions of the country. If, for example, those working, those who are administrators, are not motivated, by being not motivated we mean the conditions of work are not made good for them, they will not do their work properly. Many good teachers have resigned, **many** good teachers.[2] Only myself, I have remained behind because I vowed to God to be a teacher until I die.*
>
> *And the teaching materials, if they are not there, the buildings and so on, will begin to decay. You see, all these things contribute to the indiscipline of the students. The economy began to be run badly in this country [referring to the socialist period under President Nyerere]. It wasn't bad in those days [1950s and 1960s]. Now, we feel economically that we are very poor, and we cannot afford to make our institutions look attractive in such a way as to make students believe that whatever they are learning is good enough for their lives. So naturally you will find some students don't take too much attention for their education, you know, because they feel that no one is ever serious enough about it. It is as if they are not being cared for very much by those authorities, so they will do whatever they like. There is so much more laissez faire today than in the past.*
>
> *I, for one, I don't believe in caning. I don't say I have not caned. I have caned. Actually, when I was the headmaster at a government secondary school, I used to cane, but it was the last resort. I would not use a cane to educate my students. If my students did not understand, I would not use a cane. If I failed to teach him, then I should look for other methods to help him. And if I could not get other methods to help him, it is I who has failed. I think it is our duty to be sympathetic for the students rather than using a cane and hitting them.*
>
> *I remember during our course in teaching in this country and outside this country, much attention was given to child development. Teaching meant to develop a child, to develop a child to be a man. That was the theme of the education we had in those days. And those who received this education were happy about it. And if they were happy, and if they knew they were obliged to do it, it was their duty and they came to school knowing that they were going to develop the child ... You see, unless a teacher is concerned with his child [student], we cannot, and I say we can never, discipline our students. Even our children at home, if we are not concerned very much, they can never grow up properly. They can't! You have to know their needs. You have to know their problems and how to help them solve them.*

Mr. Lyimo's reflections on punishment, pedagogy, and the working conditions of Tanzanian administrators and teachers point to a neglected but critically important area of research as to how education and economic policy that affects conditions in schools also influences classroom practice. When buildings need major repairs, teachers' salaries remain very low, teaching and learning materials are extremely limited, and large numbers of students in the classroom make it impossible for teachers to attend to their different needs, teachers are understandably unmotivated and even downright angry. Under these stressful conditions, I began to understand how corporal punishment could be a response to teachers' intense frustration with their situation and a more expedient means for dealing with acts of indiscipline (see Tao 2015). Although I had more material resources—books, magazines, training, and time—at my disposal than most of my Tanzanian colleagues, I still felt less equipped to handle unruly students under these conditions than I did in the United States.

Such circumstances are not limited to Tanzania. For instance, in a study of teachers' lives in two former Soviet states in Central Asia, Niyozov (2017) established a connection between teachers' ill-tempered behavior toward their students and "their disempowerment in the face of the increasing intensification of their working lives" (99). As one teacher in his study explained, "I become rude because life and work conditions make me get out of control, when I prepare myself and my students don't" (99). Similarly, in research conducted in South Africa, several scholars have documented how material conditions, including water shortages, the absence of electricity, and very high teacher–student ratios, profoundly affect teachers' everyday classroom practice in historically disadvantaged Black schools that continue to face these challenges (Johnson, Monk, and Hodges 2000; Weber 2007; Weller-Ferris 1999). And in research that I conducted more than a decade later with a Tanzanian teacher educator, we also found a high level of frustration among secondary school teachers who taught at schools with poor working conditions. They consistently reported that their authoritative, teacher-centered pedagogy was a reflection of their large classes and limited time to spend on lesson preparation owing to their many additional duties at the school (Vavrus and Salema 2013). As Mr. Lyimo would have predicted, teachers who work under poor conditions tend not to do their work "properly," be it the use of child-friend teaching methods or disciplinary practices.

*****

The interview with Mr. Lyimo and our digression into the political economy of punishment revealed how far I had wandered by the end of the year from my dissertation topic on girls' schooling and fertility decline. My intention had been to focus on the formal curriculum and any direct influence it might have on female students' desired number of children. As the year progressed, however, I found myself fixated on the hidden curriculum—on the implicit lessons that convey dominant cultural values and social norms—and how everyday classroom practices like corporal punishment may be more instructive for students than anything in the national syllabus could be (Apple 1990; Bourdieu and Passeron 1990). What had happened?

Looking back at this period two decades later through field notes, letters, and interview transcripts, I can now see how Gus figured into my research in many unanticipated ways, as this chapter and the previous one reveal. In 1996, compared to 1993, I was much more interested in childhood as an area of inquiry. As Gus grew and became the focus of comparative analysis by adults in the neighborhood like Mama Anna and Mama Eric, I sought to engage with them to understand how and why their views on child development were quite different from my own. Moreover, my observations of Eric, Gus's constant companion, and other children as they were being disciplined and punished led me to think more deeply about questions of authority, intergenerational relations, and the cultivation of "educated persons" (Levinson, Foley, and Holland 1996; Stambach 2000).

These intersubjective interactions beyond the walls of the school led to a shift in my gaze from a narrow focus on schooling to the broader social practices of education, and from the certain to the serendipitous. I spent less time reviewing the neat columns and rows in my colleagues' schemes of work for clues to girls' views on childbearing and, instead, started to explore unscripted lessons about discipline that might shape students' dispositions and, eventually, their sense of themselves as educated persons with putatively greater control over their fertility or other aspects of their futures.

The experience of parenting Gus in Old Moshi was undoubtedly instructive for my research, and so, too, was the year in the classroom as a teacher myself. The certainty with which I began the year in January regarding practices like corporal punishment gave way to a more contingent, socially situated stance. Even though I did not ultimately employ it, I could understand the appeal of swift, expedient discipline when teachers had limited alternatives by virtue of the conditions in their schools and were deeply frustrated by their circumstances. These were lessons I carried with me as I wrapped up the research project in December, said farewell to colleagues and neighbors, and returned with Tim and Gus to Wisconsin for my final year as a PhD student.

Interlude:
From Doctoral Student to Assistant Professor

There was a three-and-a-half-year hiatus between the conclusion of my doctoral fieldwork in December 1996 and my first trip back to Tanzania in the summer of 2000. This gap was due to twin births: Oscar, my second child, in January 1998, and my dissertation five months later. Oscar's birth was not nearly as dramatic as Gus's had been, though the timing of it threw me into a state of panic. I had carefully planned to finish all but the final chapter of my dissertation before Oscar's due date at the end of February so that I could defend my dissertation in time to go through the University of Wisconsin graduation ceremony in May. I had managed to stick to this tight timeline even through two months of debilitating morning sickness and many days spent preparing application materials for assistant professor positions. By late January, I had only one chapter to conclude, and I still had three weeks before Oscar's birth.

What a shock, then, on the morning of January 30 to feel a gush of water between my legs that could only mean one thing: this baby has his own timeline, and the time for his birth is now. Thankfully, there was no C-section this time around; two days later, I was back home and at the computer. I remember feeling euphoric that I could hold Oscar in one arm as he drifted off to sleep and type with the other, allowing me to reestablish my writing schedule.

By the end of March, I had finished a draft of the entire dissertation, all 435 pages of it, and delivered copies to my three primary readers. While my committee members scrutinized the dissertation during the next few weeks, I turned my attention to a postdoctoral fellowship application. I knew it was a long shot: a fellowship at Harvard that supported anthropologists to get training in demography. I was already insecure because my degree was in education, not anthropology, but Stacie, who had secured a fellowship to work with the same professor, encouraged me to apply.

For the fellowship, I proposed a longitudinal study in Old Moshi that would follow a cohort of youth from the end of primary school through the next six years of their lives, or even longer. This would be the period when a minority would begin secondary schooling and, if successful, finish A-level studies, continue to university, and delay child bearing until their schooling was complete. The majority, I suspected, would find informal employment or perhaps receive some vocational training, and many would get married and have children. From my doctoral research, I knew gender relations and certain family characteristics, such as parents' level of education, employment, and household wealth, would influence these opportunities, but I wasn't quite sure how. I also had a hunch that geography would matter, especially for youth living the farthest north on the mountain, but I didn't know whether this was, in fact, the case or how residing in the middle and southern altitude belts might affect life after primary school (see Chapter 12). Finalizing the proposal to explore the interplay of gender, class, and geography, I continued to wait on word from my committee members. If they thought the dissertation was solid, we would schedule the two-hour oral exam, the "defense" of the theory, methods, and findings in the dissertation.

There are few phrases more discouraging to a doctoral student than "not yet ready to defend," but these were the words I heard from one of my committee members during a meeting in his office in early April with Oscar in tow. After the niceties about the beautiful sleeping baby, we got down to business. It seemed that the dissertation was not as theoretically sophisticated as he thought it could, and should, be. The rich ethnographic material was fine, no comments, but the interpretation of my observations and interviews needed to draw more fully on the great French theorists whose work was all the rage in the US academy in the 1990s. With this devastating news, Oscar awoke from his slumber with a howl, channeling my feelings at that moment because it meant a significant amount of rewriting and no graduation for me in May.

It took nearly two months to rework the chapters, not so much because of the difficulty of the task because I could channel Pierre Bourdieu and Michel Foucault when need be; rather, it was my mounting fatigue, with Oscar nursing more and sleeping less, that left me dragging. When the big day for the oral examination finally arrived in June, I was more nervous about my milk letting down during this ordeal than I was about the questions I might be asked.

Fortunately, academic adrenaline kicked in and kept me sufficiently focused on the queries from my committee. At one point, the professor who had asked for more theory and the professor who wanted more empirical data went at each other, so I sat back quietly and hoped they would carry on until time was up. As the two-hour mark approached, my advisor told me to leave the room so the committee could deliberate; within a few minutes, he was calling me back to the conference room.

"Congratulations Dr. Vavrus!" What golden words, and what a relief to hear that I had passed without the need for further revisions. Warm hugs followed from each of the professors, and off they went, bringing to a close five years of doctoral work with this eminent, and generally very supportive, group of scholars. Sitting down in the conference room, alone for the first time in months, I savored the moment, whispering the title "Dr. Vavrus" to myself. I only had to deposit the dissertation with the university before I could obtain my long-awaited diploma and officially be known as a "Doctor of Philosophy."

After spending a couple of days proofreading the chapters, I placed Oscar in his car seat and drove to the Graduate School to formally file the manuscript. It was my birthday, which foolishly made me anticipate rainbows and balloons rather than the heavy rain that started to fall as we neared Bascom Hill. Juggling Oscar, umbrella, and dissertation, I walked carefully across the quadrangle as I wanted to make a good impression on the official overseeing this momentous event. Much to my surprise, the building directory led us not to the top of a grand staircase but to a basement, a dark, dank room with a very bored staff member sitting behind the counter. He took the dissertation from the box, flipped through a few pages to make sure the formatting looked about right, and then tore a perforated tag from an index card.

"What's this?" I asked, wondering about the little slip of paper he handed to me with a few numbers and the date on it.

"It's your receipt," he replied. "It's proof that you've deposited your dissertation. You're done. You'll get your diploma in the mail in a couple of weeks," and then he turned his back on us to attend to another matter.

It took a few minutes for the full depth of this anticlimactic moment to sink in, enough time to get back to the car and buckle Oscar in the back seat. But I could not drive anywhere; I could only cry. I let loose with all of the tears that had built up over the past few months and unleashed themselves at that moment with unexpectedly powerful force. I cried because this two-by-two-inch piece of faded orange cardstock was all I had to show for years of work on the dissertation. I cried because I had missed graduation to rewrite chapters that would appease my committee but displeased me—the Njema students' stories had been eclipsed by dense social theory, and this had not been my plan. I cried because I had no certainty about a job in the future as not one of the many universities to which I had applied had contacted me for an interview. I cried for having been so focused on finishing the dissertation for the past few months that I had not spent sufficient time with Oscar or Gus. And I cried because I was so goddamn tired, both mentally and physically, and didn't know when I would get a full night of sleep again.

From the back seat, Oscar began making his favorite new sound, a guttural *gyah* to add to his repertoire of bilabial *ba* and *ma*. His chubby, round face widened with a delightful smile that seemed to be saying, "Hey Mom, at least you've got me," and, of course, I did. A more rational voice reminded me that I had two healthy children, a roof over my head, and a completed PhD degree, graduation ceremony or not. Moreover, I had spouse with a decent, though not high-paying, job to tide us over until I eventually launched my career, a decision he supported even though he had left academia himself. This was not a bad list of accomplishments for a thirty-three-year-old, so, blowing my nose, wiping my eyes, and gaining a bit of perspective on the situation, I grabbed the steering wheel and drove home following the slow, circuitous route along John Nolan Drive. I took in the majesty of Lake Monona and admitted to myself that I was, in fact, quite content to stay here for a while. Who knew, maybe this was *mpango wa Mungu*, God's plan, after all.

*****

The rest of the summer and fall seemed leisurely by comparison to the previous year, with a comfortable routine of child care, more job applications, and a bit of editing work on the side. I began to wonder whether being a stay-at-home mom might actually suit me because I knew from observing my committee members that an academic position would require not one book but several, along with journal articles, teaching, and a daily barrage of meetings. Was this the kind of life I wanted to lead? I had spent thirteen years, from freshman at Purdue University to doctoral student at Wisconsin, preparing for a career in academia and striving to get good grades, fellowships, and a couple of publications before entering the competitive job market. And still, here I was, with no commensurate employment and not sure how I felt about this unexpected turn of events. I had the immense privilege of a partner with a salary and health benefits for the family, and no student debt weighing me down because of fellowships, teaching assistantships, and the much lower cost of public higher education at the time. This fortuitous situation granted me time to figure out my next steps; nonetheless, it was a disorienting period of uncertainty marking the transition from successful doctoral student to floundering graduate.

As fall turned to winter, I began developing a list of Plan B options that included teaching English as a second language and searching for an administrative position at the university. Yet before the ink had dried on this document, I received an offer as a part-time lecturer in Wisconsin's International Studies program to begin with the new term in January 1999. And no sooner had I begun teaching this course than I received calls from not one but two of the universities to which I had applied for tenure-track positions: Columbia's Teachers College and Harvard's Graduate School of Education. After months of *Goodnight Moon* and *The Cat in the Hat*, I quickly had to throw myself back into reading academic texts and preparing for on-campus job talks.

I asked my female professors and former classmates for practical advice about how to broach the subject of children during the interview process because I was still nursing and would need time between meetings and presentations to pump. One friend with a new assistant professor position told me that I should not mention having children, or even being married, as this might indicate I was not a dedicated scholar. Another assured me that leaving on my wedding ring was fine, but I should avoid any talk of motherhood. But I *had* to tell someone about breastfeeding as they planned my itineraries, yet not one colleague could offer any advice on how to discuss this taboo topic for women on the job market. In the end, I told the chairpersons of the search committees the truth: I had a baby and needed breaks during the day to dispose of my breastmilk. Both mothers themselves, they graciously accommodated my request and did not seem put off by it in any way.

Despite the positive interviews on both campuses, weeks went by with no news from either university. I now badly wanted one of the positions, if only to assuage my tender ego. The pain of having no job prospects had been intense, but the feeling of failure after two on-campus interviews had an even sharper edge. Finally, in late April, I received a call from Harvard, but it was not from the education school. Instead, it was the School of Public Health offering me the postdoctoral fellowship for which I had applied the year before. I was ecstatic because it meant two years during which I could turn my dissertation into publications and start the longitudinal project in Old Moshi. Tim, too, was pleased because he had grown up a few blocks from the Harvard campus, and we had decided that if the postdoc were to come through, he would stay at home with the boys, at least for the first year before Gus started kindergarten. I said yes to the offer right away and cheerfully chalked up the two on-campus job interviews to experience.

Yet fate is a fickle friend, one day foiling our every move and the next blessing us with abundance. A week after accepting the postdoctoral position, who should call but the chair of the search committee at Teachers College? She apologized for the delay in responding but hoped I would be pleased with an offer of a tenure-track assistant professor position. I was dumbfounded. Less than a year ago, I was stifled by uncertainty with only a pile of rejection letters to my name, and now I had both Harvard and Columbia inviting me to join them.

Back I went to my professors and friends for advice: Should I rescind my acceptance of the postdoc and say yes to the tenure-track position, or should I decline the latter in the hopes that in two years I would get an even better professorial position? Most recommended the more secure, long-term position at Teachers College, but a few pushed for the postdoc because it would provide time for writing and research that assistant professors rarely have. It was Tim who suggested taking them both: Tell Teachers College that I needed a minimum of one year at Harvard and request a deferment, *and* propose to Harvard that I keep the second year of funding for the postdoc research project while starting the position in New York. Why had I not thought of this option? Why, because such a risky move seemed too bold, too confident, and I did not feel deserving of more than what these institutions had already offered. Striking a decidedly unfamiliar stance, I proposed this alternative to both schools. Lo and behold, they readily agreed.

Thus, it was time to begin packing away our memories of Madison and planning the move to Massachusetts. A pivotal chapter of my life was drawing to a close, and, like the approach of the final pages of a book, I did not want it to end even though I anticipated an equally engaging sequel. Yet I knew it was time to embrace the journey, and this next phase of life as Dr. Vavrus.

*****

Once at Harvard, I began refining the research project as I learned more about demography, longitudinal studies, and survey design. The study would now involve students in their final two years of primary schooling—Standards 6 and 7—at four of the eleven primary schools in Old Moshi, and a parent or guardian for each student (see Figure 6). The first round of data collection would start in July 2000, and I would return to Tanzania in 2001 and 2002 to see who among the primary school students actually started secondary school. Six years later, in

2006, there would be a second round of extensive data collection comparing the lives of youth who had gone straight through secondary school and those who had followed other paths during these critical years from childhood to young adulthood.

Not only did Mr. Mweka, my good friend and colleague from Njema, help with the selection of the four schools, but he also offered to be the local project coordinator to help with logistics, data collection, and data interpretation. He assembled a very dedicated research team of local teachers rather than professional enumerators from the university. He sensed that the intimacy of some of the questions on the household survey, such as the number and causes of death in a household, might be more sensitively posed by Old Moshi residents themselves. Finally, after many months of planning in Moshi and Massachusetts, I felt ready to launch the longitudinal project.

As the departure date for my month in Tanzania drew nearer, however, I became increasingly nervous about leaving Oscar and Gus. This would be the first time we had been apart for more than a couple of nights, and I felt unexpectedly worried about their care in my absence. I awoke several times from frightening dreams about Oscar being in an accident on his tricycle or Gus disappearing in the big city without a trace. Of course, parents leave their children for much longer periods all the time, and in many cases, such as military service and incarceration, they have no choice over such separations. This departure was fully under my control, but it also felt compulsory if I were to reach my professional goal of job security as a tenured professor.

Whenever periods of worry or despair arose in my youth, my wise mother counseled action and not stasis. Therefore, I decided to engage in an ambitious art project to keep me busy, making a calendar for the boys with a different activity for each day I would be gone. After they went to bed each night, I would pull out my large piece of poster board, marking pens, scissors, and glue stick and go to work. With Tim's tacit approval to help in implementing these plans, I marked days when they would go to Emack and Bolio's ice-cream parlor and others when they would take the dollar tucked under the flap on the calendar and buy a piece of candy from the drugstore on Boylston Street. It was quite a project that kept me ridiculously consumed when I should have been reviewing my Swahili grammar books and revising the training manual for the research team in Old Moshi. Instead, I was coloring and gluing and purchasing gifts in an effort to reassure myself that Oscar and Gus would not forget me over the course of my thirty-day absence, or resent me for leaving them.

Once in Tanzania, the calendar project faded from my mind because the pace of research activities was so intense that it allowed almost no time to fret about the boys. There were also many former neighbors in Old Moshi to visit after nearly four years away, and they wanted news and pictures of the family. In addition, Amina and I had not seen each other since December 1996, and we tried to spend as much time together as we could. She was in her final year of O-level coursework at Njema and had to study hard in preparation for the Form 4 exam at the end of the year. As my mother would have predicted, the frenetic pace of the trip kept sadness and concerns about Gus and Oscar at bay.

When I returned to Boston in July—just in time to start packing for our move to New York City—the boys could not have been happier to reunite with their mother. There were none of the "Why did you leave us?" questions I had feared. Instead, Oscar and Gus seemed thoroughly excited about the adventures they had had with "Pop and Gee," as they called their paternal grandparents who had come to Boston to help in my absence. My uncertainties about this separation were completely unfounded, as I had realized intellectually from the start. Nevertheless, I had felt them intensely and had newfound empathy for students and colleagues who struggled as parents to decide whether to act upon professional opportunities when it would mean extended separation from their children.

Fortunately, this experience showed me that I could return to Tanzania during the next few years even though I carefully restricted the weeks away to avoid unnecessary absences. I did so in the summers of 2001, 2002, and 2003 to work on the longitudinal study and to teach a study abroad course (see Chapter 7). In 2004, our family spent a summer in Old Moshi so that I could work on an AIDS-related project (see Chapter 8). By 2006, when the boys were eleven and eight, we were ready to spend an entire school year in the country so that Gus and Oscar could experience a different way of life while I started a new line of research on comparative pedagogy and teacher education (see Chapters 10 and 11). Owing to forethought and good fortune, I have returned to Tanzania every year thereafter—for research, teaching, and friendship.

Part Four

AIDS and the Ordinariness of Crisis

Schooling, Sponsorship, and Social Contingency

The buzzing of Amina's cell phone so early in the morning startled her from a deep slumber, and she fumbled around in her bed trying to find it somewhere beneath her sheets. "*Eh, jamani, iko wapi?*" she muttered to herself, asking where it had gone as she dug her hand between the foam mattress and wooden bed frame, eventually pulling out her little Black Nokia. Still a novelty in 2003, Amina did not like to be far from her phone in case a friend from her Form 6 class had sent her a text message. She had finished her A-level studies only a few weeks before, and her close-knit classmates from the girls' boarding school she had attended stayed in near-constant communication through the inexpensive mode of texting. For now, she was helping me with a study abroad trip for ten graduate students from Columbia University's Teachers College, where I was in my third year as an assistant professor. I had known Amina for seven years by this point, first as our neighbor in Old Moshi and now as my fictive younger sister and *profesa msaidizi*, the professor's assistant.

Lying in our twin beds at the YMCA in Moshi, I had awoken much earlier when the roosters started crowing outside our window and the smell of bacon and toast began to waft in from the kitchen below. Amina may have thought I was still sleeping because she tried to muffle the call with her nightgown. She quietly whispered into the phone "*Shikamoo,*" a greeting indicating she was speaking to someone older than herself. After listening for a minute or so, she followed with a series of fact-finding questions: "When did it happen?" "Who was with him?" "What time will you arrive?"

In an attempt to give Amina some privacy in our small, spartan room, I climbed out from underneath my mosquito net and went down the hallway to shower in the communal bathroom. When I returned, Amina was off the phone and sitting solemnly on her bed.

"*Shikamoo, Dada*," she called out to her "older sister" as she had done each morning during the past three summers we had spent together.

"*Marahaba*, Amina," I replied, using the term an older person always gives in response to *Shikamoo*. "How are you this morning?" Under normal circumstances, this back-and-forth with our greetings would have continued for several minutes as custom dictates, but this was clearly not a typical morning.

"I'm fine," Amina replied, asking no further questions about how I had slept or my plans for the morning. After a brief pause, she stated matter-of-factly, "*Dada*, my father has died. He passed away last night."

"Oh my, I'm so sorry, Amina," I cried, sitting down next to her on her bed.

Before I could think of anything more comforting to say, Amina blurted out: "Don't be sad! I said my goodbyes to him when I went home a few weeks ago. He was so sick that he could barely sit up in bed. Oh, I can still see those red marks covering both of his arms, and he had lost so much weight. Seeing him like that truly made me cry. But *Dada*, I'm not sad now. I can never forget that he killed my mother, and I loved her so much. Remember, he was the one who gave her AIDS."[1]

*****

Overnight, Amina had become an AIDS orphan. Her mother had died several years earlier when she was a student at Njema Secondary School, a traumatic event that still left her unsettled. With the death of her father, she joined the 1.1 million youth in the country who, by the mid-2000s, had become orphans due to the disease (UNICEF 2006).

HIV/AIDS was first identified in Tanzania in 1983, and by 1995 the country had reported the most cases to the World Health Organization of any African country. At the time of my fieldwork in 1996, the adult prevalence rate was around 9.4 percent, well above the average of 7.4 percent for sub-Saharan Africa as a whole (Setel 1999). The epidemic reached its peak in 1999 with approximately 16 percent of the adult population infected, including Amina's parents (U.S. Census Bureau 2008). However, it was youth, especially young women, who were facing the brunt of the health crisis, with fifteen- to twenty-four-year-olds accounting for 60 percent of new HIV infections (UNICEF 2000). Life expectancy fell from fifty-one to forty-three years from the mid-1980s to 2003 (World Health Organization 2004).

Today, the prevalence rate for adults stands at 4.6 percent, a dramatic decline since the late 1990s; 24,000 people died of the disease in 2018, compared to well over 100,00 per year in previous decades; and about 1.6 million people are currently infected with HIV (UNAIDS 2018). Despite this progress in curbing the mortality rate, HIV/AIDS continues to place a heavy burden on families, particularly on children when a critical adult in their lives falls ill and passes away. For young adults like Amina, they have no surviving parent to turn to for support as they strive to continue in school, open small businesses, and start their own families.

This chapter and the one that follows highlight the experiences of youth and their families in Old Moshi to show how the uncertainty introduced into their lives by AIDS is part of a much wider landscape of precarity formed by the stratification of social, economic, and biomedical crises. Berlant's (2011) notion of "crisis ordinariness," discussed below, serves as a useful apparatus with which to explore this landscape. Equally important is the recognition that youth actively navigate this terrain in a "quest for certainty," as Dewey put it (1929), often by developing and expanding connections with relatives or fictive kin whose support might allow them to gain employment or continue in school. Whyte and Siu (2015), in their research on people's responses to HIV/AIDS in Uganda, explained how "social contingencies" serve as a kind of buffer against the most extreme hardships for individuals and their families (see also Bledsoe 2002; Johnson-Hanks 2006). They contended that "to be contingent is to be related: to people, institutions, happenings, circumstances" (19). As we see in this chapter and Chapter 12, some of the most important relationships youth seek to cultivate are with *wafadhili*—sponsors—whose presence in young peoples' lives grants them a degree of certainty regarding schooling, but whose untimely death often leads to the abrupt cessation of formal education.

*****

I did not set out to study HIV/AIDS when I began my doctoral research in 1996 on schooling and fertility decline. However, I gradually became aware of the growing health crisis in the Kilimanjaro Region. During interviews, students would occasionally mention *ugonjwa huo* ("that disease"), and once or twice a neighbor in Old Moshi confided that someone had died of *UKIMWI*—AIDS— knowing the cause of death would be identified as a less stigmatizing disease (see also Setel 1999). There were also the occasional visits to Njema by AIDS educators during my year at the school, but in teaching the so-called "ABC" approach to sex education, these educators only discussed the A (abstinence) and B (be faithful) part, not the C (condoms). In these ways, AIDS hovered around the edges of my research, but I tried to remain focused on girls' views of pregnancy and marriage rather than on *UKIMWI*.

Over time, the impact of AIDS on life in Old Moshi, and especially on opportunities for schooling, became more evident to me. The death of Amina's mother in 1999 and its effect on her studies clued me in to the ways that the loss of a family member might lead to the termination of formal education. And when Mr. Mweka, my friend, colleague at Njema, and future research collaborator, lost his sister to AIDS, he decided to adopt her daughter and raised her as one of his own. Over the years, I witnessed the financial hardship he and his wife faced to feed, clothe, and send another child to school despite their evident love for her.

My observation of, and participation in, Amina and Mr. Mweka's lives have helped me to understand that AIDS is rarely the only misfortune faced by Tanzanian families. It is, in fact, one crisis among many, especially for young people like Amina whose economic circumstances are already highly precarious. As discussed in Chapter 4, HIV/AIDS arrived in the country at a time of sharp economic decline across the African continent, a situation that was made worse by "cost sharing" policies in the education and health sectors (Turshen 1999). The effects of these policies on the lives of Tanzanian youth were particularly pronounced. As one researcher studying AIDS in Kilimanjaro noted: "For young people, this alignment of structural forces proved to be a fatal and paradoxical bit of serendipity. At the moment environmental conditions for youth had reached their worst and many became enrolled in ... informal sector activities, HIV arrived" (Setel 1999: 147).

These aggregated crises, I contend, belie the view that success in school depends solely on learning the prescribed content and developing certain dispositions, in Tanzania or elsewhere. The stories in this chapter make clear that many bright students cannot get into O- or A-level programs in the first place or cannot stay there until the national examinations because the person paying for their education becomes ill or passes away. Without other social contingencies, neither intelligence nor grit alone is sufficient to succeed in school.

Rather than treating HIV/AIDS and schooling as two distinct domains, I want to consider how their conjuncture intensifies extant conditions of uncertainty. Despite the terrible pain of losing a loved one to the disease, AIDS is not the only source of anguish and anxiety afflicting poor and middle-income families. Likewise, failing the national exam or losing one's school sponsor is often one more difficulty among many that Tanzanian youth face. I argue that AIDS can better be understood in terms of "crisis ordinariness," a useful way of conceptualizing the imbricated conditions in which many young people find themselves. As Berlant explained:

> A traumatic event is simply an event that has the capacity to induce trauma. My claim is that most such happenings that force people to adapt to an unfolding change are better described by a notion of systemic crisis or "crisis ordinariness" … Crisis is not exceptional to history or consciousness but a process embedded in the ordinary that unfolds in stories about navigating what's overwhelming … The extraordinary always turns out to be an amplification of something in the works, a labile boundary at best, not a slammed-door departure. In the impasse induced by crisis, being treads water; mainly, it does not drown.
>
> (2011: 10)

As we shall see, most youth have, indeed, learned to keep themselves afloat on very choppy seas amid the psychological and material upheaval of the AIDS epidemic. They have been buoyed by a number of forces, including their faith in God, but most notably by the family members and fictive kin with whom they have established "creative collaborations" and in whom they have made a "broad and deep investment in social relations" (Cooper and Pratten 2015: 3).

*****

It was July 2001, and five former students from Njema were seated comfortably around the coffee table, sodas and cookies in hand, as Amina and I explained the purpose of the focus group discussion. We were gathered in the well-worn living room of a house that sat next to the school and was used by visiting teachers from the UK and the United States. Mr. Mweka had arranged for us to stay there for the two weeks when we had scheduled focus groups with youth who, in 1996, were attending Njema or Safi, a nearby secondary school. Now, five years later, I wanted to talk with some of them to explore how these former secondary school students' lives had changed from 1996 to 2001, a period when most of them had left school without graduating while others had matriculated to A-level programs or, in a few cases, to the university (Vavrus 2003).

In 1996, I had asked students at both schools to give me their addresses if they were willing to continue in the research project, and nearly all 225 of them had agreed to do so (see Appendix A). Thus, when I returned to Tanzania in 2000, I sent these former students a letter summarizing the findings of the 1996 research, inviting them to complete a short questionnaire, and asking them to write an essay about the most important changes in their lives during the past four years. It was, to my knowledge, the first mail-in questionnaire of its type in Tanzania, and I was pleasantly surprised that 125 people, which was more than half of those who received the letter, actually responded. This response rate likely reflected the fact that I knew many of these youth or was known to them, an advantage of long-term engagement with the community where one conducts research. However, as I explain below, this familiarity with one another also opened the door for requests from some youth for financial assistance, which may have also been a reason some responded to the questionnaire.

"Thank you very much for coming this afternoon," I began, glancing at my notes because my Swahili was still rather rusty after returning to the country only a few days before. "I have asked you here today because you wrote very interesting essays last year when I sent you the questionnaire about your lives since 1996. Amina and I would like to have a discussion about some of the themes that came up in many of the essays that were mailed back to me, and one of them is AIDS."

Amina jumped in at this point to restate my point more eloquently and to make sure the three men and two women gathered around the table did not think I wanted them to disclose their HIV status. "What Prof. (Professor) means," using my new moniker, "is that she wants to know what you think about AIDS education. In the questionnaires, most men said they were sexually active but only about half said they used condoms, and only about twelve percent of women said their partners used condoms at all. Why do you think this is so? Do young people need more AIDS education or a different kind of AIDS education?"

As soon as Amina finished her question, the youth at the table jumped in to respond. James, who started us off, worked for a Christian nongovernmental organization (NGO) involved with AIDS education in East Africa. He had traveled widely in Tanzania, Kenya, and Uganda as a youth educator but had grown dismayed by the poor responses from youth to the NGO's safe sex message even though it reinforced the government's own AIDS education campaign.

"When they hear on the radio or see in a magazine that AIDS kills so use family planning to protect yourself, it's like talking to people who are deaf," James explained. He became more animated as he described the meetings he had had recently with students at secondary schools in Kilimanjaro.

"At one of these schools, a girl told me that she was more afraid of getting pregnant than getting AIDS. 'If I get pregnant, I will have a problem because I will have a child who has no father,' she retorted. Or the boys are worried about getting a girl pregnant while they are still dependent on their parents. So I asked them about AIDS, and they said, 'Oh, it's like an accident at work.'"[2]

Another Njema graduate, Mary, jumped in: "Yes, they say they will die later." She then added her views on the reasons why some girls are especially vulnerable to AIDS: "A big thing that causes people to get AIDS in Tanzania is prostitution. If you ask them why, they will say that they don't like it but they do this to get money. So this decision isn't bad," Mary stated with sympathy, "because they do it to get out of poverty."

Nodding in agreement, Amina and I encouraged others to comment until everyone had had a chance to give an opinion. "Well, maybe we should share with Prof. some of the 'AIDS slang' that you hear on the streets," and the former students laughed uncomfortably as they uttered a few crude terms.

"What about this one I heard a few days ago?" As Amina started to speak, the others joined in to indicate they had heard this expression, too. "**Ache Iniuwe Dogodogo Siache**," they called out in unison and then broke up laughing, leaving me to try and figure out the connotation of this expression. James, recognizing the look of confusion on my face, offered an explanation: "Prof., I guess in English you would say something like, 'Leave AIDS to kill me, but I won't leave my young lover!' So you see, it's not like we don't know how to prevent AIDS. People know it! It's just that they have a lot of other problems in their lives, and *tamaa* (desire) makes them feel a little bit better."[3]

*****

These "other problems" in youth's lives turned out to be prominent themes in the essays the former Njema and Safi students wrote about changes in their lives since 1996. Many of the essays began like a letter, with warm greetings to Gus and Tim followed by a statement of appreciation for inviting them to continue with the research project. They then typically noted something positive that had occurred in their lives, such as getting married, having a child, or being accepted to a training program or to college. A few ended at this point, but most of the essays continued for several more paragraphs describing or simply listing the painful events that had unfolded during the past few years. It was here that death and its consequences for their lives became clear.

In some cases, the former students noted their sadness at the death of someone who was not a member of their family. For instance, several mentioned the death of the former president Julius Nyerere in 1999, and others recalled the mountain-climbing accident that had killed an American teacher who taught at Njema after my family and I had departed. A few former Njema students described in agonizing detail a tragic fatality at the school when a Form 3 student was accidentally kicked in the stomach by an older student while playing soccer. The younger student was taken to the hospital but died nonetheless in the intensive care unit. And one of my former Form 2 students, Emmanuel, brought back memories of the incident described in Chapter 4 when Albert, his classmate, died from an asthma attack:

> *I would like to tell you a very sad and moving event that has happened to me in my life. It's about the death of my most beloved friend, Albert, who was among the students you taught and who died in 1996. He was my dearest friend because we were so close to each other: We lived in the same dormitory; we actually shared the same bunk bed. He slept in the lower bed and I slept on the top one. That is why I felt so sad when he died. Asthma is a disease that attacks the lungs and chest cavity ... Until this day, I grieve the death of my beloved friend. I don't think I have much more than this. I only hope I will get a positive response from you so that we may stay in touch.*

Yet it was the descriptions of family members' deaths, and the frequency of them, which stayed with me long after data analysis was completed. The deaths of grandparents had an impact on many former students, an issue I address in the next chapter. Reginald, for instance, called his grandfather's death "a sorrowful event," and he continued by noting that he had also lost an aunt and three other close relatives in the past four years. Similarly, Victoria wrote that her grandmother's death in 1999 "really shocked me, and I was so sad to lose her."

In most cases, though, it was the relative paying school fees whose death most affected these youth. For example, Martha had been living with her uncle, and he had promised to help her with school fees until she finished school. Upon his death, she reported that there was no one in her family to pay the rest of her fees so she dropped out of school. In Elibariki's case, it was his aunt's death that most affected his schooling. She had been paying half of his fees and his parents paid the rest, but her death was a "major blow" because "now I continually miss classes because of school fees." And Samuel wrote that his sister's death was the "major experience in my life." He continued:

> *My beloved sister ... suffered from chronic malaria that eventually led to her death. It was my sister who was supporting me financially for my education by working as a tailor and selling clothes, which were her major activities. When she died, I got*

a really big shock. Fortunately, for now, my parents and relatives are struggling to help me pay for my school fees. I am now in Form 6 at Njema.

Due to the stigma of AIDS, I did not expect to see many references to the disease, and, indeed, there were more instances of innuendo than explicit discussions of it. However, a few former students did mention AIDS specifically in their essays, with Frank and Godfrey being two of them. They spoke directly to the pain of death they observed and to the grief they felt as a friend or family member passed away:

> [Frank] *Among the significant events that happened to me since 1996 is the excellent result I got on my Form 4 examination. I got Division I, the only one [at Njema] who got Division I ... I expect to join the University of Dar es Salaam next month, where I'll be studying law. A sad event is that I lost my beloved friend and neighbor this month, July. He wasn't sick for a long time and it's said he was suffering from AIDS. This is proof that a lot of us, Tanzanian youths and African youth in general, will perish if we don't change our sexual habits.*

> [Godfrey] *On November 12, 1998, I lost my uncle who was an OCD [high-ranking police officer] in Dar es Salaam. He started complaining of headaches in June ... My uncle was thus forced to go back home to Moshi so his relatives could help him after his treatment at the hospital, but he became unresponsive. Our family elders held meetings, thinking the cause of his ailment might be family conflicts [meaning a curse might have been put on him by a relative], but there were none. It wasn't until an analysis of his blood was done that it was confirmed he had suffered from AIDS. After that discovery, there was little that could be done except keeping him comfortable until he finally died at 2:00 p.m.*

Although death and AIDS were predominant features of the context in which these young people found themselves in 2000, sponsorship, lack of decent employment, and sexual risk were frequent and interconnected themes in the essays, as they had been in the focus group discussions. For instance, Jeneth wrote about her disappointment when her parents couldn't continue to support her schooling, which necessitated asking her uncle to sponsor her:

> *When I completed Form 4 in 1998, I wasn't lucky enough to be able to continue with further studies, and my parents could not afford to pay for my upper-secondary education [A-level]. I then tried to ask for help among my relatives, most of whom are also poor. Luckily, my uncle volunteered to pay for me for the first stage of my secretarial course. At present, I am in Dar with my uncle ... Life is really tough, and we have no alternative except begging for help from relatives and friends.*

Lightness, who did not complete secondary school, conveyed a similar tone of frustration owing to her exploitation, and possible abuse, working at her cousin's hotel:

> *Six months after being idle at home, my cousin came and took me to work in Arusha, where he had just opened a hotel. I stayed in his hotel, where he hired me for a very low salary. From the meager pay, however, I saved a little money and bought myself a bed and a mattress and rented a room because he really mistreated me while I stayed at his hotel.*

Despite their troubling circumstances, Jeneth's and Lightness's essays also suggest another feature of uncertainty as it was experienced by these youth: It can become a "productive resource" that compels action (Cooper and Pratten 2015: 3). In contrast to the many youth who reported being "idle" after Form 4, these two young women took steps, often painful ones, to change their circumstances. Jeneth begged for assistance from her relations, and Lightness scraped together the money to move into her own place where she felt more secure.

Another form of action on display in some former students' essays was the direct appeal to me for money to support their studies or their younger siblings' education. In terms of social contingency, this is an agentic way by which people engage in a "kind of watchfulness for positive possibility" (Whyte and Siu 2015: 28). Perhaps they had heard that Tim and I were serving as sponsors for some students at Njema and hoped that we would do the same for them. Ahmed's essay exemplified this attentiveness to potential support by way of our relationship: "I would like you to give me whatever help you can. I need that so that I can take a course in mechanics. It is better to have this skill than to remain without it. I also ask you to help me get a better life. I know that it is easier to get a sponsor to help me from that end [the United States] than it is here." Repeatedly, these youths expressed the view that relationships, including with yet unknown sponsors, might play a critical role in making their lives better and more secure.

Although I understood the youth's strategy, these appeals created a dilemma for me because I was clearly privileged relative to them and could have paid school fees for several more students, but I didn't know how to do so in a manner that felt ethical and fair. Should I consider only those youth who asked explicitly for support? Should I restrict funding to young women as they were under-enrolled relative to boys? Who ought to make such decisions in the first place as I no longer lived in Old Moshi and could not claim to know what community members valued? In the end, I worked with Mr. Mweka and a committee of Njema teachers to select female students with financial need and academic potential, and, each year, my family and friends would contribute what they could to this informal fund. There are no easy answers to questions about privilege, obligation, and ethics in long-term research because every context is different. Nevertheless, I have been aided in my deliberations on these matters by several thoughtful accounts of radical collaboration that extend conventional notions of community-engaged research (Nagar 2019).

In addition to sponsors, the other relationship that these youth frequently described as propelling action and granting hope for a better future was the one they had with God. In this largely Christian, and increasingly evangelical, community, the belief that God had a plan for their lives seemed to mitigate disappointment when unanticipated events arose. It also appeared to help youth chart a life course they believed would protect them from sexual "temptations" and HIV/AIDS. The phrase *mpango wa Mungu* was used repeatedly in the essays, which were also sprinkled with thanks to God for good fortune and declarations that God had other designs on one's life when things were not unfolding as intended. The latter was particularly common when someone had failed the national exam, as in Judith's case:

The first event is a personal event. I count this as the major event in my life. The event is that I failed my Form 4 examination. This was a very painful event that saddened me very much because I did not expect to get Division 4. I expected to get Division 3 [the lowest passing score]. By getting Division 4, I determined that God had a different plan for me, and therefore I shouldn't be disappointed for He is Almighty.

Miriam, who had passed Form 4 but had no formal employment in 2000, explained that she was not worried because "I think God has a good purpose for me." She described how she decided to get involved in activities that would keep her on a Christian path:

I think you know how tempting it is for a youth to stay idle. I have tried to join various groups to run away from such temptations. For example, I have joined the choir group and also learned sewing. At present, I sing with the main Lutheran choir in Arusha.

Judith and Miriam's faith in God offered them a sense of hope and possibility that tempered their disappointment about failing the national exam and not having other appealing options at the moment (see also Turner 2015). If God had different plans for their lives, they and other youth reasoned, then the good life, or the better life, they imagined through schooling might not be the only one to which they should aspire. This view may have helped to temper the "cruel optimism" of contemporary life in Tanzania in which secondary and tertiary education is unfeasible for most youth even though they remain deeply attached to it. In an era of AIDS, the cruelty of a young woman's "compromised conditions of possibility" can, indeed, prove "toxic" if one is so deeply attached to the fantasy of schooling that she engages in high-risk sex to pay for it, as some did (Berlant 2011: 24).

*****

It seems as though I have faced some kind of hardship at every stage in my education, as though the devil is trying to keep me from improving my life. So far, though, I've been more clever than him.

—Amina Omari, June 23, 2012

Amina's life story provides another perspective on social contingency, sponsorship, and schooling in the midst of the economic and health crises that confront many Tanzanian youth. In her telling of the tale, it is not so much God's plan that she has followed but rather the devil's she has thwarted—through the relationships she has formed and through her own sagaciousness.

When I met Amina in 1996, she was a skinny, fifteen-year-old house girl working for our neighbor, Mama Eric, who was a primary school teacher at a nearby school. Amina spent her days caring for two-year-old Eric; washing, cooking, and cleaning for him and his mother; tending to a small garden she planted between our two houses; and selling her greens as well as secondhand socks at the market once or twice a week. Amina's beaming smile, keen intellect, and consistently upbeat spirit made her a pleasure to have at our home. She spent many hours on our porch entertaining Eric and Gus, and educating me about the many uncertainties in the lives of girls from very poor families like her own.

As we became more acquainted with each other, I learned that Amina's cheerfulness masked a profound disappointment about schooling that was not uncommon in Tanzania at the time. She had been one of only three students in her Standard 7 class to pass the Primary School Leaving Exam, which should have guaranteed her admission to secondary school. Instead, a wealthy family bribed an education official in her district and "bought" her spot on the roster, effectively ending her chances of attending a government secondary school, and a more expensive private school was out of the question for her impoverished family.

Amina's principal had been notified of the examination results and had shared the good news with her, as he explained to me when I inquired about the story. She, in turn, told her parents, but when Amina went to the district office to get official documentation of the results, her name was no longer on the list of students who had passed. In this era before computers were widely used, hand-written lists of names could be easily altered, especially for children from families where the changes were not likely to be contested. Amina's parents had only finished primary school themselves and had little financial or social capital, which meant they had no well-connected relatives or friends who could help them to press the case. They decided to give up and sought instead to find work for their daughter with one of their relatives.

Eventually, Amina found her way to Mama Eric's tiny, two-bedroom house and a steady, if very low-paying, position earning less than $10 a month for seven days of work each week. Occasionally, Amina would return to her parents' home to attend a wedding or a funeral, but she had no formal agreement with Mama Eric for days off or for time to herself in the evenings. Such ceaseless working arrangements are typical for the house girls I have met over the years, and their young age—often starting when they are ten or eleven years old—coupled with their isolation in many homes, make them particularly susceptible to verbal and sexual abuse (UNICEF 2004).

And yet, in the seven years between 1996 and 2003, Amina had transformed herself from a house girl with a primary school education to a mature, increasingly confident young woman who had completed Form 6 and would soon gain admission to the most prestigious university in the country. Upon graduation, she would rise through the ranks and eventually become the principal of a government secondary school.

How did this transformation come about? Amina had done well in primary school, but it was not due to her intelligence or determination alone that she was able to proceed. Instead, she developed social ties—with Mr. Mweka, with teachers and professors at every stage in her schooling, and with Tim and me. It was serendipity that brought us together in Old Moshi, but it was social contingencies—the cultivation of "interdependencies with others"—which enabled Amina to have a shot at a more stable, secure future denied to thousands of bright youth in the country (Whyte and Siu 2015: 21; for details on barriers to secondary schooling in Tanzania today see Human Rights Watch 2017).

By the end of our year in Old Moshi in 1996, Tim and I had decided to become Amina's sponsors, using some of the remaining funds from my Fulbright fellowship to pay for Amina's tuition at Njema. We both cared about her a great deal and felt a strong friendship emerging between us. The agreement was that Amina would continue to live with Mama Eric because the girls' dormitory had not yet been built, and she would help with some domestic tasks but at a greatly reduced level. So, in January 1997, Amina became a Form 1 student, and she quickly proved herself to be one of the smartest and most ambitious girls in her class.

Despite this strong start in school, Amina began to struggle academically in Form 3 and did not score high enough on the national exam at the end of Form 4 to get selected for a government school for A-level. Thus, we continued to sponsor her at a private school for Forms 5 and 6, a much more expensive option but the only one available given her test scores. Fortunately, Amina rebounded during her two years at this school and was selected to the University of Dar es Salaam to pursue a bachelor's degree in education. Her score on the Form 6 exam fell just below the cut off for a scholarship, which meant our sponsorship continued to the university. After her first year, however, the government changed its scholarship priorities as it desperately needed more secondary school teachers for an ambitious expansion of this sector (see Chapter 10). Thus, Amina's final three years were funded by the state rather than by her sponsors, Tim and me.

As the years went by, this financial relationship with Amina turned into a more familial one as the moniker *Dada* (older sister) suggests. The role of Mr. Mweka in her life also changed, transformed from a teacher at Njema who oversaw Amina's sponsorship funds to a beloved father figure. By 2007, when Amina decided to get married, it was Mr. Mweka and I who met with her future husband and counseled both of them on matrimonial matters as family members typically do. This responsibility changed my relationship with Amina yet again, from older sister to *Mama Mlezi*, an adoptive woman who has raised a child, often by paying her school fees and providing counsel over many years. More recently, in 2017, I stayed with Amina, her husband, and their two young daughters, and the girls referred to me as *Mama Mkubwa*, the term children use to identify their mother's older sister.

*****

Returning to the study abroad trip in 2003, Amina and I would frequently retreat to our room in the evening to reflect on the day's events and prepare for upcoming outings, leaving my students to linger over dinner and beers without their professor to bother them. At the end of a day when we had visited two primary schools with a large number of AIDS orphans, Amina opened up as soon as we sat down on our beds. She began filling in some details about her life that helped me to understand how deeply her mother's death had affected her.

"You know, *Dada*, I've been thinking about those children at the schools today whose parents have died of AIDS. They will probably have no way to continue to secondary school, even if they pass the national exam in Standard 7, and some may not even want to if they can. I never told you, but I came very close to quitting Njema after my mother died."

"You did? But you knew Baba Gus and I would pay for your schooling until you finished, and you were always so determined to get as much education as you could. What happened?"

"You know, I was so happy when you and Baba Gus decided to send me to school because I thought I would just continue to be a house girl, so I was very thankful to God for this opportunity. After I finished Form 2, I proceeded to Form 3 and moved to the girls' dormitory. It was at this time that my mother became ill, but when I went to see her one day she seemed to be getting better, so I didn't believe that she had AIDS as I had suspected. Also, whenever I communicated with my relatives at home, they told me she was doing well, so I continued to stay at school even though I worried about her."

"One night in the dorm—it was a Monday night—I had a vivid dream that my mother had died. In the morning, I talked to my good friend, Edith, about my dream, and Edith reminded me that it was only a dream and I should not worry about it. I put it out of my mind; this was on Monday, so I continued with my studies on Tuesday. On Wednesday at about 10 a.m., one of my brothers came to the school. When I heard he had arrived, I knew he had come because of the death of my mother; I was confident of this so I got my things together to go home. But when I asked my brother why he had come so suddenly, he told me that our uncle had died. I thought, 'Could it be so about my uncle?' When I arrived home, I discovered that our uncle had indeed died, but so too had my mother, in the same week.

After my mother's death, I did not want to go back to school. I stayed at home for three weeks or more and felt that there was no one for whom I was studying. After some time, Miss Mushi [one of the teachers at Njema] called me and encouraged me to return to school. She told me to stop this foolishness and that I was not only studying for my mother's sake but also for my entire family, for you and Baba Gus, and for me. Finally, I realized this was the case and that education was the only way for me to have a life different from my mother's. I didn't want that kind of life: Getting pregnant at 16, having nine children, and being left by the man who gave you AIDS. And now look at my life, Dada, but it could have so easily turned out very differently. I have faced some kind of hardship at every stage in my education. My mother's death from AIDS was only the most recent of them."

*****

The social contingencies that enabled Amina to change her trajectory share similarities with those of other Tanzanian youth I have come to know during the past twenty-five years. When her spot at a government secondary school was taken from her and her parents did not know how to intervene, Amina faced the kind of "compromised conditions of possibility" that often lead young women to engage in high-risk behavior, including unprotected sex, to get the resources they need for further schooling or employment (Berlant 2011: 24). In an era of HIV/AIDS, these good-life fantasies in which further schooling is often implicated can be deadly. It was Amina's relationships with a few strategic others, most centrally with Mr. Mweka and me, that helped to shield her from this potentially lethal possibility. In the case of other youth, it was typically a relative or a stranger connected through formal or informal sponsorship arrangements who helped move forward the young person's plan for further education. When these relational networks were thin or without someone with sufficient financial or social capital, youth's options were far more limited, and they were often left trying to decipher God's plan for them because their own designs had failed.

On the other hand, there were undoubtedly youth in Old Moshi who had sufficient resources and still engaged in high-risk sex, and I have personal knowledge of several students from Njema and one in the longitudinal study where sponsorship still did not result in their successful completion of secondary schooling (see Chapter 12). As Amina's story illustrates, social contingencies that support schooling are still inadequate without agency, without sufficient capacity on the part of a young person to think, plan, and act to effect change in her life. No sponsor or fictive kin can fully safeguard another from the multiple, overlapping crises she may confront; nevertheless, the absence of such support might just prove fatal.

The Burden of Care: Grandparents and the AIDS Crisis

If anthropology has anything to offer the modern world, it is the insistence that the effort to understand the Other—any Other—is one worth making, even if that understanding can never be achieved with a level of completeness.

—Alma Gottlieb 2004: xvi

I did not set out to write an ethnography of HIV/AIDS as a professor any more than I had planned to study the anthropology of the disease as a doctoral student. Yet when the opportunity arose to spend the summer of 2004 with one of my graduate students investigating AIDS education in Tanzania, I jumped at the chance to work with her and on my own research. The timing was also ideal because Tim and I wanted to explore the possibility of spending a year as a family in Kilimanjaro, and we thought a shorter summer trip would allow us to see how Oscar and Gus, now six and nine years old, respectively, would handle the transition from Manhattan to Moshi.

I further wagered that the boys would provide more than companionship in that their presence might advance my understanding of two "Others" who were becoming particularly important in the longitudinal study I began in 2000: girls and grandparents. The analysis of the data so far showed that female students at the four primary schools in the study generally had stronger literacy and numeracy skills than boys. However, they scored well below their male counterparts on questions about HIV/AIDS and ways to prevent its spread (Vavrus 2006). This lack of basic sexual health knowledge concerned me because it was likely part of the toxic mix that compromised youth's "conditions of possibility" for the future in highly gendered ways (Berlant 2011: 24). I figured Gus and Oscar, though a bit younger than the girls in the study, might become friends with children in this age group and, in so doing, provide me with additional insights into these youth's lives.

In addition, the ongoing analysis of data from the longitudinal study revealed some interesting patterns for youth living with their grandparents. Nearly 20 percent of the former Standard 7 students were doing so, and those who resided with grandparents when their parents had died generally had lower transition rates to secondary school than youth who lived with both parents. However, when both parents were living but the child resided with grandparents, the family generally had above-average household wealth, and the children transitioned to secondary school at higher rates. The quantitative data could not explain these patterns, and I particularly wanted to know more about the grandparents caring for orphaned youth. A summer in Old Moshi with Gus and Oscar, living with Mama Ephraim, a grandmother we knew well, would likely deepen my understanding of grandparents' roles in youths' lives.

The importance of social contingencies—of relationships with "people, institutions, happenings, circumstances"—was no less significant for us as a family than for the former Njema students discussed in the previous chapter whose lives had been affected by HIV/AIDS (Whyte and Siu 2015: 19). For instance, it was Mr. Mweka who arranged for Oscar, Gus, Tim, and me to stay with Mama Ephraim in her guest house. And Amina, who was on mid-year holiday from secondary school, insisted on helping us when we arrived and worked it out to stay with Mama Ephraim and her daughters in the main house for the duration of our visit. Amina assisted us in every way, from watching the boys when Tim and I went to town to helping me interview grandparents, which she continued to do after I returned to the United States. This tremendous assistance strengthened the bonds between us and generated greater reciprocity and equity in our relationship, which might have otherwise been absent if we had served solely as Amina's *wafadhili* (sponsors) without any way for her to reciprocate by supporting us.

This chapter, then, builds on the previous one by delving more deeply into the HIV/AIDS epidemic and its impact on families in Old Moshi. Although I learned over the course of the summer that grandparents were caring for their grandchildren for a variety of reasons, AIDS carried with it additional complications because it often meant that the elderly needed to provide care for their adult children—the parents of the youth in the longitudinal study—along with tending to one or more grandchildren. Through interviews with some of these grandparents, as well as by observing the lives of youth with whom Gus and Oscar interacted that summer, I came to appreciate more fully the systemic nature of crisis, or what Berlant (2011) called "crisis ordinariness," owing to its banality rather than its exceptionalism (10). As Berlant cleverly described it, "Under a regime of crisis ordinariness, life feels truncated—more like doggy paddling than swimming out to the magnificent horizon" (2007: 779). The grandparents I met that summer had adjusted their lives to the uncertainty the disease had brought to their households. They were coping with their additional responsibilities, even if not always so well. And they employed a variety of strategies to deal with these unexpected changes, including soliciting food from their healthy adult children and from NGOs, enlisting grandchildren in domestic labor, and relying on social networks in the community tied to their clan or church.

In most cases, these tactics appeared to work because the social networks for families that extend from the mountain to the rest of the country (and overseas in some cases) are still relatively strong. There is usually someone, or several people, who can send a little more money each month or have another bag of rice delivered to help feed the additional people in the grandparents' home. However, as discussed below, the additional weight on some families whose safety net was already threadbare meant that a few grandparents could not manage the responsibility for all of their grandchildren. Berlant's notion of "slow death," or the "physical wearing out of a population ... that is very nearly a defining condition of their experience and historical existence" (2007: 754), is an apt description of this collective of the poorest grandparent-headed households in this community.

These insights into grandparents' lives were furthered by my close relationship with my own parents and with Tim's, who were nearly fifteen years younger than my mother and father. The co-temporality of Oscar and Gus's grandparents, in their seventies and eighties at the time, with grandparents in Old Moshi helped me to envision in a very personal way the myriad challenges the elderly face in caring for young children (Fabian 2014). Even though our parents were much wealthier than almost any of our Tanzanian neighbors, my parents and in-laws' lives were also socially contingent. They, too, would have needed support from their other adult children and from community institutions to meet their grandsons' physical, emotional, and financial needs. That summer, I looked at the morbidity and mortality associated with HIV/AIDS through different lenses than I had in the past, tinted by my own children's experiences and by the hypothetical circumstances in which my parents and in-laws would have found themselves had something dire happened to Tim and me.

*****

Calamitous thoughts were not on our minds as we readied for the trip to Tanzania. A few months earlier, I had been promoted to associate professor, a very unusual outcome of the three-year review process for an assistant professor and one that indicated a high likelihood of a successful tenure review in two years (see Chapter 9). Therefore, I wanted to start applying for funding for a year-long, post-tenure sabbatical leave, assuming Gus and Oscar fared well during this summer in Old Moshi. If they did not, it still might not have made a difference; Tim and I were determined to find a way to spend time in East Africa as a family, which meant the boys would be coming along.

The preparations for the trip could not have been more exciting for them. We spent the weeks beforehand discussing the merits of each book, ball, and Lego set they wanted to take in their suitcases, packing and repacking to see what would make the cut. They were less thrilled by the many vaccinations the trip required, but they were old enough to understand the purpose and accept the pain as part of the process. On the big day of departure, it was difficult for them to do anything but roll their little carry-on bags up and down the long hallway in our apartment and count down the hours until we would depart for John F. Kennedy Airport. Once on the plane, Oscar and Gus were thrilled by Bluey, the anthropomorphic airplane that adorned the boxes filled with stickers, crayons, and games they received from the friendly KLM flight attendants. The personal television screens on the seats in front of them added to their entertainment options, but it also meant they tried to fight sleep and watch cartoons throughout the fifteen-hour journey.

When our sleepy family landed at the Kilimanjaro airport, we went straight to the Danish language school and training center near Arusha, where we spent the first week studying Swahili and acculturating to Tanzania. The extensive campus was comprised of color-coded buildings, with some set up like dormitories for individuals and others laid out as compact apartments for families completing intensive Swahili courses before starting postings as missionaries or staff with international development agencies. With meals and laundry provided, and entertainment in the form of a troupe of gallivanting monkeys swinging in the treetops, we didn't need to leave the campus and could devote ourselves to language study.

Gus and Oscar's class was taught in a combination of English and Swahili by their delightful teacher, Grace. A middle-aged woman who dressed in vibrant blue and green *kitenge* (waxed-cloth) dresses laced with gold trim around the neckline, Grace exuded dignity and style as she led the boys around the campus, teaching them the proper way to greet older people as they would need to do in Old Moshi. She also took them on daily excursions, such as a visit to the outdoor market where she instructed them on the Swahili names for the different fruits and vegetables grown in northern Tanzania. They were both fascinated and disturbed by the sight of freshly slaughtered cow carcasses hanging from the rafters from which the butchers would chop off chunks of meat for customers with their machetes. It was a far cry from the Apple Tree, the twenty-four-hour grocery and deli across the street from our apartment in Manhattan where even the apples were ensconced in plastic wrap, leaving the trees from which they were picked a distant memory.

While the boys were engaged in these real-world educational experiences, Tim and I were in the classroom reviewing grammar rules with *Mwalimu* (teacher) Ester, a warm but demanding woman with years of experience as a language instructor. There was no caning and no disparaging words in this class as one finds in Tanzanian secondary schools, but *Mwalimu* expected Tim to work especially hard because his Swahili was quite rusty after being away from the country for seven years. With only the two of us in the class, we had to remain attentive during our six hours of instruction each day—no daydreaming, no talking with a neighbor, only conversation practice and vocabulary exercises from morning through the mid afternoon.

By the end of the week, Tim had grown more accustomed to using Swahili again and was anxious to get back to Old Moshi. Oscar and Gus were equally excited to see Mount Kilimanjaro and the house where Gus had lived as a baby. What I had not conveyed in advance to Tim and the boys was a detailed description of our accommodations on the mountain. I knew Tim would revel in this opportunity to rough it a bit, but I was not so sure about our sons.

The previous summer, I had talked with Mama Ephraim about renting her guest house. I had seen how she had laid it out attractively for one person, a former student of mine who was going to stay there for several months, but I could not quite envision it for four individuals. She, however, assured me it could be done, and it was certainly our best option because the house where we had lived previously was unavailable. I could already see that it was going to be a stretch to squeeze our family into this space, but I had learned a lot about my needs when traveling since my experience in 1992 in Dar es Salaam and Chekereni (see Chapter 1). The size of the accommodations mattered far less to me than privacy, cleanliness, and an indoor toilet, all of which Mama Ephraim's place would provide. And although there was no kitchen in the guest house, our rent would include three meals a day prepared at Mama Ephraim's nearby home and delivered to our door.

Another appeal of the guest house was its location vis-à-vis my research project. The house abutted the large field on the Njema campus where students played soccer in the evenings, and Mama Ephraim's front yard served as a community gathering spot because she operated a small shop where sodas and sundries could be purchased from dawn to dusk. In addition, she always had a few young women or men staying with her, often students at Njema, and I hoped to get to know these youth. And, during the school year, Mama Ephraim ran a booming *maandazi* (fried dough akin to a doughnut) and tea business whereby Njema students could purchase food and drink during the morning tea break at 10:30 a.m. to supplement the *uji* (thin breakfast porridge) they were served at dawn.

The opportunities for engaging with youth and others in the community afforded by the guest house were a big plus, and so, too, was its location atop a crest overlooking a vast grove of banana trees. This made for breathtaking views of the undulated mountain ridge stretching far into the distance, which, I admit, led me to romanticize about sitting on the small veranda in the late afternoons, typing up field notes and sipping a warm bottle of Safari, my favorite of the Tanzanian beers. Intoxicated by this imagery, I agreed to rent the guest house for the following summer, letting my initial concerns about its size and condition slip from my mind.

Yet when we arrived as a family in July 2004, it was immediately evident that I had rented a tiny one-bedroom house without a working shower or tub. Mama Ephraim had the two young men who helped her run the *maandazi* business, Steven and Moses, move two twin beds into the living room to create a bedroom of sorts for Oscar and Gus. The only proper bedroom was almost completely filled with the large king-sized bed that Tim and I used, so there was no option for the four of us to sleep in the same room. Even with the boys' beds tightly flanking the walls of the living room, there was only space for a small table and chairs that we used when eating our meals. It was cozy, to say the least, but we grew accustomed to it far faster than I would have anticipated given the size of our spacious apartment in New York where each of the boys had his own bedroom.

Learning to bathe, though, took a bit more adjustment. Each morning, Steven or Moses would carry two five-gallon plastic drums of piping hot water from the main house to our bathroom. Through trial and error, we finally figured out that it worked best if we filled a third drum to the half-way point with the ice-cold water from the spigot and then poured in the hot water to the brim, resulting in several buckets of warm water for the four of us to use to wash ourselves. The boys eventually mastered the art of bathing under these circumstances: They would scoop water from the warm water bucket with a large plastic cup, pour the water over their bodies, and then rub soap on themselves a few steps away from the water buckets lest the soapy mix slip into the drums, resulting in no clean, warm water for rinsing. After being forced to rinse a time or two in icy water after the soap fell into the hot water drum, Oscar and Gus learned how to bathe in a very mindful matter with nary a drop of water wasted. It gave them a very different perspective on the daily lives of children in much of the world, where water cannot be drunk safely unless boiled, where it does not flow freely from the tap, and where it must be carefully conserved if everyone in the family is to clean themselves each day.

*****

We had barely settled into the guesthouse when, on our first morning, Oscar heard the roosters crowing and bounded out the front door even though it was still dark outside. I could hear him closing the door behind himself, and I quickly scrambled to get dressed because I did not want him to go tumbling down into the valley or tripping over a fallen banana tree branch. But by the time I stepped onto the porch, Oscar had a *maandazi* in his mouth and was watching with great interest as Steven gently ladled the fried doughnuts out of the giant vat of cooking oil and onto a wicker mat to dry (see Figure 8).

"*Shikamoo*, Mama Gus," Steven called out cheerfully.

"*Marahaba*, Steven. I see you have a helper," pointing to Oscar who was now counting the *maandazi* laid out in front of him.

"Yes, yes, and he can help me whenever he wants. Don't worry, I'll keep an eye on him."

And so began the bonding of Oscar and Steven. Every morning, Oscar would get up before the rest of us, quietly open the front door, and run outside to "help" Steven as he prepared *maandazi* for the Njema students' tea break. Some mornings, he would be met by Amina, who was often up at the same hour making tea or washing clothes. During our second week, Oscar came running back into the house as we were starting our bathing routine and insisted we come outside to see "the grossest thing," which I knew had to be something scatological as only poop could possibly be of greater interest than a doughnut to a six-year-old. Sure enough, Oscar had been chasing some of Mama Ephraim's chickens as he often did throughout the day, and he had discovered one with a string dangling from

Figure 8 Oscar and Steven making *maandazi*, 2004.

its backside. For days we discussed how the string might have gotten inside the chicken and whether a string could find itself only partially eliminated from the bottom of a little boy, too. At this point, I knew I did not need to worry about Oscar finding entertainment for himself, and between Steven's *maandazi*, Mama Ephraim's chickens, and the afternoon soccer matches with Njema students to which Oscar—and particularly his new soccer ball—were always invited, he stayed very active and cried the day we had to leave Old Moshi to return to New York.

Gus, on the other hand, had very different interests from his brother, and he had no desire to join a soccer game or chase wildfowl through the fields. He did, however, enjoy spending time with Amina, and this included helping her wash clothing every day and hang it up to dry. They would fill buckets with warm water and laundry soap, stir the water with their arms until the soap formed a frothy head at the top of the bucket, and then they would start scrubbing away.

Gus refused to touch Oscar's mud-stained clothes, preferring instead to wash easier garments like his own T-shirts, and he took pride in staying far cleaner than his more rambunctious brother. When Oscar would run outside with his soccer ball in the afternoons to play with the Njema students, Gus would instead grab one of his books and sit in the grass on the edge of the field reading, occasionally looking up when play approached his vicinity. It was in this way that he met Haika, who shared his aversion to sports and love of learning.

*****

Journal Entry: July 30, 2004

For some time, I have been wondering about the family of the very small 14-year old girl who has befriended Gus. Unlike Oscar, who has found many friends through his soccer ball, Gus has remained largely alone, or at least without kids of his own age, for most of our stay. He doesn't seem troubled by this, however, as he comfortably shifts from working on his elaborate plans for his own airline company to visiting Mama Ephraim's daughters in their house.

This little girl, Haika, speaks remarkably good English for a child living in this rural area. The first time I met her, I could hear her giving Gus a Swahili lesson, explaining to him that "mparachichi" means avocado, "machungwa" are oranges, and on and on she went. However, in contrast to most children who speak English as she does, Haika is always rather unkempt and wears tattered clothes, even when she is not playing outside. In a country where sending one's children to an English-medium primary school is a sign of wealth and status, it is incongruous to find a child speaking English so well who is not also wearing clothes that signal the family's status.

I finally learned about Haika's situation during an interview with her grandparents. Her grandfather, Mr. Ringo, told Amina and me that Haika is one of nine young children who live with him, a 72-year old man, and his wife, who is suffering from breast cancer. There are three other adults in the household too, including the wife of his son, who was an engineer but who died of AIDS. This, then, explains the more prosperous days that Haika's family may have had when she started school. The son's wife, Haika's mother, is also sick with the disease as I could tell when we met.

As I looked around their very modest home, I kept asking myself how two elderly people could possibly take in nine young kids. There is, though, a house girl and a young adult son who was holding a baby for most of our visit and who was possibly infected with HIV. I had the same feeling as when Amina and I did the first interview with a grandparent a few weeks ago, namely, a sense of incomprehensible awe, if that is the right word, for these grandparents who are shouldering a huge responsibility. Almost all of them used the word "mzigo," meaning burden, to describe the situation of caring for their grandchildren who are either single- or double-orphans.[1] Yet they also talked about the great love they have for the children, even when they cannot provide for them very well.

*****

Prior to our trip to Tanzania in 2004, I had been reading the literature on child fosterage and child care by extended family members in sub-Saharan Africa because I thought it might help to explain why nearly one in five of the primary school students in the longitudinal study were living with their grandparents (Bledsoe 1990; Kilbride and Kilbride 1990; LeVine et al. 1994; Swadener 2000). I also homed in on studies about African children orphaned by HIV/AIDS given what I had been learning during the past four years about the impact of the disease on older youth as discussed in the previous chapter (Ainsworth and Semali 2000; Deininger, Garcia, and Subbarao 2003; Guest 2001).

In addition, I reviewed the much older anthropological literature on Chagga families that I had first encountered as a doctoral student (Dundas 1924; Gutmann 1926; Raum 1940). I knew from this material, and from my conversations with neighbors in 1993 and 1996, that it was common for grandchildren to be named for their grandparents (as Gus had been for my father) and for them to live together once a child reached adolescence so that the child could help care for his or her older relatives. In Raum's *Chaga Childhood* (1940), one of the most comprehensive of the colonial ethnographies, grandparents held positions of great respect and authority. They performed ceremonies upon the arrival of a grandchild's first tooth; they took care of their granddaughters for three months after "circumcision"; and they provided instruction to youth on everything from inheritance to sexuality (see also Mosha 2000).

Yet I also found these studies—and much more recent ones—frustrating to read because of the striking distance between the authors and the local residents among whom they lived. True, these older texts were written during the colonial era with its very problematic race-based political economy, but the authors resided in Moshi and Old Moshi for years, if not decades. Despite this proximity, it was as though Dundas (1924), a British colonial official; Gutmann (1926), a German missionary; and Raum (1940), an anthropologist, were describing inanimate figures in a museum rather than dynamic, living people. I remained acutely aware of Fabian's critique of anthropological time and Othering as I wrote my own field notes and considered how extensively to rely on colonial or contemporary sources in my own analysis:

> On the one hand, we dogmatically insist that anthropology rests on ethnographic research involving personal, prolonged interaction with the Other. But then we pronounce upon the knowledge gained from such research a discourse which construes the Other in terms of distance, spatial and temporal. The Other's

empirical presence turns into his theoretical absence, a conjuring trick ... to keep the Other outside the Time of anthropology.

(2002: xli)

Fortunately, children have a way of bringing the Other inside their own Time, creating the conditions for co-temporality that often elude the adult social scientist. Through my sons, I could peek into the world that Tanzanian children inhabit from a different vantage point than the one the classroom had afforded me a decade earlier. And as the daughter and daughter-in-law of Gus and Oscar's grandparents, I felt a resonance with the stories of the elderly caring for their grandchildren that I might not have had otherwise.

*****

Haika and Gus spent afternoons sitting outside and talking about stories they had heard or read, with each one helping the other with vocabulary. When Haika didn't know a word in English, Gus provided it and explained its usage; when she deemed a term in their conversation worthy of further explication, Haika would translate it into Swahili and have Gus repeat it a time or two to ensure proper pronunciation. Haika rarely stayed long, but her regular visits seemed to please Gus and provided him with a friend of his own.

Oscar came to know the names of many of the Njema students with whom he played soccer, but there was only one other younger boy who was also included in the afternoon games. William, who was a year or two older than Gus, was the younger sibling of Ester, a young woman in the longitudinal study and a former student at Miti Primary School (see Figure 6). William, like Oscar, was significantly smaller than the young men who came each day to borrow the soccer ball, and he, too, was fast and plucky so earned a spot on the pick-up teams. William was also very aggressive on the field, a trait that may have been there from birth or one that had developed more recently in response to the difficult circumstances in which he, Ester, and their other sibling were being raised by their paternal grandmother.

Like Haika, I first met William through my sons and then made the connection to their older siblings who were part of the research project. This situation provided a valuable context for interpreting the conversations with their grandparents, but this knowledge also made the grandparents' stories more personal and painful because of the comparisons I could not help but make between their grandchildren's lives and the lives of their playmates, my sons.

The interview with William's *bibi* (grandmother) was one of the first that Amina and I conducted, and it opened our eyes to the toll that parental mortality and morbidity took on families. It also shed light on William's aggressive play on the football pitch, or at least this was my interpretation:

> *Yes, I'm the mother who bore Ester's father, and I have many grandchildren who live in Dar es Salaam along with the three who live here with me. Traditionally, grandchildren went to live with their grandparents to help them. But today, grandchildren may stay with their grandparents because their mother may begin some business, and she comes home late at night [indicating prostitution and indirectly referencing her daughter-in-law]. I did not want to see my grandchildren suffering like this, so I took them to stay with me. And when the parents have already died, who will the grandchildren stay with but the grandparents?*
>
> *Ester's parents were infected by HIV/AIDS. Now, her father, my son, is still alive but her mother has already died. Her father is sick and he can't do anything. [She wails] He can't do **anything**! He has been prescribed drugs to give him strength, but there is nothing there, he is just waiting to die [...]*
>
> *It's more difficult today to raise children and grandchildren. The economy is different because we need more money but don't have it. And even when we cultivate our farms, the harvests of the past were much better than today [...] The main problem I face is sending these grandchildren to school, in educating them. How can you bear this burden when you don't have the money? Ester is in secondary school and her two younger siblings are at Miti Primary School. They all depend on me; where can I get enough money to educate all of them?*

Ester and William's grandmother's use of the word *mzigo* (burden), like many other grandparents we interviewed, referred to the financial weight of caring for grandchildren but not in the absence of love. In fact, this *bibi* told Amina and me how much her grandchildren assisted her in tending the garden and with other domestic tasks. They also helped her cope with the impending death of their father, her son, a very upsetting prospect. When we asked how she was managing to pay for her grandchildren's schooling and other expenses given their mother's death and father's illness, Ester and William's grandmother indicated that her other children had good health and good jobs. It was they, she informed us, who took some of the weight off her shoulders for their nieces and nephew. In fact, the family home was in a very good state, indicating that even though this *bibi* was undoubtedly bearing a burden, her social contingencies buffered her from the brunt of her new responsibilities.

The situation was quite different for one of the last grandmothers we interviewed. This *bibi* was also a paternal grandmother of a girl in the longitudinal study, a bright young woman named Aisia who had done well at Bonde Primary School. Aisia had had an interrupted path to secondary schooling because there was, initially, no one who could pay her school fees. However, at the time of our interview, an older sister had taken her in, and Aisia was, in 2004, attending secondary school in Dar es Salaam. We knew from the longitudinal study that Aisia's mother had died, and her father, who had remarried, did not want her to live with his new family. Instead, Aisia had been living until recently with her *bibi* and with her cousin, the daughter of one of this grandmother's other children who had died of AIDS. Aisia's *bibi* was particularly frank in her assessment of the situation for many grandchildren and grandparents in the community, with the issues of child neglect and the "slow death" of the elderly prominent in her comments (Berlant 2011). Yet so, too, were her expressions of the deep connection between many grandparents and grandchildren:

> I am the guardian for my grandchild, Aisia, even though she is now living in Dar es Salaam. I took Aisia away from her parents when she was in Standard 1 because she was facing a lot of problems after her mother died. I have eight other grandchildren, including this one, Sioni [pointing to the girl in the next room], and the grandchildren from my neighbor's home also come and stay with me so that I can have someone to talk to in the evenings.
>
> When I was a child, we lived with my grandparents after my father died. My mother, a widow, grew very tired, so we stayed with my father's parents and helped each other a lot. I stayed with them until I got married, and then my three sisters and one brother left once they started their own families. It's different today, though, because it's very hard for grandparents to take care of grandchildren without sufficient land and with other economic problems. It's even hard without grandchildren because most of us depend on our grown children for [financial] support, and that has become quite uncertain. No one is assisting me in caring for these children because my sons are busy sending their own children to school, and one son does not have permanent employment but his child just finished Standard 7 and wants to go to secondary school. That's the way things are. We no longer have the energy we need, and we use what little energy we do have to tend to our farms.
>
> It's difficult, but I love my grandchildren, and I don't even know why I love them so much. I love them even more than my own children, and I really try to take care of them, better care than their parents provided. Parents don't have the time to laugh with their children, but we grandparents have such a good time, and that is why our grandchildren love us. When I see them happy, laughing, I become

very happy myself. When we wake in the mornings, we take tea together even if we do not have anything else to eat. When Aisia was around, I really enjoyed it. We worked hard together, and we persevered.

"*Bibi*," Amina interjected, "what if the President summoned five grandmothers in this village and asked for ideas to help them take better care of their grandchildren. What would you advise?"

Bibi laughed at the thought of this preposterous situation where a national figure would ask the views of elderly women in Old Moshi, but she answered nonetheless:

There are grandmothers who really enjoy taking care of their grandchildren, but families are not the same. Some have deep pockets and others do not. These [the latter] are the ones who should be helped so that the grandchildren can improve their chances for a good life in the future.

Pausing, and chuckling again, she concluded:

But I really don't know what to say because these grandchildren are brought to us, so what can we do? You cannot refuse to care for them, whether their parents are alive and running around with other women or men, or whether they have already died of that disease.

*****

Without a doubt, AIDS has compounded uncertainty in the lives of many families in Old Moshi and around the world. The lives lost and bodies weakened mean that there are fewer people remaining who have the physical and financial strength to care for the children and youth who seek food, shelter, schooling, and love. The grandparents who are left to care for these children, particularly those with the fewest financial resources and most limited social networks, are "wearing out" under the conditions of "slow death" (Berlant 2007: 754). As Aisia's *bibi* put it, "we no longer have the energy we need." I could see this most starkly in the thin, weathered bodies of some of the grandparents we interviewed in their homes made of wattle and daub, without electricity or piped water. In contrast, grandparents in cement-block houses with these amenities often had a grown child or two in Dar es Salaam or Arusha, or living abroad, sending money back home to support them and any grandchildren for whom they were caring.

The imbrication of the disease with other difficulties of everyday life created a particularly problematic situation for some grandparents, but this does not mean they were passive in the face of the challenges that had befallen them. Calkins

(2016) reminded us of Dewey's pragmatism in her analysis of uncertainty in Sudan, arguing that "when people experience something as problematic, they are already outlining what is problematic and thus are beginning to articulate a path to a solution" (5).

This may have been the case for Haika's grandparents, who were finding it very difficult to cope with the care of so many grandchildren and needed to find a path toward a solution. During the last week of our stay, I expected Haika to come and say goodbye. Gus had told her when we were departing, and we had a book selected for her as a going-away gift. Yet Haika did not appear. Finally, I asked Mama Ephraim about it, and she told me the story she had heard from a neighbor. It appeared that a distant aunt had come to take Haika to live with her, promising Haika's grandparents that she would receive better care under her roof.

"*Mungu akipenda*," Mama Ephraim said with a heavy sigh, God willing.

She and I both knew that the odds of Haika receiving good care and returning to school were slim. It seemed more likely to both of us that Haika would become a house girl in her distant relative's home and not a secondary school student. Yet it was also clear that Haika's grandparents could barely cope with the burden of care for the young and the ailing members of their household. It was a problematic situation, a crisis of care intensified by HIV/AIDS but not defined by the disease alone. Her grandparents were wearing out; they may have seen this path as the best one toward a solution.

*****

I have thought many times over the years about Haika and William and the paths available to them in relation to those open to my sons. Childhoods are unequal, even within the same family, but the impact of AIDS atop acute poverty and gendered patterns of children's domestic labor makes schooling even less likely for some children than might otherwise be the case. Haika was a bright girl, no doubt about it, and had her parents been healthy, she would have had a good chance at secondary school and even college, following a path not so different from Gus's own trajectory. When I inquired about her in later years, no one seemed to know where she was living, suggesting that Mama Ephraim's suspicions were correct.

The uncertainty—financial and psychological—that disease introduces into a family was evident in my conversations with grandparents; for those in the most difficult circumstances, it only accelerated the sense of slow death of this generation (Berlant 2007). In other families, social contingencies enabled grandparents to provide sufficient support for their grandchildren and even for their own ailing children. In Amina's case, as discussed in the previous chapter, her parents' deaths due to AIDS did not affect her ability to pay for schooling because they could not help her even when they were healthy. Instead, it was her relationships with others, most notably our sororal bond, that enabled her to return to school and stay in it even though her parents were no longer alive.

There is another side to my relationship with Amina, though, that reveals one of the dilemmas of inequality that makes coevalness so difficult to establish. The profound difference in our incomes has ruled out absolute equality between us because I will very likely always have more financial resources than her and will be the one offering monetary support when she and her family might need it. Nonetheless, there exists a powerful reciprocity between us as I began to sense strongly in 2003 and 2004, and it has only grown in intensity since then. Her role in my sons' lives as *Dada Amina* granted them insights into ways of living that few American children will ever grasp. Moreover, Amina's careful attention to my wellbeing on every trip and insightful assistance with each of my research projects since 2000 has allowed us to establish mutuality in the same time that lies at the heart of coevalness. It is mutuality, the sharing of profoundly important moments in each other's lives and the giving to the other what we can offer, which has enabled us to work through the dilemmas that inevitably arise in long-term ethnographic research.

Part Five

Policy Arbitrariness

Tripping on the Tenure Track

When we pull out a plum we treat it as evidence of the real order of cause and effect in the world. For this reason it is difficult for the goods of existence to furnish as convincing evidence of the uncertain character of nature as do evils. It is the latter we term accidents, not the former, even when their adventitious character is as certain.

—John Dewey 1929: 45

Tenure, the plum of the professoriate. The certainty of a job for life that almost no other profession affords. It was established to ensure professors the freedom to express controversial views without fear of reprisal from their employer, the university (American Association of University Professors [AAUP] 1940; Besousa et al. 2014). Today, it is a privilege that fewer and fewer US faculty enjoy due, in part, to budget cuts to higher education and to a degree of suspicion, or even resentment, about scholars and scholarship in the conservative political climate in the United States during which I write (Abowitz 2016; Besousa et al. 2014; Blakely 2017; Cramer 2016). In 1970, for example, tenure-track positions in the United States accounted for 75 percent of faculty appointments; some forty years later, roughly the same percentage are nontenured "contingent" faculty who typically do not have nearly the same benefits, salary, or stable working conditions as their tenured colleagues (AAUP 2014b; see also Newfield 2011). Even among tenured professors, salaries are often not commensurate with level of education compared to other professions requiring postgraduate degrees (Hamermesh 2018; Ryan 2012). Nevertheless, the flexibility of the schedule and the security of tenure are a strong pull toward the academy for many scholars who enjoy research and teaching, and I include myself among them.

This chapter takes up the question as to why doctoral students in the United States still aspire to secure a tenure-track position even though the number of these positions has decreased dramatically. It also considers how the lucky few who do obtain such posts struggle with the uncertainty inherent in the tenure review process. I seek to show how aspirations for the security and status of tenure are part and parcel of the cruel optimism of the academy today. In other words, those who strive for tenure find themselves in a "relation of attachment to compromised conditions of possibility" (Berlant 2011: 24). Along with countless others, I attached myself to the "cluster of promises" we make with higher education itself (Berlant 2006: 20). We cling to the belief that our good grades, fellowships, and publications as doctoral students will lead to a tenure-track position and that our devilish diligence thereafter will result in our promotion to tenured professor.

The aspirations that lead to attachment to increasingly unattainable tenured positions are part of what makes academic optimism cruel today. So too, I suggest, is the uncertainty surrounding the attainment of tenure itself for those who do land such positions after graduate school. As a "structure of feeling," the uncertainty of the five or so years leading up to the tenure decision is marked by "a pervasive sense of vulnerability, anxiety, hope, and possibility mediated through the material assemblages that underpin, saturate, and sustain everyday life" (Cooper and Pratten 2015: 1).[1] The material assemblage of the tenure dossier, comprised of letters of recommendation, books, journal articles, teaching reviews, and evidence of community engagement, represents the possibility of a position for life. However, it is also saturated with vulnerability because the magic number of publications, engaged activities, students advised, and courses taught is rarely, if ever, written into the guidelines given to junior faculty. In its place typically lie vague criteria like "academic achievement," "intellectual distinction," and "significant publications" (University of Minnesota 2013). And intensifying these feelings of indeterminacy for pre-tenured faculty is the often conflicting advice dispensed by senior colleagues. Their views may differ widely on issues like the merits of books versus articles, conducting research on domestic or international issues, and the importance of stellar or simply satisfactory teaching evaluations. These preferences are based on the norms of different disciplines and personal predilections rather than any absolute standard; their variability creates a sense of unease among many young faculty about the priorities they should establish during the years before the tenure review.

In short, no matter how determined or persistent a junior faculty member may be, it often feels like it is not enough to satisfy the senior staff or the "greedy institution" itself, and it may not be (Ward and Wolf-Wendel 2012: 41). It is these hierarchical social relations that generate profound feelings of uncertainty during the years preceding the tenure decision. At the same time, it is relationships with kindred colleagues, particularly other junior faculty who are also experiencing these conditions of indeterminacy, which may enable aspiring academics to employ uncertainty more productively, "as a source for imagining the future with the hopes and fears this entails" (Cooper and Pratten 2015: 2).

*****

My experiences as a professor at Teachers College resembled those of many pre-tenure faculty members in the United States, and I had added advantages of an academic family and a cadre of faculty friends to help me navigate the tenure process. Nevertheless, it took an inordinate amount of energy and time to keep up the pace along the tenure track, from the time I started as an assistant professor in 2000 until I was granted tenure in 2006. My sister, Mary, was one of my primary advantages. She had successfully gone through the tenure process a few years before me at the University of Minnesota and offered constant guidance along the way, from how to respond to a "revise and resubmit" request from a journal editor to tips for writing a successful book proposal. Doctoral seminars rarely cover strategies on how to succeed as a professor, so most graduates are left to figure it out on their own without sororal or fraternal advice only a phone call away.

I also had an advantage in the strong and enduring friendship I established with the other junior faculty member in the department, Lesley, who arrived at Teachers College eighteen months after I did. We commiserated with each other when we encountered professional setbacks and attempted to make some sense of the arbitrariness of the administrative decisions that deeply affected our lives. We also established a pattern of reading each other's work and giving copious developmental feedback on it, and we spent considerable time together with our families as the mothers of young children.[2]

Many Friday nights were spent at Lesley's faculty apartment or ours, where boxes of Chinese takeaway provided comfort at the end of a grueling week that often felt more like hazing than professional development. As Lesley's babies and my boys entertained themselves, our spouses, who were not academics, would, for a while, listen with bemusement at our tales of turbulence within our institution. They would then stridently steer the conversation away from the workplace, their assurances that we would both sail through the review process serving as a segue to talk about lighter topics. Although Lesley and I did not want the college to colonize our lives, the ceaselessness of uncertainty on the tenure track meant that we could not so easily suspend our anxieties on the weekends. Our need to discuss these common experiences, even over dinners of dumplings with our families, demonstrated how stubborn social uncertainty can be. It was through our relationship with each other that we sought to allay the precarity of the tenure review process (Bledsoe 2002; Cooper and Pratten 2015).

These critical relationships with Mary and Lesley helped me to cope with the unforeseen challenges of life on the tenure track, which felt particularly acute owing to my aspirations to emulate the faculty life I had observed in my youth. My expectations were profoundly influenced by my father's career as a professor, who taught in the foreign languages department at Purdue University from 1960 until his retirement in 1988. As a child, I eagerly anticipated my visits to campus on the days when he, rather than my mother, picked me up early from school for a doctor's appointment and swung by his office before returning home. In the early 1970s, the male professors—and they were the absolute majority—still wore suits and ties, and their pipe smoke emanated from the faculty lounge on the first floor of Stanley Coulter Hall. It permeated the corridors lined with bulletin board covered with alluring posters for study abroad courses in France, Mexico, and the USSR, which may have subtlety influenced my decision to go into the field of comparative education.

Trailing my father into the lounge, my seven-year-old self listened in awe as Professor Vavrus greeted his colleagues in one of the eight languages he spoke, often pouring himself a cup of coffee from the communal pot and sitting down on an overstuffed chair to join conversations about the latest news from Russia on Leonid Brezhnev or on Francisco Franco's dictatorial rule in Spain. If my father needed to pick up a few books or papers from his office, I would skip along behind him, smiling at the students who greeted the professor respectfully, imagining that I, too, might receive such reverence as a professor one day. It appeared to be a life spent leisurely sipping coffee while talking in tongues with friends, doing a bit of teaching, and reading books of interest late into the night. In this era, there was little pressure on faculty, at least in his foreign languages department, to publish as a means of securing tenure; it was simply granted at some point whether one was ever promoted from assistant professor, where my father ended his long career, to associate or full professor. For a child who loved to read and dream about the wider world, the professorial life I saw before me could not have been more enticing.

These memories were etched early and deeply, and they did not give way when the academy began to change dramatically in the 1980s. The neoliberal policies of President Reagan's administration included market-driven demands that trickled down to universities, which began to measure more aggressively faculty research as a means of assessing productivity and performance (Broucker and De Wit 2015; Deem and Behoney 2005; Newfield 2011; Shore 2008). These new forms of institutional governance and managerialism meant that Professor Vavrus, who had devoted his career to stellar teaching and service, was now informed that he would not get promoted or receive much of a raise each year unless he began publishing journal articles and books.

My mother, who earned a very low salary as a part-time ESL teacher in an adult education program, worried a great deal about our family's finances with three children quickly approaching college and little in the bank to fund them. Like many women of her generation, she had supported my father's graduate schooling and had abandoned her own educational aspirations when she became pregnant even though she had been a brilliant student from the time she started school. In my mother's case, pregnancy meant ceasing her doctoral studies in Spanish literature to be a stay-at-home mother for more than a decade until Steve, the youngest in our family, began elementary school. She assisted my father with editing and typing when he did occasionally work on a journal article. Pulling out her manual typewriter, carbon paper sandwiched between onion-skinned sheets, she would work the hard rubber eraser whenever Professor Vavrus changed a word here or there. Yet this attempt at publishing did not last long: My father opted to tighten the family's financial belt rather than succumb to this pressure to publish for the sake of promotion. This resulted in significant marital discord and a single option for college for my siblings and me—Purdue—because it was the only institution our family could afford without taking out loans, a route my Depression-era parents were loath to follow.

Despite this change in my father's attitude toward the academy, it did little to sour my taste for professorial life, nor did it affect my sister or brother's palates. Both of our parents continued to encourage us to "get an education," and as much of one as we could, even though they knew firsthand that publishing had superseded teaching as the primary criterion for advancement at top-tier universities. The academy had certainly changed dramatically, and Mary, Steve, and I knew when we completed our PhDs that the pressure to publish could not be ignored if we hoped to retain faculty positions.

We also knew that there would be no spouses waiting to type our papers and manage the household and children as our mother had done. In my case, Tim certainly shouldered an equal share of the labor in raising our sons and managing our domestic affairs. Nevertheless, this still left me needing to do far more than my father and the male professors of his generation had done. The coffee and conversation with colleagues I recalled from my childhood had given way to lunch in front of my computer every day, hammering out one manuscript after another to submit to a top-tier journal in the hopes that it would lead to a determination of "significant publications" in year six on the tenure track.

*****

The lengthy process of preparing for my tenure review coincided with writing a proposal for a Fulbright fellowship to return to Tanzania with my family during the anticipated sabbatical year that would follow a positive review. During the summer of 2005, I took another group of students from Columbia University to Tanzania, and I visited Badiliko Teacher Training College (TTC), which would serve as my host institution if the Fulbright application were successful. It was inspiring to learn about the active, participatory approach to teacher education guiding the staff at the college, a private, church-affiliated institution at the base of Mount Kilimanjaro that had been established only four years earlier. The principal (akin to president of a college) and other administrators were eager to have a visiting professor who could help with professional development for faculty members, most of whom held bachelor's degrees in their content areas but sought master's and doctoral degrees. Moreover, the college offered a house on the faculty compound on campus where we could live, which greatly appealed to me as I envisioned the rich cultural experience it would provide for Gus and Oscar. Tim was itching to return to Tanzania as well, and the location on the outskirts of Moshi, surrounded by coffee farms and fields of corn and sunflowers, appeared ideal for his long morning runs when he could explore new areas on the mountain. Thus, I worked intently on both the Fulbright application and the detailed personal statement about research, teaching, and service that serves as one of the pillars of the tenure dossier.

My sense of the university as a greedy institution always felt particularly acute between June and August. Most faculty appointments in the United States, including my own, are based on nine-month contracts, not twelve, meaning we're not paid to work in the summer and yet we do. Only Wonder Woman might be able to complete her necessary research and writing during the same nine months when she is teaching, advising students, reading multiple drafts of dissertation chapters, writing grant proposals, and attending a steady stream of meetings. For the rest of us, summer is the primary time we devote to the demands of research and publishing, and it is also the period when faculty with children need and want to be with them.

The attempt to achieve the elusive work–life balance affects parents across professions, but researchers who study this issue have found distinct gender differences between male and female university professors that may make women more likely to succumb to the demands of their institutions. Mary Ann Mason and her colleagues, for instance, ask "do babies matter" in their research on higher education, and their conclusion is they certainly do: "Compared with her childless female counterpart, a woman with a child under six is 21 percent less likely to land a tenure track position. This same mother is 16 percent less likely to get a tenure-track job than is an otherwise comparable father" (Mason, Wolfinger, and Goulden 2013: 28). These findings bear out what female doctoral students have already surmised about life at R1[3] institutions: Less than 30 percent believe a career at such a place would be "family-friendly" compared to 46 percent of male doctoral students (Mason, Goulden, and Frasch 2009). And being on the "mommy track" at a university may mean publishing less than colleagues who are not losing sleep nursing babies during the night or taking sick children to the doctor. Many universities still do not have maternity leave policies, and none, to my knowledge, make allowances in the productivity expectations for tenure to account for the hours spent parenting and/or caring for sick or elderly relatives.

Although Oscar had ceased nursing and Gus was entering kindergarten when I began the race down the tenure track, I rarely felt fully focused on my research and teaching because the demands of parenting are as relentless as those of the profession. The interrupted sleep when one of the boys had an ear infection or a bad dream; the events at their schools that inevitably fell during department meetings; and the boys' class projects that always seemed to be due the same day as a grant proposal or recommendation letter often left me feeling as though I could barely keep up with these demands. During the first few years, in particular, when the boys needed the most care and the pressure to publish was greatest, I often felt like I was treading water, not actually setting my own professional course. Yet I refused to give over more than the occasional Saturday to work, rarely, if ever, going back in the evenings or pulling out the laptop on a Sunday afternoon. While I took pride in pushing back against institutional greed and savored the time with Oscar and Gus, I nonetheless worried a great deal that I was not publishing enough, not securing enough in grant funding, and not agreeing to serve on enough committees to be deemed a good college citizen by my senior colleagues when it came time to vote on tenure.

The phrase "governing of the self" aptly applies to many junior faculty members. It's a term associated with Michel Foucault to mean "the way in which an individual questions his or her own conduct ... so that he or she may be better able to govern it" (Dean 2010: 19). By the time a disciplined doctoral student becomes an assistant professor, it has already become extremely difficult to put limits on the amount of time she spends at work or to cease thinking about research or teaching when she should be off the clock. It's no wonder that relationships start to strain when the focus of conversation around the dinner table turns to Foucault and not the family, or when one partner feels slighted by the time and energy it takes the other to finish a manuscript or fellowship proposal. I hasten to acknowledge that many institutions make similar demands on their employees as do universities, and with no possibility of tenure. That is, I admit the privilege in the promise of tenure even as I recognize that precarity and vulnerability are increasingly central facets of faculty life in the United States and beyond.

*****

If anthropology has saliency for understanding policies as political and administrative processes, the converse is also true. Policies are inherently and unequivocally anthropological phenomena.

—Cris Shore and Susan Wright 1997: 7

After the taxing summer of 2005, I was exhausted but satisfied with what I had accomplished by the time classes resumed in September. I had submitted a strong proposal for a Fulbright research/teaching fellowship that would, if successful, support the continuation of my longitudinal research in Old Moshi and enable the initiation of a research seminar with the Badiliko faculty. In addition, I had completed a solid draft of my personal statement to share with my sister, Lesley, and a few other trusted colleagues at Teachers College for their feedback before submitting it in final form with the rest of the tenure dossier.

The tenure process and the policies governing it vary somewhat by institution, but the core features are quite similar, and all of them involve evaluation of one's work by esteemed others. If ever there were a period in a person's professional life wrought with uncertainty, it is this year in which scores of senior colleagues stand in judgment of the corpus of scholarship one has developed as an assistant professor. It begins at least a year before the final decision will be made by the university's president, provost, or dean, starting with the selection of professors from peer institutions to serve as external reviewers of one's scholarship. Their letters are often considered the linchpin for a positive review. These notable scholars, who are not supposed to know the junior professor very well, if at all, are asked to assess the significance of the person's line of inquiry, the quality of the venues where the work has been published and presented, and whether the professor would likely receive tenure at their institutions.

At Teachers College, eight external reviewer letters were needed, whereas at other institutions five or so might suffice. Four of the names were to be selected from the list of possible reviewers I submitted, and Lesley and I discussed for many months who among the senior scholars in our field might be favorably inclined toward my work. The other four names came from the list the tenured faculty in my department had identified, and these could be people whom they thought would also give a positive review if they wanted to keep me around, or they could be professors known to write critical or, equally damning, very brief review letters. I was not to know the names on the department's list or who was ultimately selected to review; it was a selection process shrouded in secrecy.

While the external reviewers were working on their letters in the early fall of 2005, I was digging through my files to complete the rest of the dossier that would be reviewed by the tenured faculty in my department and the College's powerful Promotion and Tenure Committee (hereafter "the Committee"). Besides the publications in the dossier, the second most important section is the evidence one submits of good teaching and advising. The prioritization of research over teaching may be reversed at undergraduate-focused institutions like liberal arts colleges, but R1 universities, not infrequently, grant tenure to outstanding researchers with less-than-stellar teaching records. However, Teachers College, as the name suggests, demanded a rigorous accounting of one's skills in this area, too. In the era before online course evaluations, I needed to keep the paper course evaluation forms from every course I had taught during the past five years along with the email addresses of the hundreds of students in these classes who would be asked by the department chair to write letters about my teaching.

Unbeknownst to me until the process of compiling my dossier had begun was that I should have also been saving a paper record of every activity listed on my curriculum vitae to prove that I had done this work. I recall spending an entire Saturday morning in my office pulling physical files from my cabinets and opening files on my computer to make a desperate attempt to find some kind of documentation for professional activities that did not, at the time, seem to warrant their own files. I was swearing up a storm when I failed to find my talking points from a workshop for teachers I had held on comparative conceptions of childhood at Oscar's preschool, irrationally convincing myself that a positive tenure review hinged on this single line on my CV.

As my frustration mounted, so too did the sense that such documentation was a form of surveillance, another form of power described by Foucault that is not repressive so much as it is "productive" in that it generates certain kinds of dispositions and ways of being (Dandeker 1994; Hornqvist 2011). In retrospect, my behavior was astounding, produced as it was by sincere belief that tenure might rest on finding evidence of speaking to these preschool teachers. Yet it was a feeling spawned by a sense of being surveilled, a sense that I might inflate my record of accomplishments if I did not have proof of every guest lecture I had given in a colleague's class or every community organization I had spoken to during the past five years.

With each piece of documentation deposited into my tenure file, I could feel myself growing ever more attached to the *need* to receive tenure. This is the cruel optimism of the tenure process because, by clinging to this vision of the good life, I was clearly inhibiting my flourishing, at least in the short run (Berlant 2011). I was spending far too many hours tracking down notes from talks and formatting my CV in just the right way rather than actually carrying out research, preparing better lesson plans, or counseling my advisees.

This striving for success, this effort at pacifying the precarity of the tenure review by abiding by rules and regulations that are continuously in flux, meant that I had, by the end, assembled far more material than necessary. I lugged to the department secretary's office two huge cardboard boxes containing neat, clearly marked files of every journal article I had published, the book I completed, printouts of PowerPoint presentations at conferences, the many applications for funding I had submitted, evaluations for some twenty courses, cards and email printouts with words of praise and appreciation from former students, and anything else I thought would help make the case that I was worthy of tenure. With a supportive smile of solidarity, and a shake of her head at how ludicrous it all was, she showed me where to leave the materials for the tenured faculty to review in advance of the upcoming department meeting, where the first of the two high-stakes votes would occur. The second vote, a few months later, would be with the Committee.

*****

The unanimous vote in favor of tenure by my senior department colleagues buoyed my spirits, and their acclamation boosted my confidence that the rest of the review process would go smoothly. I also learned through back channels that all eight of the external reviewers' letters were stellar with not a single one wavering on their recommendation that I be awarded tenure. In addition, I heard good news from the Fulbright office shortly before the Committee's vote that I had received the fellowship, and I immediately submitted this information to them because of the prestige such external validation carries.

The assurances from colleagues, family, and friends that the Committee vote would also be unanimous mounted in the days before they met, yet there was still something niggling at me. Some call it the imposter syndrome whereby one assumes that she is not worthy of an honor or accolade because she "attributes achievements to external factors" despite evidence to the contrary (Parkman 2016: 51). This is particularly common among professionally accomplished women. As Kate Bahn writes, "What's alarming is that the more education and professional skills women acquire, the less confident we seem to feel" (2014: para 4). In my case, I began to wonder whether my early promotion to associate professor had simply been a fluke, a freak academic accident by the Dean that would soon be recognized and reversed. I also couldn't stop thinking that the positive reviews of my work by senior professors were based on collegiality rather than qualifications, or on my hard work as they knew I would carry my weight, and some of theirs, if I were granted tenure.

The intensity of this self-doubt surprised me given the burst of confidence that had followed the department vote, and I kept it largely to myself lest it seem as though I were seeking praise rather than honest assessment of my work. Tim could not understand my uncertainty because he firmly believed the reviews to date, and the Fulbright award, ensured a positive decision; moreover, he was impatient with academic politics and stood ready for us to move to Tanzania regardless of the outcome of the vote. He eagerly awaited the adventure that lay ahead for our family whether or not I had a position to return to after the year abroad. Therefore, it was Lesley's sympathetic ear that heard me out because she could empathize with my feelings better than anyone else. She had also shared with me concerns about her own tenure review the following year. Nevertheless, she boosted my confidence and encouraged me to start planning for the long-awaited sabbatical in Tanzania.

On the beautiful spring day on which the College's Promotion and Tenure Committee met, I sat in my office trying to concentrate on grading papers while I awaited a call from the Dean about the outcome. The morning dragged on as I stared at the phone on my desk that remained curiously silent long after the Committee should have dispersed. Finally, the call came through, but the Dean's news was nothing I had prepared to hear. I had braced myself for a negative vote, but I was optimistic that it would be a unanimously positive one, as my colleagues had assured me it would be. The Dean was characteristically upbeat, leading me to assume the next words out of her mouth would be affirming. Instead, she informed me there had been a "split vote" among the members of the Committee. For this reason, she said, she needed further information before making a decision. Such committees, it should be noted, are only advisory to a dean or provost at most institutions; a dean can side with the majority or, in unusual cases, overrule the committee's decision and grant or deny tenure regardless of the faculty committee's vote. In my case, the Dean was neither granting nor denying me tenure. Instead, she asked me to write a few paragraphs summarizing my research and its significance. After reviewing this short statement, she told me she would make a final decision.

I was dumbfounded. How could any member of the Committee have gone through those enormous boxes filled with numerous publications, eight positive letters from external reviewers, glowing letters from former students, and a lengthy statement detailing the impact of my research and still not understand what I had been doing for the past five years and why it mattered? Why would the Dean have been persuaded by the hesitation of a few people rather than the affirmation of other committee members, my entire department, and eight external reviewers? How could five years of toil and my family's future boil down to "a few paragraphs"? If I had been in our (college-owned) apartment and not in my office, I would have let out a scream of indignation that would have rattled the windows of buildings across Manhattan. Unfortunately, I did not have that option at the moment. Instead, I calmly replied to the Dean that I would get the explanatory paragraphs to her within the next few days as requested. I then sank into a stupor until tears of frustration began to fall.

Then, as I had done since childhood whenever my confidence began to quake, I called Mary and let my big sister rant and rave on my behalf until I could articulate the anger myself. As a recently tenured professor herself, she knew how precarious the process can be, even at the University of Minnesota where faculty have the right to read every letter of review in their dossiers and write a rebuttal when they believe the assessment is unjust. Mary gave voice to my outrage, but she also wisely suggested that I write the paragraphs as quickly as possible and put this humiliating experience behind me.

Lesley, anxiously awaiting my call about the vote, was equally incensed and similarly astute about the importance of responding quickly and concisely to the Dean's request. Thus, taking a few deep breaths and opening a new document on my computer, I started a list of key terms to describe my research and another summarizing its significance. By the day's end, the paragraphs were done, but I did not send them immediately to the Dean. Recalling advice I had recently read about how to avoid regret for sending hostile email messages, I decided to let the paragraphs sit until morning before hitting the "send" key, giving myself time to reread them in a calmer state and modify the tone if it seemed inappropriate.

However, I could not go straight from office to home because Tim was anticipating a celebration, and the boys, at ages eight and eleven, were far too young to understand my troubled mental state. Rather than turning toward our apartment, I headed in the opposite direction toward Riverside Park, where I often sought solace from the compound demands of parenting and professing. The sight of the Hudson River had the intended calming effect, helping me to recognize that a negative tenure decision would not lead to my demise. We would go to Tanzania regardless of the outcome, where Amina, Mr. Mweka, and other friends would undoubtedly point out that it was *mpango wa Mungu*, God's plan, for things to work out this way. Feeling somewhat better about the day's unexpected events, I wended my way home to share the news with Tim of a contingent tenure decision and to play with boys as though nothing else mattered.

*****

In the light of morning, I looked again at the prescribed paragraphs and decided to remove a few curt adjectives before sending to the Dean. Clicking the critical key, I said a little prayer and hoped for the best. And lo and behold, who should I meet on my way home later that afternoon than our neighbor across the hall, the president of Teachers College, who gave me a hearty congratulations on getting tenure! It seemed that he had already approved the decision, and so, by May 2006, I had received tenure at this prestigious institution (though officially it still had to be approved by the president of Columbia). *Now* there was cause for celebration.

Yet the tumultuous past few days had left me in no mood for celebrating. The uncertainty surrounding the final decision about tenure after so many years of hard work left me soured on higher education with its archaic, secretive conventions, policy arbitrariness, and apparently intentional obfuscation of expectations for junior faculty. My sense of dissatisfaction with the whole damn institution was compounded when I later learned more details about the decision of the Committee. It turned out that there had not been an evenly split vote as I had imagined; rather, there had been one person on the committee who had apparently not reviewed the materials thoroughly or had not understood the theoretical foundation upon which my work rested, and this had been the only person who had voted to deny tenure. The rest of the committee was upset that I was going to be asked to provide additional clarification about the importance of my work when its significance was evident from the reviewers' letters and my publications. It reinforced for me the fragility of the process and the arbitrary nature of institutional policy, or the lack of transparent policy altogether.

With this furtive information, I felt desperate to leave New York and spend a year on sabbatical in Tanzania. I longed to have more time with my family by basing myself at an institution where I could work at a slower pace without any expectations to publish or teach. My only duty per the Fulbright fellowship was to advise my Tanzanian colleagues on their research proposals while I continued with my longitudinal study nearby in Old Moshi. Alas, higher education institutions are greedy the world over, and what I thought would be a quiet year of research and writing turned out to be far more demanding than I had anticipated.

Aspirational Equality and the
Precarity of Policy

We arrived in Moshi on August 1, 2006, and it felt like a deep exhalation after the tumult of the tenure review a few months earlier and the frenzied activity to prepare to leave New York for the year. The apartment had to be readied for the subletters; the boys wanted to visit each of their friends one last time; and I needed to finish preparations for the continuation of the longitudinal research project and for the research seminar I was to lead for faculty at Badiliko Teacher Training College. The pace was incessant until we boarded the plane and, two days later, stepped back onto the red clay soil of Kilimanjaro to begin our year at the college.

After settling into our cozy cottage on the Badiliko campus, it did not take long for us to meet our neighbors in the other houses and duplexes that compromised the faculty compound. There was a British couple who had taught at the college since its inception and took in the four of us, and there was another American, a Peace Corps volunteer, in one of the duplexes. Our other neighbors were Tanzanian lecturers at the college, one with young boys who liked to play soccer with Oscar, and others were single or had families who lived elsewhere in the Kilimanjaro Region. Several of these neighbors became good friends, and three of them worked with me to develop and lead the teacher professional development program discussed in the next chapter.

For the next eleven months, we integrated ourselves into two distinct but occasionally overlapping social spaces: the expatriate community in Moshi and the predominantly Tanzanian community of educators at the college. Although we did not live in Shantytown, the ironic name for the wealthy part of Moshi where most expats from Europe and the United States live, we would take our well-worn Suzuki Escudo down the narrow paths that cut through the cornfields surrounding the college until we met up with Lema Road, the hard-packed dirt thoroughfare that terminated a few yards from the International School, where

Oscar and Gus spent third and sixth grades, respectively. During the dry season, we could make it in fifteen minutes; when it rained, and it was a particularly wet year, I would take the much longer but less treacherous paved road between the college and the school to get the boys to their classes by 7:30 a.m.

Gus and Oscar quickly got to know their classmates from Tanzania, the UK, Germany, and other countries, and they made friendships that endure to the present. With many birthday parties to attend and weekend "hashes"—runs and walks organized mainly by expats—we found ourselves in a very different social world than we had experienced living in Old Moshi, where there might be only one or two other non-Tanzanians for miles around. As the boys established their school routine, Tim found friends with whom to go on long-distance runs. He also worked closely during our initial months with the Peace Corps volunteer, who helped him figure out how to deal with long, frequent power outages and limited internet connectivity that slowed down the completion of his computer programming assignments sent from his workplace in New York.

My days were spent primarily at the college, and I became far more enmeshed in the everyday lives of my colleagues than I had anticipated. My primary responsibility, according to the terms of the Fulbright fellowship, was the continuation of my longitudinal research project in Old Moshi, a forty-minute drive from campus. I had proposed to carry out a second round of surveying with the nearly 300 adults whose children were in the study and to interview about forty of these youth who were now in their late teens and early twenties. The faculty research seminar at Badiliko was supposed to be a secondary responsibility with a session every week or two and individual consultations as needed for lecturers developing proposals for their master's theses or dissertations.

However, this balance of research and teaching reversed course even before classes started owing to staffing shortages at the college. When the administration approached me about teaching the English methods course for students in the two-year diploma program, I had some reservations because it might detract from the research project. At the same time, I was intrigued by what I might learn about the preparation of secondary school teachers after working as one at Njema a decade earlier. Thus, I agreed to teach the twice-a-week course, dusting off my ESL degree and turning from the design of the household survey to the preparation of a scheme of work for the year.

Now that I was spending tea breaks in the staff room and lunches in the dining hall with my colleagues, I began to pick up on a theme I would see emerge a few months later in my interviews with youth in the longitudinal study: aspirations and the ways that policy often thwarted them. A number of the Tanzanians lecturers had studied abroad for their bachelor's or master's degrees, and quite a few had close relationships with foreign friends whose professional lives often served as a benchmark against which they assessed their own. They also compared the college itself to higher education institutions abroad and often expressed their frustration at its limited resources, especially the size of the small library and the absence of reliable internet. They also lamented policies about teaching and supervising pre-service teachers in schools far from Moshi, which they felt prevented them from flourishing as young scholars who needed time to conduct research and get published in international journals (Thomas 2018; see also Chipindi and Vavrus 2018). Their exasperation became palpable when, as discussed below, a national education policy was changed abruptly during the 2006–2007 academic year, which several lecturers held up as further evidence that the country would never reach an "international standard" when poor planning and undemocratic decision-making abounded.

In this chapter, I seek to unpack these poignant assessments through a consideration of the ways that aspirations for equality and a striving for certainty through schooling form a relation of cruel optimism for Tanzanian teachers and teacher educators. Recalling Berlant's definition that this is a "relation of attachment to compromised conditions of possibility" (2011: 24), I contend that *kuhakikisha maisha*, to make life certain, frequently falls short for those most tightly enmeshed in the education system, namely, teachers and teacher educators. This is due to multiple factors, especially inter/national[1] and local institutional policy that undermines their aspirations and leaves them feeling like they have failed (Bartlett, Oliveira, and Ungemah 2018).

The Badiliko students—all aspiring secondary school teachers—and the lecturers themselves were well aware of Tanzania's place in the international economic-education order and the structural challenges they and their nation faced. Nevertheless, many held closely to their aspirations for professional development in the hopes that it would enable them to advance in their careers (see Chapter 11). As the chapter illustrates, this optimism is cruel because these educators, like those in many parts of the global South, face difficulties in their working conditions that are almost unfathomable to their colleagues in the global North and reflect a globally unequal playing field upon which scholars aspire to compete (Chipindi and Vavrus 2018; Thomas 2018; Vavrus and Salema 2013).

*****

Journal Entry: August 23, 2006

*The differences in material conditions are evident all around us, and Gus and
Oscar are far from pleased by this perceived decline in their standard of living.
The dust blowing in their faces when driving in the midday heat along bumpy dirt
roads; the hassles of doing homework while sharing our kerosene lantern whenever
the electricity goes out; and the inconvenience of getting water from the communal
tap inevitably lead to questions about why the Tanzanian government can't pave
more roads, improve the electrical supply, and train more plumbers.*

*Too often, my response to their whining about why Tanzania can't be more like
the US seems like a harsh one: "Get used to it, kids, because this is how most of
the world lives." Yet their laments are also a window into my Tanzanian friends
and colleagues' complaints about their own country. The faculty on campus are
similarly incredulous about the government's stated rationale for the recent round
of power cuts, due, the public was told, to insufficient water for the hydroelectric
dams even though there have been especially heavy rains this year.*

*These complaints strike me as an affirmation of [anthropologist] James
Ferguson's argument that material aspirations among Africans toward sameness
with the global North should not be interpreted as mimicry but rather as resolve
for gaining material equality with the West. He contends that "yearnings for
cultural convergence with an imagined global standard … can mark not simply
mental colonialization or capitulation to cultural imperialism, but an aspiration to
overcome categorical subordination" (2006: 20). In other words, there is a strident
call for "aspirational equality" that anthropologists, myself included, have failed to
hear, maybe because it points to an uncomfortable, enduring hierarchy between the
living standards across much of the North Atlantic and most of Africa. (2006: 22)*

*****

Living and working in the interstices between Tanzania and "the West"
repeatedly reminded me of Ferguson's (2006) argument about the materiality of
"aspirational equality" in contemporary Africa. At no point did I feel this more
acutely than during this year of teaching at Badiliko and in the following eight
years when I continued to work closely with some of these colleagues at the
college. Ferguson employed this concept to make sense of conversations with
people he had come to know through his years of fieldwork in southern Africa.
Reflecting on one such conversation with a man he had met in the 1980s in
Lesotho, Ferguson explained, "The aspiration to a 'European' house, he forced
me to see, was not a matter of blind copying; it was a powerful claim to a chance
for transformed conditions of life—a place-in-the-world, a standard of living,

a 'direction we would like to move in'" (2006: 19). Ferguson went on to argue that anthropologists, and others in development studies, need to recognize more fully that the impulse to regard different "cultures" as equal has not adequately addressed the profound socio-economic inequality acutely recognized by Africans who experience every day "their low global rank in relation to other places" (2006: 186).

My colleagues at Badiliko TTC, especially those who had studied abroad or had friends from Europe, Canada, or the United States, conveyed repeatedly to me that their frustrations with college-level and national policy had to do with the direction they wanted to move in, the transformations in the conditions of their professional lives that would enable greater certainty and security for their families. It was not, as Ferguson explained, a desire to copy policies from the global North and implement them in Tanzania; rather, they wanted more resources, such as more journals and generators on campus, and opportunities for teaching reductions and research leaves as faculty typically have in wealthier countries to help them reach their aspirations as scholars and teachers.

To provide some context, Badiliko had been established five years earlier as a residential, coeducational college offering a two-year diploma in education for Form 6 graduates. It had been elevated from a teachers' college to a university college shortly before we arrived in August 2006, which meant they could now offer a three-year bachelor's degree in education in addition to the two-year diploma. While the diploma program provided the credentials to teach at the O-level—the first four years of the secondary cycle—the degree program qualified graduates to teach at the A-level, the final two years of secondary school. A few years later, Badiliko became a full-fledged university offering bachelor's, master's, and doctoral degrees. Most of the students, who numbered under 100 in 2006 but more than 5,000 today, studied two academic subjects, such as chemistry/biology, English/geography, or physics/mathematics in recognition that Tanzanian secondary school teachers often teach more than one subject.

With the change in my plans to teach the English diploma students, I found myself on campus nearly every day rather than the one or two days a week I had initially envisioned. For the English methods course, I developed lesson plans, teaching materials, and schemes of work for the first- and second-year students. The faculty research seminar met once every two weeks and comprised five Tanzanian and one British staff members. Based on a teacher-researcher model (Zeichner and Liston 1996), we read and discussed current educational research conducted by teachers and teacher educators, prepared research proposals, and presented each staff member's year-long research project at a college-wide symposium at the end of the academic year.

In addition to these activities, I also observed some of my colleagues' classes, interviewed several of them to understand more fully the intricacies of college-level and national education policy, and conducted in-depth interviews with six of the nine second-year English methods students after they graduated. With this immersion in everyday life at Badiliko, my primary focus for the year shifted from the longitudinal research project to an ethnography of this TTC (Vavrus 2009). Nevertheless, with Mr. Mweka's unwavering encouragement and role as the head of the Tanzanian research team, we also completed the household surveys and youth interviews by the time my family and I returned to the United States in June 2007. This change in the direction of my research was only one of several unexpected events that occurred throughout the school year. The most dramatic, though, had little to do with my research and everything to do with the contingencies of inter/national policy.

*****

Journal Entry: October 26, 2006

We are enjoying three days at the beach during the boys' week-long midterm holiday. Peponi, which means "paradise" in Swahili, is a modest resort along the Indian Ocean popular with expats in the northern part of the country. The bandas [small thatch houses] are basic but comfortable, and each has a little porch looking out at the ocean, a comfortable spot for me to write this work-related note before I get distracted by the palm trees and the mesmerizing Black and white-speckled guinea fowl grazing on the grass that forms a pathway from the bandas to the beach.

Right now, I'm missing a staff meeting at Badiliko that was called to discuss how we will cope with the change in policy the government just announced regarding two-year teacher education diploma programs like ours. Students in these programs will now need to be finished by February rather than by May [2007] as we had planned. This means no BTP [Block Teaching Practice, or student teaching] during February-March and a greatly expedited period of instruction and examinations between now and then. The meeting today is intended to sort out how to change the timetable to accommodate this abrupt policy decision. I want to get the details on why this action was taken without any apparent input from teacher training colleges. I assume it is all part of the government's push to get more teachers into secondary schools ASAP, but without advanced planning, it will definitely affect quality.

*****

Why did the teacher education policy in Tanzania change so abruptly in October 2006? The 2006–2007 school year happened to fall during a period of massive expansion of Tanzania's secondary education sector following the establishment of the Secondary Education Development Programme, a World Bank–funded expansion effort launched in 2004 that ran through 2009, with a second iteration 2010 to 2015 (MOEVT 2010). SEDP, as it became known, helped to boost the matriculation rate in Tanzania from around 5 percent—one of the lowest in the world—to around 30 percent today (UNESCO 2018). A huge increase in student enrollment occurred at this very time, from approximately 148,000 secondary school students in Tanzania in 2005 to just over 400,000 by 2007, a mere two years later (International Budget Partnership [IBP] n.d.).

A change of this magnitude does not happen overnight, as though government officials suddenly decided in 2004 that secondary schooling mattered to the nation and its economy. Instead, the decision to dramatically bolster enrollment reflected a pronounced shift in the late 1990s and early 2000s among international development organization, especially the World Bank, toward post-primary schooling (Mulkeen et al. 2007). In 1996, when I began my research at a Tanzanian secondary school, the World Bank was not making any loans for secondary schooling—in Tanzania or elsewhere in Africa—but by 2004, this sector constituted nearly 40 percent of its lending (Secondary Education in Africa Initiative [SEIA] 2007).

One reason for this change of priorities had to do with the way World Bank economists calculated returns on investments in education. Some of the leading figures at the Bank had developed "rates of return" analyses that documented how money invested in primary schooling produced the greatest economic and social benefits to a society (World Bank 1999). By the early 2000s, however, economists were declaring secondary schooling to be a "threshold" for the productive use of direct foreign investment (SEIA 2007: 10; see also Bloom, Canning, and Chan 2006). The same international institution was now arguing that without a secondary education, African youth would not be able to contribute sufficiently to their countries' economic growth because of limitations on "human capital" as those with an education are often known (Schultz 1961). So, with nearly $150 million in loans and grants from the World Bank, Tanzania launched SEDP in 2004, a policy that aimed to transition rapidly more than half the nation's primary school students to the secondary level (Ministry of Education and Culture 2004).

To reach such a bold target, the government quickly began building classrooms to add to existing schools and building schools themselves. The prime minister at the time promised a school in every one of the country's 2,500 or so wards by 2010 (Wedgwood 2005). The country began building like crazy: Nearly 1,000 schools were built between 2003 and 2006 with partial support from the government and in-kind contributions of labor and money from communities (Mafuru 2011). However, much like the half-built "World Bank schools" that residents of Old Moshi had shown me a few years earlier when primary schooling was expanding under a similar policy, many of these new secondary schools were barely schools. Called "ward schools," they often had only two or three rooms in total that served as classrooms and administrative offices. As HakiElimu, the Tanzanian educational rights organization, emphasized in a critical review of the SEDP policy:

> Curiously, recent developments notwithstanding, policy attention and implementation in Tanzania (and many other countries) continue to equate education progress with the erection of school buildings. Buildings are of course important, but teachers matter more. When you cannot have everything and trade-offs need to be made, priority should be given to teachers over buildings. Many will agree that the most important thing in education is the interaction between motivated, competent teachers and their students. Therefore education policy, as well as programs, budgets and political exhortation (including photo-ops) should hone in on this fact.
>
> (Sumra and Rajani 2006: 4)

National education policy did acknowledge that more teachers were needed, but it did so by truncating teacher education to expedite the placement of student teachers into the classroom. Some government colleges implemented "crash programs," one- to nine-month trainings that came to be known as *VodaFasta*, a riff on the Vodacom mobile carrier's quick recharging system. Badiliko, as a private institution that prided itself on its high-quality teacher education program, did not participate in the *VodaFasta* effort. However, the faculty were still forced abruptly to reduce the teacher preparation program by four months to accommodate this change in policy.

The consequences of this truncation reverberated across the curriculum. For one thing, the Badiliko lecturers needed to decide immediately what topics to cut from their schemes of work and what to include in the end-of-term exams that would now be administered in mid-November rather than mid-December. I decided to give my students a short questionnaire asking them to specify the topics they felt were the most important for our remaining month of class. Although I had hoped to see the areas they had struggled with the most, such as how to use active, participatory methods to teach speaking and listening, the results of the survey were consistent: grammar won, hands down. These future English teachers specified on the survey that they wanted to study "grammar pattern [*sic*] particularly concession, inversion" and "how to teach the grammatical structures in form II and those found in form III." When I asked them why grammar when there were many topics we might explore, their views were similar, if not unanimous. They firmly believed the assessment of them as "good teachers" by their students, peers, and school administrators would depend on the scores their students received on regional and national examinations. And because the exams emphasized English language structure, they aspired to become good teachers by learning as much as they could about the proper usage of "although," "despite," and "in spite of" rather than how to build conversational fluency or critical reading skills.

Another consequence of the shortening of the teacher preparation program was the pressure it placed on the faculty and the resentment among some of my Tanzanian colleagues that the college expected more of them without any additional compensation. With the compression of the school year for the second-year students, the faculty quickly had to prepare and mark the exams for the abbreviated first term of the school year while immediately beginning to teach the second term classes before the Christmas holiday. This was done in an effort to complete two short semesters of instruction before students graduated and started their careers as teachers. Although the Badiliko administration had no choice in this policy matter, its enforcement sparked tension during a few staff meetings and complaints shared with me outside the walls of campus.

One notable example I coded in my field notes as "aspirational equality" involved one of the Tanzanian lecturers who had completed a master's degree abroad and sought to share information during a staff meeting about a UNESCO fellowship he thought might be appropriate for his colleagues who were looking for graduate programs themselves. He and another Tanzanian colleague also wanted to discuss news about a Norwegian grant that might support Badiliko lecturers to do research. Although the request to discuss these fellowships and grants seemed innocuous to me, the administration official chairing the meeting responded in a curt tone and told the faculty they would have to wait until the next meeting when the Principal was present. At that point, another Tanzanian colleague who was exceptionally enthusiastic and rarely made waves interrupted to say that it seemed like a "dictatorship" not to allow the discussion of these opportunities for faculty advancement. This appeared to upset the administrator further, who then declared the staff meeting adjourned and left hastily.

On my way back to the faculty compound with the two colleagues who had tried to discuss the Norwegian funding, they expressed great frustration, saying that a person would "go crazy" if they didn't get a break from teaching to do research. They complained that the administration did not support the completion of their advanced degrees by giving them teaching reductions or money to do research, which they knew to be the case in many other countries. On the other hand, neither of my colleagues conceded that a small institution like Badiliko might be struggling with staffing and covering its costs from the modest tuition paid by students. Herein lay the tension between the aspirational equality of individual faculty and the struggle to maintain quality teaching by the college itself.

*****

The condensed academic year for the second-year diploma students meant they took their final exams at the end of January, and many immediately began teaching. Despite the pressure on their time, they readily agreed when I asked to interview them. We met in Moshi or the surrounding communities depending on the schools where they had been placed, and each of them had a great deal to say about their reasons for going into teaching, their experiences at the college, and their views about the future of their profession. Yet the question that sparked the lengthiest responses had to do with the strengths and weaknesses of the Tanzanian education system, and this may have been due to the impact of policy changes on their lives.

One of my former students was Stefano, a quiet but insightful young man whose mother had only finished Standard 4. After primary school, he had attended a technical school to get a certificate in electrical installation before eventually finding a sponsor to cover his expenses through secondary school and Badiliko. Stefano had a job as a high school English teacher awaiting him, but he was troubled by the shortening of the teacher education program and the growth of ward schools with little attention to how these changes affect educational quality:[2]

> What I think is that the Tanzania education system is not consistent. For example, the diploma in education takes two years, but when I joined this college, I completed the first year and was about to complete the second year. Then we received information that we have to shorten the period of staying in the college. So it is a problem for the teachers and the students to finish the syllabus. And also it will affect the schools because what was planned for us to be taught will not be possible

to be covered. So the teacher will have less knowledge, and also implementation of the knowledge they have got in the colleges will have some problems.

And another thing is that education system in Tanzania, it is not forecasted, it is not forecasted. Because there are these teachers' crashing [crash] programs, those who had just completed a Form 6 education. So they are taken to the college for almost one month, and they are sent to the schools to teach. So what I think they got from the college was like introduction about teaching profession. But they don't have any knowledge to teach students. And as you know, many schools are located in the towns. They have enough teachers simply because teachers are pushed, are pushed to the town because there are good social services and they can engage in business activities in order to help them make a living. So the schools which are faced with the problem of teachers are the schools which are located in the rural areas, and there are many, many, many new schools which are established in rural areas, the undeveloped areas [...] And at the same time, at the end of their O-level program, these students are going to be assessed equally, with the same examination. So automatically, the students who are coming from town will pass more than those who are coming from local areas.

And also there are lots of new [ward] schools in Tanzania. So you can find a school, it has just four classrooms or three classrooms—nothing else. So students will enter the classroom, but there is no library there, there is no laboratory there—it is only teachers and students. I think it is not a school. I can say that these schools are like tuition centers. So the government has to look first at the necessary things to be a school before it opens them. For example, there is a secondary school that I was teaching at during my vacation. Almost each and every thing that I had to teach in the class I had to come with there. There were no things in the school, there was nothing in the school [...] Yeah, almost every ward has a school, yeah. But necessary things that are important in schools are not there. Even teachers are not there. So sometimes you may be compelled to teach other subjects than you have knowledge of ... I think it is not professional because there is not a teacher for every subject. So there will be no equality between those students who are facing those problems and those who are learning in good environment or in good schools.

Stefano was not the only student critical of the rapid expansion of the secondary school system without adequate planning for teachers. Anneth, for example, had attended a hastily built government secondary school even before the SEDP policy went into effect, and her schooling was interrupted due to the death of her grandfather because he had been paying her school fees. Even though she managed to pass the A-level exam, her mother claimed that she could not pay for her daughter to attend college, an argument Anneth disputed because she and her mother had a strained relationship. Thus, Anneth sought assistance from her relatives, and a Catholic priest in the family paid for her to do a one-month computer course that led to a job in an office in Moshi. After some time, the priest helped her to apply to Badiliko and get a scholarship from foreign sponsors. At the time of our interview, she had started teaching at a school run by the same sponsoring organization. Anneth told me that she could relate to the students at this school, who were selected due to their status as "vulnerable children," because of the challenges she had faced as a youth:

> *Anneth: We were the first intake of students at the school. We started with ninety students, yeah, but we completed thirty-five only, thirty-five, thirty-five! And within those thirty-five, we were three who were selected to join A-level; two girls and one boy.*

> Fran: Wow, what happened between the ninety and the thirty-five? What happened to those other students?

> *Anneth: There were no books. There were two teachers only—the head of the school and the academic teacher. Those two teachers were the ones who were the teachers of all subjects. So the parents who were able to pay for the private schools or to find a chance for their children somewhere else, they just took it. So some students went to other schools nearby or far away, but thirty-five remained and took seven subjects, only seven subjects we were taught [out of the thirteen in the national curriculum]. We couldn't get physics, never chemistry … You know, when I was doing my O-level, we were very troubled because sometimes you can fail to get tuition [tutoring]. During Saturdays we were supposed to go to school with 500 shillings [about thirty-five US cents at the time]. Every Saturday. But I did not get to go because my grandfather was old, he had no money to pay that tuition fee the whole year […]*
> *Yeah, even in Arusha where I teach, there are schools which have only the head of the school and one teacher who is from crash program, just from crash program. Just two of them.*

Anneth, like Stefano, had ample reasons for opposing the crash program and the building of schools before a sufficient number of teachers had been prepared to teach in them. The Badiliko lecturers, both Tanzanian and expats, were equally cynical about the sudden policy change and the uncertainty it generated. Most attributed the change to government incompetence, citing a long list of other examples when policy fomented rather than dispelled uncertainty. I cannot say I disagreed, especially when I thought back to the 1990s, when students at Njema and schools across the country were sent home on several occasions to collect more school fees because fees were hiked by the government in the middle of the year with no advance warning, affecting both public and private schools.

It was Edmund, one of my second-year diploma students, who provided the most sophisticated explanation for these changes. He often sat quietly during class until he had something insightful to say, whether it was his critique of "spoon feeding" as a teaching method or his challenging of his classmates' views on examinations as the best measure of a person's intelligence. Edmund's father had been a teacher who later got a degree at the University of Dar es Salaam and became a school inspector. He described his father as "a teacher in the heart" who highly valued education, and so, too, did Edmund's mother even though she did not have the opportunity to attend secondary school.

Edmund stood out from his classmates in several respects, from his father's background as a teacher to his decision to get a diploma in education at Badiliko even though he had been admitted to the more prestigious University of Dar es Salaam. His critical eye on education was sharpened even further after he asked to borrow my copy of Paulo Freire's *Pedagogy of the Oppressed* (1970), which he devoured in less than a week. For the rest of the semester, Edmund used Freirean phrases like "the banking model of education" to explain his opposition to rote memorization and to the teacher-centered approach to teaching found in most Tanzanian classrooms. He also expanded upon Freire's analysis of class-based oppression in education to include a critique of postcolonial relations as reflected in the production and dissemination of knowledge around the world.

For these reasons, I looked forward to the opportunity to sit down with Edmund and ask him some of the lingering questions I had from my observations at Badiliko regarding the rationale behind Tanzania's education policies and how they affected practice in secondary schools and TTCs. I began by asking Edmund the same question I had posed to his classmates regarding what he had learned during the diploma program that would be of greatest use to him as teacher. He quickly expanded my query and directed it toward his critique of inter/national relations as they affect the content of schooling in Tanzania and the United States:

> *Edmund: We learned the importance of counseling, the techniques of counseling, and generally the whole procedure, but the procedure is somewhat western, you know.*

> Fran: Sure, I mean, it will be interesting to see how you modify what you have learned here in your real experience. You said it was also kind of western. What does that mean?

> *Edmund: The thing is, there are topics which are very good things, but the problem is if you try to put them in a Tanzanian context or, if I can generalize, into an*

African context, it's not the way that it has been shown there. There are many, many things that you cannot really put into, I can say, into a Tanzanian context and then they fit. Lots, lots of things.

Fran: Can you give me an example of something you think just wouldn't fit here that you've learned about, maybe regarding counseling or something else that you know from experience is going to have to be modified?

Edmund: Yes, in counseling, they want you to go into a room somewhere, away from noise, with a table, a coffee table, maybe two chairs, you know, things like that. And in Africa, when we are counseling, we usually don't go in, yea, we usually talk outside anywhere. And sometimes it's difficult you know, I don't know how I'm going to do this but to me, I've found it not easy. The thing is you don't just go straight and say, "Today we're going to talk about your problem, you've been irresponsibly drinking," and things like that. In our place, we don't say things in Black and white; you put in some green and yellow. You don't just say the thing as it is. It's not our way [...]

I think we can take this as an African problem: After independence we had this colonial education which everybody said was an irrelevant education for us, and some countries tried to change that but many did not. It remained just the same that formal education prepared people for white-collar jobs, and that's the same thing in Tanzania. In the past it was not very difficult when you were in Form 4 or Standard 7, you could get a very good job somewhere. We had few people who had gone to school, and I don't think the administration made efforts to make sure that people get secondary education. Due to this trade liberalization and all, free market and things of that kind, now everybody wants a well-trained person, you know [...] I don't want to only blame colonialism, but I think it's the detrimental effect of the colonial education that people think you go to school to work in a government office. That's the thing.

Fran: And today, now that it's forty-plus years past colonialism and twenty-plus years past Mwalimu Nyerere's retirement, would you say this mentality is as strong as ever or has it decreased or increased?

*Edmund: It is **very, very** strong. In the past it was ... I think Mwalimu was very clever about this. He emphasized primary education but not secondary education. So many people could go to primary schools but not secondary schools. After 1980s now, people wanted to have the degrees and BAs, you know, so now everybody is in school, he's doing anything to get a good job, many things like forging or using other people's certificates. Now people are in school but not doing anything for the sake of education but only to get the job. And there are people who are trained to be this [profession], but you wouldn't find them doing that. They're doing another thing. Our economy is not set up so that if you are trained to become a technician,* *you'd always be that. You can train to become a veterinary officer and, in the end, you end up teaching agriculture in secondary school.*

I don't know, but there are some advantages of specialization. You know, that's why we're having some people doing things that they did not train to do, only doing the job half way, you know, they're not doing it the way it's supposed to be done. Some people would say you employ yourself, but before employing yourself, there must be some conditions that will enable you to employ yourself. You don't just come out of the college and say, "I have this plan. I'm going to employ myself." How? So I think we have put all our efforts in telling people "go to school," but we don't tell them what to do after school. Now we know that more than half of those who finish Standard 7 do not go to secondary schools. What do you do about them? Then you have this few who go to A level. They go to A level; after A level, only a quarter will probably go to university. And after university, what are they going to do after university? It's not known again. So it's this chain: You aspire to go to school; you go to school, but in the end of school there is nothing.

Edmund's comments capture the relation of cruel optimism in Tanzania today: Inter/national education policy during the past fifteen years has led to a dramatic increase in opportunities for O-level schooling, fueling aspirations for youth who would have been shut out of school after Standard 7 in decades past. This, in turn, stimulates attachment to A-level and university education even though there are "compromised conditions of possibility" for the increasing numbers of college graduates to gain employment in the fields for which they were trained (Berlant 2011: 24).

When I asked Edmund to elaborate on the shortage of jobs for college graduates, he argued that trade liberalization policies following the Nyerere years have brought significant foreign investment to the country, especially in mining and other export-oriented sectors. However, he averred that the education system has not changed to develop the kinds of skills—often called "21st century skills" in the international development literature (OECD 2018)—needed for these positions. Thus, Edmund gave examples of employers recruiting Black and white employees from Kenya, South Africa, and Zimbabwe, making it difficult for Tanzanian graduates to find white-collar jobs in the private sector.

Moving to the final question in the interview, I asked Edmund, as I had his classmates, what he most wanted people to understand about secondary and tertiary education in the country and where he wanted attention directed to improve the education system. As he had done throughout our conversation, Edmund answered my question but broadened it well beyond Tanzania to consider global inequalities and the constraints they pose for achieving the equality to which many young Africans aspire:

Edmund: So we're having lots and lots of schools. My young brother went to secondary school from Form 1 to Form 4, but he did not know what a pipette is, what a Bunsen burner is. So there was chemistry and physics and biology, but he never went to a laboratory. So I think we are having this big problem. I don't know whether it is people not being serious about it or whether there isn't enough money. I don't know why.

And again, the curriculum and the content of our education, my problem again. I don't know where this curriculum came from, and I studied and I know that the curriculum, its views and ideas, should come from the Ministry of Education, from the Tanzania Institute of Education, from NECTA [the National Examinations Council of Tanzania], from parents, from learners, from teachers, the philosophy of the nation, the psychology of learning, and all these things. But I know and I'm very sure that the needs of the learners, the ideas of the parents, the ideas of the teachers, are not included when preparing for curriculum [...]

And that's a big problem because there are these historical problems, I mean, for instance, language. In Tanzania, I am glad I was born in town, but a Pogoro [an ethnic group in south-central Tanzania], maybe when he or she is born, he will first learn Pogoro and then Kiswahili at school, primary school, and at secondary school she or he will have to speak English. Now, the problem, it's a very, very big problem, because now you are having to transform your knowledge of Pogoro into Kiswahili and then into English. So it's very difficult, and you are switching from five vowels into 20, and lots and lots of other things in the English language. And you will only speak English in the classroom. You go out, Kiswahili; in the classroom, English. So you will find pupils cramming how to write "crust" while they don't know even the meaning.

Most of the content in our education system is not Tanzanian by nature. It's from somewhere else and imported to us. I just want to give this example. I'm diabetic and went to KCMC, and I was given this leaflet about what's right to eat. One of the things that they wrote is oatsmeal [sic]. Oh my goodness! I've never eaten oatsmeal, and I don't know where to find oatsmeal. So I think it's like this doctor just read from a book by an American, and what she did was just translating from English to Kiswahili without even thinking that this oatsmeal for Tanzanians cannot be found. So I think now that's the big problem: People go to the library, read books about the Americans who have done the research, the Britons and everything, and you know what they did? They transformed that from America, they bring it here. They change the names, they change the pictures, instead of really going into the field and trying to see what people understand about things. Because I think if you are really going to ask people themselves what they think, they're going to give you very, very good answers. Now let's go back: People really want to sit in their offices; they don't want to go into the field and know in the reality how is this thing being perceived by the people out there.

What we are studying here, I can say it's, um, I don't know if it's going to be an exaggeration, it's like a global [social] class kind of thing. I studied in my geography about everything from the Corn Belt in America to the Rhine River in Germany to rice producing in Burma to rubber plantations in Malaysia, almost everything. And then I was reading one day that there were people in America who could not find Iraq on a map, so I don't know, I've tried to picture it in my mind and see how they are teaching and still cannot find Iraq on the map while I know all the states that are in the Corn Belt in America. Because we even study about TVA, Tennessee Valley Authority!

Fran: So, would you say this is a strength of the Tanzanian system?

Edmund: No, I don't want to call it a strength. I said I don't know how to call it. I don't know if it's strength or it's just a big load, I don't know. That we learn everything about this world, almost, almost everything. Even our History Paper 2 [exam] is mostly about Europe; it's about World War Two; it's about Germany; it's about the rise of imperialism, capitalism; it's about industrialization, you know ... Paper 2, the whole of it has very little to do with Africa.

Fran: When you think about that example you gave earlier, of Americans not being able to identify Iraq on the map, how does it make you feel? How do you interpret that?

Edmund: Um, unfortunately I've never been able to learn about the education system of America. But I was uneasy that, uneasy because America is one of the donors to our education. And lots and lots of Tanzanian educators have been trained in America. And now, I cannot get the idea how it is that this is happening. I don't know. Sometimes I feel it's like, um, Americans feel that being in America is like being the world. So knowing much about what is outside the world is not important when you are in America. While I feel like I need to know more about how people are living in Russia, I need to know how people are living in the USA. Maybe, I'm not sure, it's just a proposition, but I think things are like that.

*****

Edmund's critique of the Tanzanian and American educational systems addresses relations of power and inequality that extend far beyond the classroom. His vivid account of receiving a pamphlet with advice for his diabetes listing a food unknown to this college-educated youth, and his questioning of the reasons why he had to learn about Europe and the United States, down to the Tennessee Valley Authority while many Americans cannot locate Iraq on a map, much less Tanzania, suggests a kind of aspirational equality in reverse. It's not that Edmund aspires to be geographically ignorant; rather, his exasperation suggests that he no longer wants to be held to a different standard owing to his country's low socioeconomic standing in the world.

Similar to his classmates' and lecturers' laments about the sudden change in the country's teacher education policy, Edmund drew attention to the "fantasies of the good life" that schooling fosters and to the cruelty of such an imaginary when individuals cling to it while encumbered by political and socio-economic conditions that lead to its dismantling (Berlant 2011: 1). Secondary school is challenging under most circumstances, but Tanzania's education policy that abruptly switches the medium of instruction from Swahili to English upon entering Form 1 makes learning even more difficult for the vast majority of students whose proficiency in English is extremely limited. Similarly, the absence of basic science equipment like pipettes and Bunsen burners, and a curriculum that continues to privilege European and American geography and history over indigenous languages and knowledge, makes it very difficult "to overcome categorical subordination" by turning people's aspirations for success in schooling into reality (Ferguson 2006: 20).

The anthropology of policy treats these authoritative texts as a "cultural category and political technology" (Shore and Wright 1997: 12). We see this in the tangible consequences of policy for students, teachers, and professors whose lives can be uprooted in an afternoon with the unexpected application of a tenure policy or with a sudden change in the national curriculum and academic calendar. Precarity is the doubleganger of policy, the ghostly figure that follows the "experts" who develop procedures but who, so often, may not "know in the reality how is this thing being perceived by the people out there." It is this specter that haunts the next chapter.

Part Six

The Social Life of Uncertainty

Speed Bumps on Lema Road

The thoughts and actions of "development" bureaucrats are powerfully shaped by the world of acceptable statements and utterances in which they live; and what they do and do not do is a product not only of the interests of various nations, classes, or international agencies but also, at the same time, a working out of this complex structure of knowledge.

—James Ferguson 1994: 18

Journal Entry: February 3, 2007

Book title idea: "Speed Bumps on Lema Road: An African Development Tale." The argument would be that the speed bumps being built on Lema Road are like so much development work—superfluous while more fundamental needs, such as actually paving the road, go unmet. But this title also speaks to aspirations in that those building the speed bumps on this pot-holed road may be working with a view to it being improved someday. This is not really a delusion but rather a hope for a certain kind of future.

There were two routes to get from the Badiliko campus to the paved roads leading into Moshi Town: the narrow, gravel road used by students and other pedestrians to reach the gated entrance to the college, or the wide, dirt road that leads from the former chiefdom of Kibosho on the slopes of Mount Kilimanjaro to the International School at its base. The latter route, known as Lema Road, was far more direct for those of us who lived at the college, but it required careful navigation of the road's ruts and attentive driving to avoid hitting children walking to school and women scurrying to the market with bananas piled high on their heads.

One bright morning in February, on my drive back to campus after shopping in town, I spotted a group of men piling dirt across Lema Road. At first, I thought these sweaty, bare-chested workers were filling in potholes and waved to express my appreciation as I drove slowly past their operation. The next day, however, when I spotted the work crew again, I realized they were not shoveling dirt into holes but rather piling it into long, narrow bands to build speed bumps. Although I had occasionally encountered these bumps on rural roads near schools and churches, this effort struck me as wholly unnecessary because of the sorry state of this particular stretch.

By the time I reached home, I had formulated a critical assessment that I shared with Tim about how the building of speed bumps on rutted rural roads served as a kind of synecdoche for the whole of development with its frequent waste of resources and misplaced priorities. I told him that I assumed an international NGO was funding the project, its bureaucrats likely living comfortably in Shantytown and seeking to aid the "banana ladies," as Oscar and Gus referred to them. And couldn't he imagine statements in the NGO's appeal to donors, making use of essential terms in the discourse of development like "women's empowerment" and "entrepreneurship"? Tim nodded and smiled as he, too, had many critiques of foreign aid and the representations that accompany it.

On my next trip to town, I decided to pull over and ask the Tanzanian foreman for more information about the project. Sure enough, the work had to do with development, but not quite as I had imagined. For starters, the project was being funded by the municipal government as part of its rural roads program and was not supported directly by any international aid organization.[1] Furthermore, the foreman told me enthusiastically that the bumps *were* intended to accelerate development in the area by slowing down traffic. They would attract people with some means, who undoubtedly have cars, to build homes in the area. These imaginary residents, he exclaimed, would see themselves as people who might need a reminder not to race down the road in their Land Cruisers.

Huh? This explanation seemed mighty convoluted to me with the foreman suggesting the speed bumps would accelerate, not slow down, development. It only began to make sense when I thought about critical social theory, particularly Louis Althusser's concept of interpellation, and applied it to the foreman's "complex structure of knowledge" about development (Ferguson 1994: 18). The idea is that individuals are interpellated, or "hailed," by particular ideologies, such as liberal-capitalist ideology and the consumerism that accompanies it (Althusser 1971). From this perspective, the speed bumps on Lema Road do symbolic work; they do not simply slow down traffic. They serve as ideological objects signifying success by virtue of car ownership, calling out to the growing middle class in Moshi to recognize themselves as individuals who might speed down the street.

As if on cue, the foreman gestured toward the nearby entrance to a secondary school on this nearly deserted road and slammed his left fist into his right hand to dramatize a hypothetical accident caused by cars colliding with students. Anticipating more vehicles and more students in the years to come, the building of the speed bumps made perfect sense to him and evidently to city planners. Thanking the foreman for his time, I slowly accelerated our old Escudo and gently rolled over the bourgeoning bump in the road.

The more I pondered the appearance of the (currently) superfluous traffic tamers, the more I wondered about my initial reaction to them: Why had I assumed they were another misguided development scheme concocted by "experts" whose lives are disconnected from a project's putative beneficiaries? Although I still could not fully grasp the logic of the speed bump scheme, I began to see it as a local manifestation of hopefulness and aspiration. Given the pattern of growth in the Moshi area, it was likely that far more people would be traversing the road in their cars, so why not build speed bumps in anticipation?

Moreover, it wasn't only Tanzanians who imagined a more "developed" future for the area. Gus and Oscar did the same when we would drive down Lema Road on hot Saturday afternoons with hardly a soul around, and they would shout out from the back seat what might be built there someday. Gus would point to a clearing where goats often grazed and pronounce it the future home of a Wal-Mart. Oscar liked to envision the Check Point Grocery, a tiny shop that sold beer, soda, and little else, as a McDonald's, the first in all of Tanzania. He was convinced that the meat-loving Maasai and Chagga, as well as the *wazungu* at the International School and the nearby hospital, would turn his imaginary Lema Road McDonald's into a thriving business. Though amusing for their immediate improbability, my sons' visions of the future seemed as certain as the foreman's, with Lema Road a busy thoroughfare one day. The speed bumps had aspirational significance, part of a social imaginary that made more sense when I considered it from the perspective of my neighbors whose logic about development did not, and need not, correspond with my own.

*****

This chapter forms a bridge between the previous chapter and the one that follows by connecting the themes of aspirations, knowledge production, and the certainty of development "experts" regarding their own expertise. This chapter is framed by Edmund's assertion about development that concluded Chapter 10: "People really want to sit in their offices; they don't want to go into the field and know in the reality how is this thing being perceived by the people out there." Although I concur, and exemplify further in this chapter, I contend that equal skepticism ought to be maintained regarding the certainty that significant, on-the-ground engagement will necessarily ensure *verstehen* and the generation of knowledge based on meaningful understanding of another's perspective. Sitting in one's office, whether literally or figuratively, undoubtedly contributes to the "spectator view of knowledge" about development that reveres standardization and transferability and eschews the analysis of context-specific complexity (Dewey 1929: 23; see also Ferguson 1994). This is the focus of the first half of the chapter.

Yet researchers who *do* spend significant time in the field, living in co-temporal, coeval relations with others, must still contend with the distinct epistemologies—beliefs about knowledge and what can be known—of their own and of "the people out there" as Edmund described them (see also Vavrus and Bartlett 2012). As I have argued throughout this book, spatial and temporal coevalness creates the possibility for the production of a different sort of knowledge from the standardized, replicable "what works" approach prevalent in education, development, and other fields today (Vavrus 2016b). Nevertheless, it is still no guarantee that a policy or project will satisfy the aspirations of those for whom it was intended, an issue explored in the second part of this chapter through a reflexive analysis of a teacher professional development project I helped to initiate.

The final chapter, Chapter 12, homes in on the aspirations of the youth in the longitudinal study set against this broader backdrop of inter/national development discourse, policy, and practice. The heightened ambitions of these youth are the result of decades of educational expansion, from the 1990 Education for All movement that increased access to primary schooling internationally to the past fifteen years of national policymaking to expand secondary schooling. Yet the economic difficulties for parents to support their children's educational aspirations make strategic relationships and the generation of social capital beyond the nuclear family ever more important. Cooper and Pratten contend, "As social infrastructure, interpersonal collaborations become 'a platform providing for and reproducing life' ... in the context of inadequate and unreliable official policies and economies" (2015: 8). It is these inadequate policies and programs, often but not always developed from a distance, upon which I focus in this chapter as a way of illustrating how experts' own social contingencies shape their ways of reasoning about the problems they seek to address and the solutions they offer to others.

*****

Field notes: December 21, 2006:[2] I was already drenched in sweat by the time I got to Lydia's office for our 10 a.m. meeting, but I figured she would also be suffering in the oppressive December heat as she had recently moved to Dar es Salaam from New York City. I had gone to Dar for a few days to discuss with two NGOs the findings emerging from the second round of data collection from my longitudinal research in Old Moshi. I had met Lydia a few years earlier when she was working for the same international NGO, and she had spoken in one of my classes at Teachers College about how her background as an anthropologist informed her work with this NGO. Now it was her turn to invite me to talk with her staff about my research.

Lydia was attending a managers' meeting when I arrived, so her Tanzanian colleague, Judith, welcomed me to the conference room, gave me a cup of coffee, and began unwrapping three large stacks of child labor reports. They had been very professionally produced, with a glossy photo of a laboring child on the cover and colorful graphs and charts inside illustrating the kinds of work children perform in Tanzania and the attendant risks to their health and to their opportunities for schooling.

Lydia arrived shortly thereafter, asking Judith where the rest of the education sector team had gone because several others were supposed to join us. Judith explained they had been called to a meeting at one of the new beachfront hotels north of the city to discuss the implementation of an accelerated primary school program called COBET designed for out-of-school youth returning to the classroom. It was a high-level meeting, she said, with representatives of the Prime Minister's Office (PMO), regional education officials, and other invited guests. Judith told us there was "fear" at the policy level that the government's enrollment targets set out in the Primary Education Development Programme, or PEDP, would not be met. This was due, she explained, to the fact that the Ministry of Finance determines how much money the Ministry of Education and Vocational Training (MOEVT) receives, and no money had been allocated to train COBET facilitators; there was only money for them to receive honoraria when they actually taught classes. If these "vulnerable children" did not go to school, they would impede the PEDP targets, and the MOEVT did not want this to happen. Yet Judith was clearly more concerned about the children themselves than about the policy: "They need to recognize where these children are coming from," she declared, expressing her frustration that schools are not sufficiently "child-friendly," especially for the kinds of vulnerable children the COBET program sought to reach.

Lydia jumped into the conversation at this point and began telling me about her organization's new program focused on COBET and HIV/AIDS. They planned to work in six districts in different regions of the country to monitor policy, pilot a few projects, and "build capacity." Judith added there was now a "dire need for secondary school" as evidenced by SEDP (see Chapter 10), with expanded opportunities for post-primary schooling especially important for children from poor households.

On the matter of HIV/AIDS, Lydia explained that she and her staff had met with two other international NGOs the day before to discuss a national life skills program with the goal of creating one coordinating body for the country that would develop curriculum guidelines from pre-primary onward because, at that moment, there was no national framework. Judith added that "the base of the problem are social, cultural issues," to which I responded by asking how they intended to work with teachers who are often uncomfortable teaching about HIV/AIDS. Judith confidently explained that they "start with the teachers themselves" by getting them to think about AIDS in their lives and about how they can support children in their classrooms using "participatory" methods rather than lecturing to them. She argued that "it's the methodology" that matters when building life skills.

In response, I mentioned the in-service teacher education program called Teaching in Action (TIA) we hoped to start at Badiliko to address teachers' limited understanding of participatory methods. I then queried Judith about the costs for teachers to attend the life skills training program, telling her and Lydia that school leaders often complained to me about being required by the government to send their teachers to trainings but were not given sufficient funds in their school budgets to cover the costs. Judith shrugged her shoulders, indicating a degree of resignation and noting that it had recently been reported in the papers that the government had only secured 40 percent of the budget from foreign donors needed to implement SEDP.

Lydia then asked me to discuss some of the preliminary findings from my longitudinal research, and I gave a short presentation about it, answering Judith and Lydia's questions and welcoming their feedback. They asked if I could investigate the matter of school fees at the primary level in the next round of data collection because they had heard that PEDP had not, in fact, resulted in free primary schooling as intended. They admitted that they had not spoken to any parents to verify this information even though it directly affected their work.

As we walked out of conference room, Judith thanked me for coming and especially for talking to them about my observations from rural and semi-urban communities. As we parted, she shook her head and chuckled, "We never get out of the office."

Returning with Lydia to her office, I got the same sense of a dedicated "expert" swamped by the demands of continuous monitoring and evaluation, and correspondence with staff in Tanzania and the United States, all of which prevented her from spending time in the communities affected by the organization's programs. Waving her arm at the pile of reports on her desk, Lydia apologized that she could not join me for lunch as planned. I could see the long list of unanswered email messages on her computer screen, which helped me to understand the stress she had reported the night before over dinner. Lydia had complained about the heavy workload in the office that was keeping her from doing "what I really want," meaning spending more time in communities identifying issues of concern and exploring the effects of the NGO's programs. She confessed that much of her time was taken up editing draft reports from her staff to ensure the quality was sufficient for "HQ," the headquarters in the United States.

As I stepped out of the air-conditioned building and into the stifling midday heat, I imagined the meeting at the swanky hotel where Lydia's team had gathered. They were probably sitting down right about now to a generous buffet lunch with representatives from the Prime Minister's Office, the MOEVT and Ministry of Finance, UN organizations, and bilateral aid agencies discussing important educational issues as they ate. Yet there would not be any COBET students, and probably no COBET teachers, dining with them; they were, literally, absent from the table where critical decisions about their lives were being made. Those at the table likely worked in their offices most of the time unless they were attending these sorts of meetings; they did not spend their days working and living alongside the people whose problems they are supposed to help resolve.

Looking for a bit of shade, I decided to get a quick lunch at a nearby restaurant I used to visit in 1996, when I was working at the National Archives on my doctoral research. Sure enough, it was still there, offering a full plate of beans, rice, and *mchicha* (fried greens) for less than $2. There was a breeze blowing in from the Indian Ocean that mitigated the heat, and the red and white Coca-Cola awning above the table provided sufficient protection from the sun. However, the cheap metal chair upon which I was sitting was singeing my thighs, so I downed my meal as quickly as possible before hailing a cab to take me to my next meeting.

I signaled to the old man in the taxi who had been eying me during lunch, undoubtedly hoping for some business to pay for his own midday meal. As expected, the air conditioning no longer worked in his tired taxi, and the threadbare covering over the back seat barely concealed the springs underneath. Yet I always opted in Dar for older drivers and their antiquated cars because they tended to drive more slowly and offered stories to make up for the discomfort. Ali was no exception: By the time we arrived at the offices of the Tanzanian NGO where I had an appointment that afternoon, I had learned more about the cost to parents of the so-called free primary school policy, PEDP, than I could have learned in any meeting with government officials at a beachfront hotel. It turned out that despite his age, Ali still had two children in primary school, even though his other six children had long finished their schooling. "Ha, schooling is **not** free, Mama, no matter what they say in Parliament. Instead of '*ada*' (fees), they now call them '*michango*' (contributions)!" Ali shook his head in dismay and suggested I ask my colleagues at the NGO about this matter because he did not want me to be fooled by any government declarations about free schooling. I promised to follow his advice, which proved prescient.

Gasper, the outspoken director of the NGO, greeted me warmly as I was escorted into his office. We had met years before in the United States and had seen each other the previous summer when I had brought students from Teachers College to Tanzania to talk with him about national policy. I launched right in and told Gasper the taxi driver's story about still paying for his kids to go to primary school even though the mandatory costs were now "contributions" and not "fees." Gasper let out a laugh and then became quite serious, explaining that the "domains of PEDP" were not clear, which meant that schools continued to demand contributions from parents for things like a building fund and the watchman's salary, but the actual fee for attending school had been eliminated in the cases his organization had examined.

Gasper then drew a figure to show me different decision-making levels in the country, with the national being "most significant." At the most local level are the schools; above the schools are the district and regional authorities; after that are the national authorities, which he divided into the MOEVT, the Ministry of Finance, and the Prime Minister's Office. Gasper explained that the PMO coordinates all of these other offices, and this is "part of the mess" because there are so many offices involved in PEDP.

Gasper also pointed out that the international level is critical to understand because, in 2000–2001, the education sector got a "kickstart" from the World Bank. He explained that the director in Tanzania at the time "got things done" and made sure that education was in the country's poverty reduction plan, a document known as a Poverty Reduction Strategy Paper (PRSP) that was required by the World Bank to get debt relief (Vavrus 2005; Vavrus and Seghers 2010). Gasper reminded me that this had been the "voices of the poor" period at the Bank, when they were interested in presenting poverty from the perspective of those living on the margins. Further, at that time, the Jubilee 2000 Movement, campaigning globally for the cancellation of debt, had put significant pressure on the International Monetary Fund and the World Bank to reduce the burden on very poor countries like Tanzania and to support long-term efforts to eliminate poverty, such as abolishing school fees and other mandatory contributions. "And just at the last minute [PEDP] got written into Tanzania's PRSP as a presidential decision," Gasper chuckled.

Gasper went on to tell me that once this decision had been made, President Mkapa (1995–2005) promoted it broadly so that he could say Tanzania was working toward achieving the United Nations Millennium Development Goals. Thus, there was a "huge shift" from 2002 to 2004 for primary education, and a lot of costs for parents did come down. However, their labor was still needed to help build schools. Gasper grinned when I told him about parents in Old Moshi telling me that the new classrooms and half-built structures I saw in the community were "World Bank schools."

At the end of 2005, however, Gasper saw things changing because of the costs of the presidential election, which led to a "real funding squeeze." Thus, the government stopped supporting the full $10 capitation grant per student as specified in PEDP, which was supposed to go to the schools for things like tuition, books, and other supplies. Nevertheless, there continued to be international reports on the "great enrollment leap" in Tanzania, Malawi, and a few other African countries, so the "international guys" continued to be "gung ho" about school fee abolition (see Vavrus and Kwauk 2013).

Gasper explained that the official national policy—the "standard policy line"— is that school fee abolition led to the enrollment increase; however, he noted, the government has "threatened people all over" to get their kids in school, which undoubtedly shifted the numbers. I confirmed this point by telling Gasper that Amina, whom he had met the year before with my students from Columbia University, had given me the same explanation based on her observations: It wasn't eliminating the 2,000 Tanzania shillings (~less than $1 USD in 2017), the actual school fee, which led to the increase in enrollment because parents still had to buy uniforms, notebooks, and make mandatory contributions; rather,

Amina declared, it was the threat of punishment by the state if parents didn't send their children to school that seemed to matter most.

To my surprise, Gasper defended the "international guys" driving this policy because he said they are not aware of mandatory contributions "sneaking in." It seemed, at first, like the same "we never get out of the office" problem that Edmund noted in the previous chapter and I had observed with Lydia's organization. This hardly struck me as a legitimate excuse for not being aware of a major violation of policy. Therefore, I asked whether Gasper's organization had investigated this problem in the implementation of the PEDP policy, and he confessed they had not even identified it as one of its top twenty priorities.

Gasper sighed, "Fran, you have to pick your issues." He went on to say they had worked so hard to help get school fees abolished that it would be like resurrecting a fight with the government they had already fought.

Not wanting to take up too much of Gasper's time, I quickly shifted the conversation to ask about the problem Badiliko and other TTCs were facing as a result of the sudden implementation of the secondary school policy, SEDP, and the reduction it had wrought in the period to educate and prepare student teachers. Again, he had important insights and explained that the PMO had made very public the targets for secondary schools: Fifty percent enrollment of youth in this age cohort and a school in every ward. Moreover, it was the prime minister himself who had promised that all children who passed the Standard 7 national exam would have a place in a government secondary school. "But where will the teachers come from?" Gasper asked rhetorically. He explained that his organization had pointed out this problem in op-ed pieces in national newspapers and had gotten a lot of publicity about this issue. He confirmed what I knew to be the case, namely, that two years of pre-service training in diploma programs like ours at Badiliko had been reduced to one year or less. Even then, there was still no way the enrollment targets in SEDP could be met. Gasper concluded by saying there was no certainty about where the money would come from to fully fund SEDP or how many teachers were actually needed for all the schools; furthermore, there were no assurances that teachers would stay in the schools to which they were posted.

After ignoring several phone calls during our meeting, I suggested that Gasper take this one and said a quiet goodbye as he switched into Swahili for what appeared to be the beginning of a long, heated conversation. I chatted with the receptionist, who urged me to take some of the organization's reports and posters to distribute at Badiliko, which I eagerly did. They found a new home in the staff room, on bulletin boards, and as teaching aids that students took to their secondary schools upon graduation.

*****

The uncertainties of the contemporary situation are immense, and all but the most banal predictions are more than usually impossible.

—James Ferguson 1994: 282

Back at Badiliko after these meetings in Dar, I reflected on the preliminary plan my colleagues and I had developed to initiate a short-term program for in-service teachers on participatory, learner-centered teaching (LCT) methods. It would be based on the knowledge we had gleaned out of the office, so to speak, in classrooms, observing our students during their block teaching practice, and it would draw on our experience as former secondary school teachers ourselves. I had received a small grant of around $17,000 from a US-based NGO to work with Badiliko on such a program, and we decided our priority should be the college's recent graduates who had had four months shaved off their pre-service preparation due to the change in government policy (see Chapter 10). We named this program Teaching in Action (TIA).

We knew as experienced educators that induction into the teaching profession can be bumpy, even under the best of circumstances, and these were certainly not ideal conditions for our graduates who likely needed more mentoring than students who had completed the full two-year diploma program (Lieberman et al. 2011). They would likely be struggling to figure out how to apply the coursework on LCT they had received at Badiliko to the conditions in which they found themselves, namely, schools with few teaching and learning materials, with limited or no access to the internet, and with senior colleagues who might balk at the learner-centered methods these young teachers were bringing into the classroom (see Thomas and Vavrus 2010; Vavrus 2009, 2013).

Five Tanzanian faculty at Badiliko and I worked throughout the second semester to develop this week-long program, and we spent considerable time creating materials, generating activities that would model learner-centered instruction, and determining who among us would lead which sessions. Unfortunately, the only time the college could host the thirty or so participants— both recent Badiliko graduates and a more seasoned teacher from each of their schools—was after my family's residency permit expired. This meant that I could not be present for the first year of the TIA program. Nevertheless, we worked together to prepare for and practice facilitating the sessions, and I left my five colleagues in charge to implement our plan. I anxiously awaited word from them once the program began to unfold several weeks later.

The email messages I received from Badiliko, as well as from the NGO that funded the project, deemed it a success. Therefore, the following year, we were offered twice the funding to expand and enrich the program. The Badiliko team asked that I return with additional US colleagues who could help with the parts of the curriculum they felt somewhat unprepared to develop, such as how to apply learner-centered methods to specific topics in the Tanzanian syllabus for different secondary school subjects.

The syllabi, which take the form of booklets specifying topics, subtopics, and suggested teaching methods and materials, list methods like "brainstorming" and "role playing." However, few teachers, even the Badiliko graduates, have had much if any experience with these methods, and even fewer had learned how to determine where in a lesson one method might be preferable to another and why. Even the Badiliko faculty sought more guidance on the theoretical underpinnings of learner-centered teaching as well as its practical application in Tanzanian schools. They knew from experience that there was rarely enough time to get through the scheme of work and "cover the syllabus" before the national exams approached at the end of the year. Thus, the US team, of which Lesley, my colleague from Teachers College, was a part, engaged in both faculty professional development and in leading some of the sessions with our Tanzanian colleagues.

During the years when the TIA program had an international team of facilitators (2008–2014), we discerned several fundamental differences between the Tanzanians and Americans, and between the facilitators as a whole and the participating Tanzanian teachers.[3] I prided myself on working "out of the office" through my long-term ethnographic research in Old Moshi that included teaching in a secondary school. I had also been a teacher educator at Badiliko for the year of my Fulbright fellowship, and, as an education professor, I had read a considerable amount about education in Tanzania from the colonial era to the present. I had even published a book and numerous articles on this topic by this point in my career as a tenured associate professor (Vavrus 2003, 2005, 2009).

Nevertheless, I still did not fully recognize the epistemological differences reflected in the Tanzanian facilitators and teachers' definitions of "good teaching." For many, though certainly not all, good teaching meant transferring a body of knowledge established by "experts" from teacher to students. Knowledge was produced elsewhere, by others, and transmitted from adults to youth. The more efficient and expeditious the transfer, the more knowledge from the syllabus could be "covered," helping to ensure students' success on regional and national examinations.

My perspective on knowledge, which was shared by most of the US facilitators, had emerged from a constructivist epistemology. Specific to the field of education, this view treats "knowledge as constituted by interpretation, learning as a process where there is not always a right answer, and co-construction of new knowledge by students or by students and teacher" (Vavrus and Bartlett 2012: 648). Students' scores on national exams did not square neatly with this view of knowledge production because the tests were based almost exclusively on the recall of facts and with little analysis, evaluation, or synthesis of new material required.

The US team and some of the Badiliko lecturers recognized that the exams did not assess these "higher-order" cognitive skills, and especially not the critical thinking about contemporary issues we sought to cultivate via demonstration during the TIA program (Gardner 2011). We assumed these skills would, indirectly, improve students' scores on high-stakes exams, but we, the US facilitators, deemed it more important to demonstrate teaching methods that might enable students to become more discerning adults prepared for the uncertainties they would confront in the years ahead.

To this end, we drew heavily on educational psychology because some of the Tanzanian and US team members had studied the same theorists and concepts. We incorporated into the TIA program Howard Gardner's concept of multiple intelligences and how lesson plans should tap into the strengths of visual, auditory, and kinesthetic learners (Gardner 2011). We also utilized Benjamin Bloom's model of cognitive domains and the importance of developing lessons that move students from lower-order cognitive skills like remembering and describing to the higher-order skills of analyzing, evaluating, and creating (Anderson and Krathwohl 2000).

Throughout the week-long TIA program, the Tanzanian and US facilitators engaged in meta-teaching as we put these ideas into practice in our sessions, meaning that we paused frequently to explain what we were doing and why. For example, we would use and then discuss teaching techniques like "cold calling," whereby a teacher calls on a student to answer a question without students first putting their hands in the air (Lemov 2010). We also made extensive use of Grant Wiggins and Jay McTighe's *Understanding by Design* (2005), with its advice to design topical units "backwards" by starting with what a teacher wants students to know at the end and planning in reverse, and its exhortation to use broad, open-ended "essential questions," as discussed below.

Drawing on these sources for the workshops illustrates the tension between knowledge based on local circumstances as the foundation for development programs and the utilization of general theory derived primarily from research on "what works" in the global North. As the head of the US team throughout these years of the TIA program, I was fully implicated in the borrowing of these putatively universal educational models owing to the certainty that, with a bit of tweaking, they would have as much relevance for rural teachers in Tanzania as they did elsewhere. We quickly discovered otherwise, as these two vignettes from the TIA program illustrate.[4]

*****

Vignette #1: *Whose Knowledge Counts?* One of the principles upon which we based the TIA program is that teachers should activate students' prior knowledge of a topic and build their lessons from there. This is not a difficult concept to grasp because it would waste class time and bore students into a slumber if a teacher lectured at students about material they already knew. As TIA facilitators, we assumed this to be a universally accepted principle and therefore used phrases during the program like "activating students' schema" and "meetings students where they are." We assumed Tanzanian teachers would agree that it is critical to find out what students already know about a topic before launching into it.

During the second year of TIA, in 2008, my Tanzanian colleague and I led the first session of the workshop on the concept of multiple intelligences using an interactive lecture method, which meant we wrote some of the notes from the lecture on the board but intentionally left blank spaces to model a way of promoting more active listening. I had started the lecture by asking the participating teachers what they already knew about multiple intelligences, and we noted their key terms and phrases on flip-chart paper at the front of the seminar hall. At the end of the interactive lecture, following a discussion of its content, my Tanzanian partner and I sought to engage the teachers in a meta-teaching discussion of what we had done during the session and why we had done it this way. The "notes-with-gaps" method for promoting more active listening made sense to the group, and there was a lot of nodding as we talked about how they could use it in their classrooms with only a blackboard and a piece of chalk as teaching aids.

In contrast, my explanation as to why we had asked them what they already knew about multiple intelligences was not well understood by some of the teachers. From the looks on a few of their faces, I wondered whether my American accent was causing confusion, but this was not the case. An older male teacher wearing a scowl and sitting with arms folded in a skeptical pose unfolded his right arm and raised his hand high in the air.

"Madam," he stated firmly as he addressed me, "if you ask students what they already know about a topic, they will think you do not know about the topic yourself."

"*Ndiyo, ndiyo*" [yes, yes], I could hear some teachers quietly murmuring as he spoke. My co-facilitator and I asked the teacher to elaborate, and he, joined by others, explained that students will think a teacher is "fishing for answers" by asking students for definitions of new terms or explanations of concepts at the beginning of a lesson on these concepts. They argued that it is different when a teacher asks such questions the day *after* he has taught the correct information to students because then the students will recognize these as review questions, testing their knowledge of what the teacher has already taught them.

As I listened to his logic, I drifted back momentarily to Lema Road. In this case, I was treating the activation of students' prior knowledge similarly to filling in potholes on a rutted road; it is what *everyone* knows to be the way to better learning (and to better roads). Yet here were seasoned Tanzanian teachers making a point that seemed equally obvious to them by prioritizing the maintenance of authority in the classroom and the transfer of authoritative knowledge from teacher to students.

Had the teachers in the 2008 TIA program been the only ones to raise this objection to the elicitation of students' prior knowledge, I would have written it off as a concern of a few teachers who had had insufficient opportunities for professional development since they started their careers. But similarly skeptical teachers spoke up again in 2009 and 2010, suggesting that their objections did not stem from being ill-informed about educational psychology. Rather, their comments reflected a profound epistemological difference from my own about what constituted knowledge worthy of discussion in the classroom and how teachers ought to utilize it during their lessons.

Vignette #2: What Is Essential about an Essential Question? During the years of the TIA program, teachers and Badiliko faculty themselves frequently struggled with the concept of an "essential question" (EQ) (Wiggins and McTighe 2005). It, too, assumes that psychological theories of learning are universally applicable and that "what works" in one classroom will work in others. The idea is that by posing an expansive question to students that does not have a single correct answer, the teacher is stimulating students' higher-order thinking skills and inviting them to synthesize, evaluate, and analyze information throughout the lesson as they ponder the EQ.

The EQ concept was new to most of the Badiliko lecturers because many of them had been hired as content-area experts who often had little or no teaching experience, and few, if any, courses in pedagogy. We, members of the US team, explained that EQs needed to meet certain criteria, and we provided models of questions that were "open-ended"; "thought-provoking and intellectually engaging"; "raise[d] additional questions"; and "require[d] support and justification, not just an answer" (McTighe and Wiggins 2013: 3). As we worked with our Tanzanian colleagues to prepare for the TIA week, we put example EQs on the board, such as: "Why would we as teachers want to promote active learning?" or "How can teachers promote analysis in the classroom?"

During the week of the TIA program itself, the Tanzanian and US facilitators were supposed to model the use of EQs during two types of sessions. In the morning sessions, the secondary school teachers were together in a large lecture hall discussing general principles of learner-centered teaching, and these sessions were co-led by a Tanzanian/US pair. In the afternoon, we divided the teachers into their subject areas led by a Badiliko lecturer with expertise in the same subject as the small group of teachers. The lecturers were supposed to demonstrate how to apply these LCT principles to biology or English or math, and they were to support the teachers as they developed their own "micro-teaching" lessons and taught them to their fellow teachers as though they were teaching in front of their students.

Yet the Badiliko facilitators themselves frequently struggled with the concept of an EQ because it was quite different from the kinds of questions they were used to posing to prepare their pre-service teachers for their examinations. During preparation and planning meetings in 2014, my final year of formal involvement in the program, the Badiliko facilitators described the model lessons they were going to present on the first afternoon of the TIA workshop when working with teachers in their subject area. In the case of chemistry, the chemistry lecturer proposed using the following as his EQ: "How is electroanalysis mechanism in the lab?" For the model English lesson, the facilitator suggested, "Analyze how public debate format can improve the language ability of students in secondary school."

After six years of working with different groups of Badiliko lecturers, I was not surprised by these examples. The first case was not, in fact, an open-ended question because the lecturer explained to us that in his model lesson, he sought the specific electrochemical methods by which electroanalysis can be conducted. In the case of the second EQ, it was not a question at all, and this happened frequently. Further, the facilitator was not looking for thought-provoking responses based on analysis and evaluation of debating as a teaching method; rather, she told us that she expected to hear the "right" answers from the teachers based on reasons with which they should already be familiar and which she subsequently listed in her model lesson.

During the TIA program the following week, the essential questions of the secondary school teachers took many forms. A few were provocative, open-ended, and linked directly to the rest of the teacher's model lesson. However, the vast majority of the EQs I saw on the blackboards throughout the week were factual: "Identify types of friction." "What are the major sources of food?" "What is environmental pollution?" In short, what was essential about these essential questions was that they *could* be answered by recall of factual knowledge and did *not* raise additional questions. These were questions similar to the ones students would encounter on national exams, and these teachers aspired to become better instructors by refining their skills in preparing students for high-stakes tests.

Throughout the years of my involvement with the TIA program, both the participating teachers and the Badiliko lecturers involved in it displayed a strong preference for questions of fact over analysis and maintained a degree of skepticism toward the view that students themselves might generate valuable knowledge. And I began to wonder with increasing puzzlement as to why I held so steadfastly to my views about pedagogical knowledge and knowledge production.

*****

It remains conceivable that at various points in these struggles, in various organizational locations, there may in fact be demands for specific kinds of advice or expertise. But, if there is any advice to be given, it will not be dictating general political strategy or giving a general answer to the question "what is to be done" (which can only be determined by those doing the resisting), but answering specific, localized, tactical questions.

—James Ferguson 1994: 282

What do these tales from TIA and from development organizations in Dar es Salaam have in common, and how do they help to make sense of speed bumps on a rural road on Mount Kilimanjaro? One of my intentions in bringing together these disparate stories has been to illuminate how the social contingencies of "experts" shape the problems they take up and the certainty of the solutions they propose. When such experts rarely get out of the office or do so only to attend meetings with other "spectators," in the Deweyian sense of the term, the resultant policies are unlikely to reflect the particular concerns of the intended beneficiaries. Moreover, there is a "relatively small, interlocked network of experts" engaged in planning inter/national development programs (Ferguson 1994: 258). Often trained in the same graduate programs at institutions where instrumentalist epistemologies are favored, it is not surprising that these "experts" often embrace a view of knowledge as general, transferable, and relatively context-independent rather than specific and informed by local cultural, historical, and material contexts (Vavrus and Bartlett 2012).

My other intention in this chapter has been to illustrate how the certainty of expertise, even when derived from coeval, out-of-the-office experiences, is still partial and contingent. For instance, my proximate experience as a secondary school teacher and teacher educator led me to believe that I could accurately gauge the degree of adaptation necessary to make "universal" pedagogical principles appropriate for this Tanzanian context. I believed my experience on the ground had sufficiently reshaped my foundational knowledge of education and development, giving me a privileged perspective that combined the general and the specific.

However, the resistance to some of these practices by some Tanzanian teachers and lecturers, and the transformation of TIA over the years as the influence of the US facilitators waned, pointed to striking differences in our views about the place in the classroom for the sharing of personal, experiential knowledge; for the co-construction of pedagogical knowledge; and for the transmission of general, propositional knowledge. The lead facilitators at the college continued to use many of the materials we had developed that drew on teachers' prior knowledge and called for reflection about pedagogy, but the facilitators also removed anything they deemed to have limited utility for teachers who needed to teach to the test, albeit in a somewhat more learner-centered manner. The Teaching in Action program became much more about bolstering teachers' formal, factual knowledge of specific concepts in their content areas and less about introducing them to methods for activating students' prior knowledge or developing their analytical thinking skills. In other words, the knowledge accorded the highest status by "those doing the resisting" differed significantly from the knowledge my US colleagues and I valued most (Ferguson 1994: 282).

Perhaps the moral of this chapter can best be conveyed via an epilogue to the story of the speed bumps on Lema Road. On a trip to Tanzania a couple of years after my sabbatical at Badiliko, I was driving to the college from Moshi Town along Lema Road and was anticipating the abrupt change in the road's surface from tarmac to gravel beyond the gates of the International School. Instead, to my utter surprise, the road had been paved, and well beyond the Check Point Grocery that marked the turn toward the corn and sunflower fields that surrounded the campus. Moreover, the road was dotted with nascent cement foundations for new homes, just as the foreman had predicted.

In 2007, I had not understood the logic of the speed bumps because it did not fit within the structure of knowledge that framed my understanding of development. I possessed some specific expertise about development from living and working in the Kilimanjaro Region for more than a decade at that point, but this local knowledge was overshadowed by the general theories and principles of socio-economic change I had studied as a student and scaffolded the entire development apparatus. It seemed beyond question that slowing traffic on a rural road would arrest, not accelerate, the movement of the middle class. Nevertheless, within a few years, it had come to pass; homes were being built on the edge of Shantytown by car-owning Tanzanians. I wondered what other "truths" about development I would have to reconsider when I re-interviewed the focal youth in the longitudinal study in a couple of years. It is to their stories that I now turn in the final chapter.

12

Gendered Contingencies

It was 10:00 a.m. on a Sunday morning, a time when traffic stills and church bells call parishioners to services across the mostly Christian communities on Mount Kilimanjaro. In my twenty years of traveling to this region, I had never before been invited to someone's home at this hour because we were supposed to be attending church. Yet here we were, Amina and I, standing at the entrance to the home of one of the participants in the longitudinal study of youth lives. We called out *"hodi"* to announce ourselves, though this formality hardly seemed necessary as the engine of our jeep thundered across the valley as it slowly climbed the steep, slippery mountain pass on this damp June day in 2012. When Grace, whom I had interviewed in 2007, invited us to her in-law's home at this unusual hour, I was delighted. Amina and I had been struggling to schedule our meetings with the twenty youth we wanted to re-interview because we had only four weeks for this particular research trip. These young women and men now lived across the Kilimanjaro Region and in other parts of the country, making it more challenging for us to meet with them. This Sunday morning was one of the few free times left in our busy schedule, and though pleased to see Grace again, I was puzzled as to why she, the daughter of a minister, had suggested this time for our interview.

As we called out our greeting, a middle-aged woman with a brightly colored *kanga* covering her dress came out of the house to meet us. She clasped my right hand firmly and hoisted my heavy backpack laden with tape recorder, spare batteries, notebooks, and pens over her shoulder as she led us into the house.

"Ah, Mama Gus," Grace called out, lifting herself slowly from the oversized couch and giving Amina and me warm hugs. Amina, immediately ascertaining the situation, cried out, *"Hongera dada* (Congratulations sister)!" Still waiting for clues as to why Amina was congratulating Grace, I looked around the room and spotted a pile of wet towels that hinted at the circumstances surrounding our Sunday morning invitation. Amina had once explained to me that massage with hot towels was one of the best ways to reduce a woman's soreness after childbirth. As if on cue, Grace announced that she had had a baby boy three weeks earlier and, following Chagga custom, was staying inside the home of her in-laws for three months while they took care of her every need.

After another round of hearty congratulations, we took our seats at the coffee table as Grace and Amina began to compare notes on postpartum care. Although not Chagga, Amina belongs to a closely related ethnic group with many similar traditions. These two young women began describing to me how the women on the husband's side cook soft, smooth foods for the new mother like *mtori* (a stew of beef and bananas) and *uji*, which are believed to stimulate lactation. They also concurred that postpartum women should not sit or stand for long periods of time but rather lie down as much as possible, though Grace insisted she had recovered fully and would be fine sitting upright during our visit. In fact, she seemed eager for the company and did not let us leave until the early afternoon, after we had had lunch with her and her new baby.

Though blessed with a beautiful child, Grace, now Mama Amoni, had not intended for her life to unfold in this way. Among the 146 young women in the longitudinal study, Grace seemed like one of the most likely to fulfill her dreams, which, for her, meant getting a master's degree at the University of Dar es Salaam and becoming a journalist, specifically a journalist reporting on economic matters. In Standard 7, she was ranked second in her class of 129 students at Sokoni Primary School, the most well resourced of the four primary schools included in the longitudinal study. She was also one of the few primary school students at any of the schools who, on her questionnaire, identified a specific career goal—an economics reporter—when others typically wrote down general occupations such as tailoring, masonry, or secretarial work.

In addition, Grace's family matched the local profile of those whose children tended to complete higher education: Her mother had finished college, and her father had a teaching diploma even though he was working as a pastor; there were only three children in the home compared to the average of four or five; the family always had enough food to eat; their house was made of cement and had electricity and piped water; and they could afford to hire day laborers to work on the family farm (see Vavrus 2003 for details on this household survey). In addition, Grace's father, who had been interviewed periodically over the twelve years of the study, supported Grace's choice of journalism as a career and expected her to attend the university, the same expectations he had for his two younger daughters.

In 2007, Grace was well on her way to becoming a journalist. When we met at that time, she had recently completed Form 6 at a good government school and was awaiting her results. Her tone was determined, and her goals were clear whenever she spoke about her future:

> Grace: *I want to be an independent woman. I saw my mother being a homemaker for a long time until she recently found a job. I don't want to live such a life, to depend on a man. I also want to help my community.*

Fran: Why don't you want to depend on a man?

> *You won't have a happy, full life. When you need clothes or bus fare, he has to provide it for you, and I don't think that is a good life. I want to show others that women are able to govern their own lives. That's why I'm studying hard.*

You said you don't want to be dependent to a man. Can you explain the problem when a woman depends on a man?

> *It causes conflicts and divorce. If a woman just waits to receive everything from a man, he may run away from his family. Also, if he can't provide all that his wife needs, she may go looking for other men, just for money [...]*

Can you tell me what you want to be in future?

> *I would like to be a journalist, and I also want to study economics at university because it's what I studied at A level. I also want to get married.*

When do you want to marry?

> *I want to study first until I complete my master's degree, and then I will think of getting married. I know that if I get married before I get my master's degree, it will be hard to finish, so that's why I want to study first.*

Where do you want to live in future?

> *Dar.*

Why Dar and not Moshi?

> *Because it's the place I think I will be able to practice my career.*

Meeting Grace five years later at her in-laws' home in rural Kilimanjaro with a baby but no master's degree, I wanted to know what had happened that had led to this change in plans and how she felt about it. She had married a young man barely ten months earlier who was in a four-year degree program in theology, and she reported that they had very little money because her husband was a student. Moreover, she was not living in Dar or even in Moshi Town but rather in a small house in a rural community nestled among banana trees and coffee bushes with six of her husband's relatives: her in-laws, two sisters-in-law, and two other relatives who were attending school. Although the family appeared to be middle class like her own, there were signs that they were not quite as well off: the faux leather on the couches had begun to peel and split, and the photos of grandparents in the sitting room barely covered the deep chinks in the eggshell blue walls. Furthermore, the weather in this part of the mountain was far cooler than at her parents' home, the dialect of Chagga distinctively different, and the traditions of her husband's clan unfamiliar. As Grace remarked, "I went into another family, a new environment, and it's like I had to teach myself again."

Before turning on the tape recorder and starting the interview, we could hear Amoni starting to cry behind the closed door leading to the bedrooms. "Don't worry, they'll bring the baby to me," Grace explained, and Amina chortled that this was the only period in a woman's life when she could enjoy herself because others were doing the domestic work for her. Sure enough, one of Grace's sisters-in-law brought in the baby and placed him in Grace's arms while the other carried in a platter with cups, saucers, and a thermos filled with hot, milky tea. As soon as Amoni fell asleep, he was taken back to the bedroom without a word from Grace, who settled in with her cup in hand ready to answer our questions.

It was obvious on this day in 2012 that Grace had not become a journalist, and I hesitated before asking her why she had not followed the path she had set for herself in 2000 and reasserted in our interview in 2007. I posed the question as delicately as I could, and as soon as I mentioned "journalism," Grace added that she "**really** wanted" to study it. Her voice quivered as she began to explain her story to us:

After I completed Form 4 at Asante Secondary School, they offered me a spot for A-level because of the subject combination I wanted to pursue—HGE [history, geography, economics]. It was not my wish to go back there because I wanted to study in a different environment, in another region, but I found myself being called back to my former school. So I went back … and after completing Form 6, I still wanted to do journalism. That was my dream. I had told you [laughs]. If I had been able to join university, I would have studied mass communication and journalism, but I was not able to do so. At that time, there were financial problems at home, so I was unable to continue. I could have gone to university because I passed Form 6 with a Division 3, 15 points,[1] but I was not able to go because of the financial situation at home with my younger siblings in secondary school who needed their fees paid.

This situation forced me to go for the crash [teaching] program for one month, though I initially did not want to be a teacher because of the fear of standing before students. I went there by force because of the prevailing circumstances in my family. It's not something I wished for or wanted. I would rather not talk about it. If I were studying journalism, I would …

Grace's voice faded off as she looked away from Amina and me, and in this moment I felt as though the act of interviewing had violated Grace's very being. Feminist oral historians and ethnographers have written extensively about the limits of ethical research when the questions one asks open up old wounds or lead to painful reassessments of one's life (Gluck and Patai 1991; Nagar 2014). Until this moment, I had not fully appreciated how a question about unfulfilled aspirations could inflict psychic pain through the process of remembering desires from the past and the circumstances that squelched them. I did not want to press on with the interview, so we simply sat quietly until Grace continued:

All of us who were in the crash program were Form 6 leavers who were then sent after a month [of training] to secondary schools, ward schools, which had no teachers. I then applied to three teachers colleges to do a diploma in education, and it was at one of them that I met my husband. I think I will be able to get a degree because this college offers it, and I still want to further my education by studying special education so that I can help children with special needs.

"Special education and journalism are very different," I gently pointed out.

They are very different, but I have already decided that I will study special education because I am now a teacher. I studied psychology at the teachers college, and I became interested when I saw some people taking milk to the special education students [as a snack]. I also got interested in looking for ways of assisting them. I'm less than six months into my new teaching position where I'm the academic mistress and a counselor for children. I want to stay with these children and understand their needs.

Tactfully posing one of the questions we asked each youth in the study, Amina inquired of Grace as to whether she had achieved her earlier goals:

No, my objective was not achieved, but I don't regret it that much. I have to adapt to the way things are even though earlier I was deeply hurt by this situation. I thank God very much because, by going to a teachers college, I have realized there are children with special needs for me to help.

*****

Grace's story illustrates the "adjustments to the present" necessitated when our fantasies of the good life suddenly disappear and our possibilities for the future becoming distinctly compromised (Berlant 2011: 20). In Tanzania, particularly for middle-class Chagga youth, a university degree is increasingly desired, but the "conditions of possibility" have not kept apace, even for those like Grace who have passed the national examinations and succeeded at every critical juncture in the education system (Berlant 2011: 24). Grace is not alone among Tanzanian youth today, particularly young women, for whom success in secondary school does not provide certainty that they will be able to continue to the university and achieve their personal and professional goals.[2]

During the socialist period of the 1960s to the mid-1980s, there were far fewer young people in secondary school and university, and those who qualified were assured they could continue because the state covered their expenses at public institutions. At the university level, the government assumed the cost of tuition fees and student bursaries beginning in 1974 through the early 1990s. In the 1980s, however, cost sharing, a central element of structural adjustment policies, became the centerpiece of national economic reforms (Benbow 2011). Sharing the costs of social services, especially education and healthcare, made it extremely difficult for families like Grace's to have one child in secondary school or university, much less three children who all needed money for fees and related educational expenses.

Nevertheless, there were several youth in the longitudinal study from families with far fewer economic resources than Grace's who still managed to get through secondary school and into university. In most cases, they had not done nearly as well as Grace in primary school but found a way to fund private schooling when they were not selected for the much cheaper option of government (public) school. What accounts for these differences in young people's ability to realize their aspirations?

As noted in earlier chapters, a great deal of educational research today concludes that noncognitive factors like perseverance and resilience are central reasons as to why some youth succeed in school where those from similar backgrounds do not (Duckworth 2016; Dweck 2016; Tough 2016). These qualities, along with cognitive competence, certainly matter. However, the lives of the youth in the longitudinal study demonstrate the significance of three other interlocking forces—class/wealth, geography, and gender—which affect the formation of the social relationships necessary for many youth to advance in school.[3] Even when a young person in the study embodied intelligence, tenacity, and resolve, the absence or presence of *wafadhili* (sponsors) made the difference between the youth ceasing formal education or continuing to secondary school and university. The most critical junctures in these youths' lives corresponded with the high-stakes national examinations at the end of Standard 7 (primary school) and Forms 2, 4, and 6 (secondary school).[4] These are precarious periods for nearly all students, but they are particularly indeterminate for youth whose parents cannot afford fees and related expenses, and must cultivate social relationships that will enable their continuation in school (Vavrus and Moshi 2009).

Throughout the preceding chapters, I have argued that social contingencies greatly affect how one navigates uncertainty, especially the uncertainty surrounding post-primary schooling. I have shown that the formation of social networks is a critical part of youth's efforts to make life certain (*kuhakikisha maisha*), a process that is not limited to Tanzania because state support for higher education has dwindled in many countries. "Uncertainty is entwined with social relations," Cooper and Pratten remind us (2015: 2), and the four youths' lives profiled in this chapter illustrate how the mitigation of uncertainty cannot be achieved by high test scores and persistence alone. It also demands social relationships that can serve as "social insurance and social capital" (Cooper and Pratten 2015: 4); when times are tough, these relations can be converted into the financial capital necessary to pay for schooling.

Yet the lives of the youth in the longitudinal study also reveal the contingent nature of the very terrain upon which they seek to forge these critical social relationships. It is not a solid, steady playing field at all but rather one traversed unevenly by class, geography, and gender relations. I've chosen to highlight four of these stories—two women (Grace and Furaha) and two men (Baraka and Jackson)—because they are particularly poignant illustrations of the different *structured* patterns of possibility for making life more certain through schooling, with cognitive and noncognitive skills only one part of a far more complex picture.

*****

The students in the longitudinal study, including Grace and the three youth profiled below, attended one of the four schools Mr. Mweka and I selected from the eleven in Old Moshi at the time (see Figure 6). As discussed in the Interlude, I sought geographical diversity because I suspected that proximity to Njema Secondary School and the better road, more ample electricity, and proximity to Moshi Town on the west side of the Msangachi River Valley might affect students' performance in primary school and their lives thereafter. Thus, we selected Mbali and Bonde Primary Schools from the eastern side of the valley and Miti and Sokoni from the western side.

Mbali, meaning "far away" in Swahili, was the northernmost primary school in Old Moshi and the one with fewest resources (see Figure 9). The school, in 2000, had no electricity, very limited teaching and learning materials, and some of the classrooms had no cement flooring or windows, making for very uncomfortable conditions during the cold, damp rainy season. Bonde ("valley" in Swahili) is located less than a mile south of Mbali and had significantly more resources than its neighboring school and better academic performance among its students. In many respects, it resembled Miti Primary School, which lies due west and across the valley, but this distance from the infrastructure on the other side of the river helped to explain some of the differences in students' lives at Bonde and Miti.[5]

Miti (meaning "trees") was the closest primary school to Njema Secondary School, and its prominent trees on the edge of the school grounds marked the path to the house where my family and I lived in 1993 and 1996. As discussed in Chapter 2, the school was built in the early 1940s and was the place where many older residents in Old Moshi had studied as children. During part of the twelve-year longitudinal study, the school benefited from a dynamic headmistress who had formed partnerships with organizations in Tanzania and abroad to support its work and had the best infrastructure of the three rural schools in the study.

The fourth primary school, Sokoni (or "market" owing to its proximity to Kiboriloni as described in Chapter 2), sat at the southernmost point of the

Figure 9 Students at Mbali Primary School greeting my students from Teachers College and me, 2003.

all-weather dirt road that runs along the western side of the Msangachi Valley. The road extends beyond Miti and Njema to the north and, to the south, intersects with the paved national highway that runs from Dar es Salaam to Moshi, Arusha, and westward toward the country's famous national parks. The school is semi-urban, meaning it lies on the border of the Moshi Urban and Rural districts, and it stood out among the four schools in the early 2000s for its steady supply of electricity, well-built classrooms, and a few computers.

Even though the four school catchment areas shared some striking similarities—for instance, 96 percent of the families identified as Chagga and 90 percent as Lutheran—the amenities and degree of food security afforded the families in each area varied considerably and changed proportionally over the course of the twelve years of the study.[6] For example, in 2000, about 2 percent of homes in the Mbali catchment area had electricity, and only 24 percent of parents indicated that they always had enough food to eat. Although these figures had increased by 2012 to 14 percent of households with electricity and 36 percent of families with enough food, they remained vastly different from Sokoni, where 77 percent of homes already had electricity in 2000 and 74 percent reported having enough food to eat in 2012. Similarly, there were differences across the four catchment areas in terms of the percentage of Standard 7 students in 2000 who started Form 1 in 2001: Thirty percent for Mbali, 49 percent for Bonde, 60 percent for Miti, and 83 percent for Sokoni. The rest of the youth were at home helping their parents/guardians; studying a trade like carpentry, masonry, or tailoring at a technical school or as an apprentice; working odd jobs as day laborers; or working as domestic laborers, mainly as house girls (see also DeJaeghere 2017).

*****

During the course of the longitudinal study, I became particularly interested in the lives of several young women who had attended Bonde Primary School because of the way their lives had already diverged sharply by 2007, dispelling the notion of a "single story" of rural African women and of the villages in which they live (Adichie 2009). These women left a particularly deep impression because of their difficult circumstances (in three cases) and their efforts to change these conditions, even though they had few social networks through which to cultivate sponsors. All of them had grown up in the Bonde catchment area, and each resided with a parent, parents, or grandparents of modest means who were subsistence farmers with an additional small business on the side, such as tailoring or selling produce. Moreover, these young women were all in the top half, or higher, of their Standard 7 class at Bonde Primary School, and three of them passed the national exam at the end of primary school. Two of them started Form 1 at a government school not far from Bonde, and one finished Form 4 at a private secondary school in Dar es Salaam with her fees paid by her father. The fourth, who lived with her mother in one of the poorest families in the study, did not pass the Standard 7 exam, had a baby not long thereafter, and worked selling food as a street vendor for a while and was then employed at a small restaurant in Moshi. Amina and I visited all four of them again in 2014 even though the longitudinal study ended in 2012, and I continue to stay in touch with one of them via Facebook.

Among these four focal women from Bonde, Furaha's life story was particularly compelling for the twists and turns it had taken from 2000 to 2014. Furaha, like Grace, had done very well in primary school: Grace had been ranked second in her class at Sokoni Primary School, and Furaha ranked third in her class at Bonde. Both young women had also passed the national examination at the end of Standard 7 and had been selected to join government secondary schools for Form 1. However, Grace came from a wealthier family and managed to stay in school through Form 6, even though her parents could not pay for her to attend university as she had hoped. Furaha, owing to her family's more dire economic circumstances, could not complete Form 2 and had no siblings or other relatives willing or able to support her in school. Moreover, she lived farther from relatives and a greater distance from Moshi Town, making it more difficult to communicate with them about school fees at a time when cell phones were not widely available as they are today.

Furaha relayed her story to me in 2007 during an interview over tea and *maandazi* at the YMCA in Moshi. She arrived at 10:00 a.m., dressed in a pressed blouse and skirt with an embroidered handkerchief folded neatly in her hands. Before starting the interview, she politely inquired about Gus, Oscar, and Tim, as well as my family in the United States. I did the same regarding her family even though I knew quite a bit about them from the survey her father had completed a few months earlier.

By the time Furaha and I met in February 2007, she was working as a seamstress at a shop in Kiboriloni because she had been unable to continue in school past Form 2. I had recently interviewed several other youth who had not continued to Form 3, and none of them exuded such grace and confidence. Thus, I had anticipated meeting a young woman with a similar disposition;

instead, she spoke with great self-assurance as she explained how she wanted to continue in school:

> *What was my aim in 2000, you want to know? I wanted to continue studying until I encountered a sign stopping me, inscribed with "no more school for you"! I was so happy when one of my teachers notified me that I had passed the Standard 7 examination, and so, too, were my parents, because it meant I would continue on in school. You know, only one of my sisters completed secondary [school], and there are 10 children in my family—I'm the youngest. So I started Form 1 at Ikundu Secondary School, a government school, in 2001, but I could not continue beyond Form 2 because my parents couldn't pay the fees. My father paid some of the fees for Form 1 but not all of them. When I started Form 2, he could pay nothing at all, so I was sent home frequently to get money.*
>
> *There was a village assistance program for poor students that I registered for when I joined Form 1. I tried to follow up on this assistance when I was in Forms 1 and 2, but there was never any response from this office so I gave up. My father would also go to the village office and get a letter requesting that I be allowed back in school while pledging to pay the overdue fees the following week. After the week had passed with no payment, I would be sent away again, as usual.*
>
> *I managed to finish Form 2 but was barred from taking two of the Form 2 subject exams. I was not even allowed to get the results of the exams I did take because my school fees had not been paid that year. I never went back to the school again. Instead, my sister-in-law took me and taught me tailoring, and that is what I'm doing now.*

In addition to hearing about the financial problems that affected her advancement in school, we also spoke about Furaha's aspirations because tailoring was not her ultimate goal. She noted that she had a cousin with whom she was close who had advised her to find a way to continue in school; however, he could not serve as her sponsor because he was paying school fees for his own children. With only one sibling out of nine who had finished secondary school herself, Furaha's advancement in school was contingent upon finding other relatives or adults to assist her. From the household surveys her father had completed in 2000 and 2006, I knew her brothers and sisters were in no position to help her; furthermore, her father felt stymied by the lack of assistance from the village government and did not have the social capital necessary to find other people to support his youngest child.

Furaha's enthusiasm for schooling and evident ability to succeed led me to discuss with Mr. Mweka the possibility of my serving as her sponsor to complete a special program for adults who wanted to study for and take the Form 4 examination. Furaha eagerly agreed to this plan and, for the next few years, she attended classes in Moshi Town in preparation for the exam. She finally took it in 2011, but she did not pass. During these four years (2007–2011), Furaha got married and had a baby, making it difficult to devote herself to her studies and travel from her home to town to go to school on a regular basis.

When Amina and I interviewed Furaha in 2012, her demeanor and appearance had changed dramatically. This time, and again two years later in 2014, we met in the tiny two-room apartment where she, her husband, and toddler Hoki lived. It was one of five or six apartments that surrounded a courtyard where children played, women washed clothing and dishes, and chickens pecked at scraps of food mixed amid the crushed gravel. Furaha's dress was completely different from 2007 on both of these two latter occasions: Her professional attire had been replaced by a tattered T-shirt and faded *kanga*, which is unusually casual when two guests are expected at one's home. Furaha also spoke harshly to Hoki, who turned six in 2014, as though she was frustrated at him and at the wider world.

During the interview in 2012, Amina and I pressed Furaha to talk about the changes that had happened in her life since 2007, such as getting married, having a baby, and finishing Form 4, even though she did not score high enough to continue to Form 6. Instead, Furaha repeatedly stated that nothing had changed and seemed resigned to her current situation:

Fran: Now what do you think, how has your life changed from 2007 to today?

Furaha: *From my point of view, it's the same. I'm just continuing as always.*

Fran: Have there been any challenges?

Furaha: *No, it's just the same.*

Fran: So you're saying there haven't been any big changes?

Furaha: *No, it's just the same.*

Amina: No changes at all?

Furaha: *Maybe very small ones.*

Amina: I would think that becoming a mother is a big change [laughter]!

Furaha: *No, it's just a small change.*

Fran: And to get married?

Furaha: *[she shook her head and laughed]*

When we met Furaha in 2014, her appearance and resigned tone had changed very little, but she did have a new job working as a cashier at a gas station along the highway leading to Dar es Salaam. She reported that her salary, approximately $90 per month, was far better than her wages as a seamstress, but it required a much longer commute and frequently working seven days a week. When she worked, Hoki attended school or stayed with one of her neighbors because her husband, a day laborer, was also away from home. Furaha made it clear that she was not planning to have another child right away and that she was not going to pursue any further schooling. She explained that her education helped her a lot to keep the books at the gas station and to make change correctly; therefore, she no longer saw any reason to continue in school. Instead, her aspirations were to save money—and get funds from her husband—to open a clothing shop in Kiboriloni.

The person sitting across from Amina and me in 2014 was a decidedly different person from the Standard 7 girl who, in 2000, aspired to attend university and study computer science, and from the young woman in 2007 who still eagerly sought more schooling. There is no single reason for the change in Furaha's trajectory and no solitary source of uncertainty for her future. Instead, she experienced the multiple consequences of poverty intensified by geography and gender: her father's inability to her pay school fees; limited social network of adults with financial resources; distance from the western side of the valley with more developed infrastructure; and an unplanned pregnancy. Whyte and Sui, writing about HIV/AIDS in Uganda, contended that "[s]ocial contingencies are always multiple in that you are dependent on several other people, and the sources of uncertainty are correspondingly several" (2015: 23). This was true not only for Furaha but for other youth in the study as well, including Jackson and Baraka whose stories illustrate how they were better able to overcome some of these obstacles to make their lives more certain.

*****

From Standard 1 to 7, I was always the first in my class. The teachers [at Miti Primary School] liked me because I was mature and well-behaved. Because of the problems in my family, I started school late and was much older than the other children. I was 11 years old when my grandfather came and took me from my parents so that I could go to school and live with him on our family land in Old Moshi.[7] My parents were farmers, and they put little thought into education. This is why I started school late because my parents didn't even know how to get me enrolled, and they didn't have money [for school expenses]. My mother only finished Standard 3 and my father Standard 7. I'm the fifth of seven children, and my oldest brother didn't go to school at all. The others also started school late because of the level of poverty in our home. School was not considered a priority, and all of my brothers and sisters eventually failed the Standard 7 exam.

So began Jackson's accounting, in 2007, of the influence of poverty on his life as a young man in his early twenties finishing Form 6. He was still living with his grandparents because he was attending Njema Secondary School nearby, where Mr. Mweka had taken him under his wing as had several of his teachers in primary school who worked particularly hard to help him succeed in school. Jackson had an acute sense of the importance of schooling if he were to make his life more certain, yet his academic success and determination repeatedly proved insufficient for him to move expediently to the next level. He spent years actively seeking out sponsors and cultivating relationships with teachers and others in the community to help him advance:

> *Before the Standard 7 examination results came out [in 2000], I was worried about failing because I realized that if I did, I would have a lot of problems. This is because my guardians, my grandparents, didn't have the resources to send me to private school. If I failed, I knew I would have to join them in their work. My grandfather had a son who was a mechanic, and he would have sent me to him [as an apprentice]. When I got the news that I had passed, my grandparents were happy, but my mother, who was still alive in 2000, didn't learn of it until I started Form 1, and my father had died in 1998.*
>
> *Because I passed, I was selected for a government secondary school and had a scholarship from the government [to cover additional expenses]. But after the first semester, they [the government] stopped paying my other expenses, only my school fees. I was forced to find a sponsor, a good Samaritan, who helped me with these additional expenses from Form 1 to 4.*

Even though Jackson managed to find a sponsor, a distant relative, this person did not continue to support Jackson after he passed the Form 4 national exam. Thus, he spent the next two years farming with his grandparents and doing casual labor to help cover his living expenses. He investigated government programs to support orphaned children but to no avail, and he pursued an *mzungu* he had met in Moshi, but she had left the country by the time he needed her support.

When Amina and I interviewed Jackson five years later, in 2012, he went into detail about this difficult period in his life and how he made it through owing to his faith and his social network, which eventually enabled him to make connections with a sponsorship program:

> *I stayed at home in 2005 and 2006 and continued to pray to God. "God, I pray that you continue to offer me blessings so that I get money to continue with education because I want to go to school." Imagine, someone could repeat Form 4 and take the O-level examination but fail to attain a [passing] score. Yet I passed, on my first attempt, but I was unable to further my education. I continued to pray to God, and,*

indeed, some people came from the US. They had plans to support [orphans], so I wanted to be part of this sponsorship initiative because I faced all the challenges of being an orphan. My main goal was to go to school and study. I wanted to get support to continue to study. Someone I knew connected me with these individuals from the US. [...]

Because my goal was to attain more education, I did not waste time when I went to Form 5, and I succeeded with a Division 3 with, no, I don't remember with how many points. But I saw that my score enabled me to join the university. At that time, the government was giving priority to the education sector [to individuals who would study education]. Therefore, I chose to study Swahili literature because I had long desired to become a teacher one day. When I finished Form 6, I didn't play around. I joined the university immediately.

Jackson's story serves to illustrate the multiple contingencies that may enable a youth whose life is following one trajectory to move in a decidedly different direction. Had Jackson remained with his parents in the most under-resourced part of the Kilimanjaro Region, it is unlikely that he would have succeeded in primary school, much less attended it at all. His grandparents' home, in contrast, lay close to a good primary and secondary school, and though they did not have resources like electricity in their home, Jackson told me in 2007 that he would go to his neighbor's house each night after his grandparents went to bed and study under the glow of their lights.

In addition, Jackson's gender likely played a role in his grandfather selecting him rather than one of his younger sisters to live at his home even though these girls were also missing school. Jackson's grandparents needed a significant amount of help to maintain their *kihamba* (family homestead), and his grandfather reported on the survey in 2000 that Jackson worked a lot when not in school: caring for the grandparents' farm animals, collecting firewood and water, tending the family garden, cleaning the house, and helping with laundry. Although a girl could have done these tasks too, it's likely that Jackson was considered stronger and more readily able to do this work and still succeed in school. Despite the odds, he did.

*****

It had been several years since I had been to the University of Dar es Salaam (UDSM), a sprawling campus some five miles from the city center. Established in the early days of independence, it became a full-fledged university in 1970 and remains the top-ranked higher education institution in the country (Mgaiwa

2018). Each time I had visited the campus during the previous two decades, I was struck by the contrast between the new buildings under construction for the business school and computer science program while the core of the campus, where the School of Education lies, looked little different from when I was a student there in 1990 during the Swahili language program that initially brought me to Tanzania.[8]

I recall my first reaction to the university with some discomfort today for I focused my gaze on the buildings in disrepair, the slim offerings in the cafeteria, and the bookstore with a very limited supply of books. The university, one of only two in the country in 1990, did not match my image of a flagship institution of higher education even though I knew of its renowned faculty in departments like history and law. Over the years, the contradictions of UDSM, with its many stellar scholars and students working with limited material resources, came to represent for me the education system at large. At every level, from primary school to college, some students make it, even without the benefits of many books. They typically possess the requisite combination of intelligence, perseverance, and resilience, *and* the social and financial capital necessary to stay in school.

Baraka's life vividly illustrated these contingencies, and he brilliantly linked them to the global political economy affecting teaching and learning in Tanzania. We discussed these matters in great detail in 2012, when Baraka, Amina, and I met at one of the restaurants on the UDSM campus. Of the 277 students in the longitudinal study, Baraka was the only one who had, by 2012, made it to this university. He was eager to share with us his views on many matters, from environmental conservation that had become his passion to the politics of pedagogy in postcolonial Africa.

We had also discussed pedagogy extensively in 2007, when Baraka was the only focal youth among the thirty-six who critically analyzed the global political economy and its impact on Tanzanian education. He brought this perspective to a question I posed of all of the youth about how they would recommend improving education in the country. Unlike his peers, who tended to talk about more books and qualified teachers, Baraka used terms like "G8" and "Third World" to explain the gap between how students are educated in the global South and North, and the financial burden on poor families that often prevents their children from going to school. With echoes of Edward (see Chapter 10), Baraka spoke at length about the Tanzanian education system by comparing it to other parts of the world:

To tell the truth, there's a big difference between our Tanzanian education and that of developed countries like the G8 ... We don't have an education system that challenges students to be creative ... They [teachers] would come and tell us the map is like this or that without showing us a map in class. They would tell us that the world was round without proof. We were only taught theory, and if you asked a question the teacher would criticize you and tell you to do this or that [as punishment] ... Our counterparts in the developed world, on the other hand, have a very demanding education that helps them to discover a lot. We Tanzanian students don't discover much on our own because our teaching is based more on theory.

And many families in the Third World are poor; parents are unable to take their children to school due to a lack of money to pay fees ... I was unable to join Form 1 [at first] due to my family's poverty and the high school fees.

Baraka moved from this macro-level discussion of education to his own story when he explained how this kind of teaching had affected him. Unlike Grace, Furaha, and Jackson, Baraka *had* failed the Primary School Leaving Examination at the end of Standard 7. Therefore, he was not eligible to attend a government secondary school where the fees would have been a fraction of the cost at a private school. Baraka had attended Sokoni Primary School along with Grace, but unlike her, he was ranked only forty-ninth out of his class of 129 students. Moreover, Baraka acknowledged in his questionnaire in 2000, when he was a Standard 7 student, that he had been caned by teachers for misbehaving and had not been a school leader. In response to the question about the kind of work he might like to do in the future, Baraka's broad, non-specific answer of "pastor" and "government official" were more similar to those of average students than academic standouts like Grace, Furaha, and Jackson.

However, Baraka faced financial challenges similar to the other three but not as dire as Furaha or Jackson's situations. His mother and father had divorced years before, when he was a child, and Baraka's father, who had finished Form 4, was not involved in his life by 2000. Baraka's mother had only completed Standard 7, though she served as a teacher in their Pentecostal church, earning very little and unable to pay for him to attend a private secondary school. He was the only child of his mother and father; he had many step-siblings from father's second marriage, but none had gone far in school and no one was compelled to help him. Therefore, Baraka began to pursue other adults in his social network who might serve as *wafadhili*—sponsors—for some kind of post-primary education.

Living with his mother in the Sokoni catchment area, Baraka could get to Moshi Town more easily than youth in the three more rural schools. This offered him some options for where he went to school, and he cultivated different sponsors to help him, first, get into some kind of post-primary schooling and, second, to change to a school he preferred:

> Baraka: *After the Standard 7 results were out and I knew I had failed, I went to an older aunt of mine for help because my mother's financial situation was bad. I saw this as the only opportunity … so I went to Moshi Technical with the aim of acquiring vocational education. I studied electrical engineering and installation as an introductory course.*
>
> Fran: So you did not go to Moshi Tech for regular secondary schooling?
>
> Baraka: *No, even though we studied five other subjects, technical education was the main thing we studied. It was not my wish to study technical education. It was my unstable background at home that made me decide not to just sit idle at home doing nothing. So when my aunt offered to pay for my technical education, I just agreed even though it was not what I wanted.*

Baraka had little interest in vocational training, but he went ahead and completed the course. Within a year, though, Baraka had secured a second sponsor, an acquaintance who was not a relative but who promised to pay Baraka's secondary school fees if he were accepted to a private school. Thus, Baraka took the placement exam at a private day school in town and received the top score among the applicants. He started his post-primary schooling all over again in Form 1 at this school.

A year later, Baraka received a high score on the national Form 2 examination and was selected for a government school for the remainder of his O-level studies. By this time, his mother had a boyfriend who offered to pay his expenses at a boarding school in a town in the central part of the country. Once at the boarding school, Baraka could devote himself to his studies without the domestic work at home, and he easily passed the Form 4 exam as well as the Form 6 exam two years later. The following year, in 2008, he was admitted to the University of Dar es Salaam, where he had recently completed his bachelor's degree when we met in 2012.

*****

Baraka, Grace, Furaha, and Jackson are not typical of the youth in the longitudinal study in that they, unlike their peers, completed some post-primary schooling and three of them post-secondary education as well. However, what their lives do illustrate are the different kinds of contingencies—material and social—that enable or impede the progression of youth through the education system.

The slight economic advantages that Grace and Baraka had and the geographic benefit of living closer to Moshi aided them in completing secondary school and receiving some kind of post-secondary education, even if it was not, as in Grace's case, the kind of education to which she initially aspired. In contrast, Furaha's home across the valley and her family's limited social and financial capital impeded her chances of finishing secondary school. Yet sponsorship in Furaha's case was still not sufficient to enable her to pass the O-level examination because of the demands on her time and energy once she got married and had a child. Jackson's story of moving from a place where he was not going to school at all to one where he could attend both primary and secondary school indicates the importance of geography. Moreover, his age and gender likely contributed to his academic success in school and ability to create a strong social network of adults, starting with his grandfather, who helped him succeed even though it took him a while because of his family's financial situation.

In none of these cases was continuation to the next level of schooling certain. In Baraka's case, he failed the national examination at the end of primary school; Jackson had no one in his family to pay for his schooling even though he successfully passed the PSLE and the O-level examination; Furaha could not even sit for the Form 2 examination because her fees had not been paid; and Grace's parents could not fund the degree in journalism and economics she had sought.

Despite this uncertainty, none of these youth sat idly by and simply waited for life to happen to them. They had made "adjustments to the present" at critical junctures in their young lives that meant, for Grace and Furaha, relinquishing their optimism about the future as they had envisioned it in 2000 and 2007, and establishing different goals that reflected this recalibration (Berlant 2011: 20). In all four cases, these youth strove to "enact certain visions of what will happen" in their lives by seeking out relationships that might enable them to achieve their aspirations while recognizing that these plans, be they God's plan for them or not, were different from what they had intended (Calkins 2016: 3).

This recalibration of aspirations may be the primary way in which we adjust to schooling as uncertainty: Despite academic success that demands both cognitive ability and noncognitive skills, we still may not be able to persist in school. Work as hard as we may, it may still not be enough to succeed. And yet most of us keep at it, recalibrating, re-envisioning, and rethinking the social contingencies that might help us make our lives just a bit more certain.

Epilogue

[U]ncertainty saturates the natural and social world and so frames the relative security we enjoy.
  —Melvin Rogers 2007: 101, discussing Dewey's *Experience and Nature* 1925

It took only one brief weekend in December 2017 for the relative security upon which my world rested to dissolve. On Friday, I reveled in the signing of a book contract; on Saturday, I delighted in the elegant dinner Tim had arranged to celebrate this accomplishment; on Sunday, I sat in stunned silence as my spouse of twenty-five years told me he had met a woman in Tanzania and did not intend to end this new relationship. He abruptly moved out of the house a few weeks later, and, by the beginning of March 2018, less than three months after his announcement, we were divorced. Nothing had prepared me for this moment, and no amount of education could make it go away.

The rapid unraveling of my marriage was devastating, and it profoundly changed my relationship with the preceding chapters. As I revised them after the divorce, I was forced to reconsider the years in which I had been married through the prism of uncertainty and contingency. I wondered whether my marital misgivings from decades earlier indicated a kind of crisis ordinariness, "an amplification of something in the works" to which I should have been more attentive (Berlant 2011: 10). I also felt the sting of cruel optimism even after the divorce was finalized, existing in a suspended state by "maintaining an attachment to a significantly problematic object," in this case to the man with whom I still hoped to grow old (Berlant 2011: 24). Yet, as Berlant might have predicted, he never returned home.

Even though it was difficult to eat, sleep, or envision a future without my longtime partner, there were myriad personal and financial decisions that simply could not wait. The precarity of the present became a catalyst for change, and Calkins's words echoed in my head while speaking to lawyers, realtors, and bankers. Uncertainty, she whispered, is generative, and you must act "to know, organize and govern the future and to make it more calculable" (2016: Chapter 1, Location 1153).

Thus I acted, but I never did so alone. As Cooper and Pratten reminded me, "[U]ncertainty does not exist as an autonomous, external condition. Rather, uncertainty is entwined with social relations" (2015: 2). Throughout this period of acute pain, I discovered that my wellbeing was as contingent on social ties as it was for the Tanzanians whose lives had become entwined with my own (Bledsoe 2002; Johnson-Hanks 2006; Whyte and Sui 2015). Strong social bonds stretching from Minneapolis to Moshi supported me, with friends and family coming for visits and calling to offer advice. Their presence helped to render the future more predictable, the daily pinging of text messages and buzzing of the cell phone buttressing me during this uncertain time (Calkins 2016).

One of the most vivid examples of these sustaining relationships came a few months after the divorce. From across the living room, my cell phone started ringing with the distinct sound of a WhatsApp call, which meant a friend from abroad was trying to reach me. This morning, it was Amina.

"Dada," she stated firmly, "I'm worried about you because you haven't responded to my messages for a while, and I wanted to hear your voice."

After apologizing for not returning her texts, I listened as Amina began to explain the purpose of her call. She had been thinking a lot about what had happened to Gus, Oscar, and me in the past six months and was still struggling to believe I was now divorced. "*Amelogwa*" (He's been possessed), Amina concluded about my ex-husband to explain this sudden turn of events. She went on to say that the new woman was the likely culprit, and there was little I could have done to have stopped him from leaving me. Therefore, she said, I had to toughen up and move on. I needed to build a future by living as though my former spouse had died and to focus on the blessing of two boys that resulted from our decades together. "Life is about more than marriage," Amina reminded me, resolute in her conviction that the end of this marriage did not mean the termination of the vibrant life I had built with my sons or the preclusion of happiness with another man. After we said our goodbyes, I sat and reflected on Amina's words for a very long time. She was right: Tim had, indeed, been possessed, enchanted by the adventure and excitement of a new love, and this was a potent spell I could not have broken.

Amina's astute reframing oriented me toward another way of seeing the termination of this relationship and helped me to address the cruel optimism of my circumstances. Even though I had been immersed in the concept while writing this book, I could not see how the unlikely possibility of any further relationship with the "problematic object" of my desire had become a cruel attachment affecting my wellbeing (Berlant 2006: 21). In the end, letting go of this object and accepting uncertainty as a productive force in my life allowed me to embody the thesis of this book.

*****

Uncertainty has served as the backstory for many people whose lives have been recounted in the preceding chapters, including my former colleagues at Njema. In 2015, their lives were upended by the sudden closure of the school. During a visit in 2017, Amina and I had the opportunity to speak with Mr. Mweka and a number of people who had worked on campus or earned a living selling food and provisions to its students. They described in detail the precarity of the situation and noted that it was still far from resolved two years later. As one of the former teachers explained:

> *I still remember the date very well—April 13, 2015—the day we returned from the mid-term holiday and found no students at Njema. The teachers were not told in advance that students would no longer be there. They had simply been taken away to government schools, and we were not informed.*

Another of my former colleagues chronicled the events that had led him and others to seek other positions even though it was difficult to do so:

> *The teaching and non-teaching staff hired a hiace [minivan] to go to Moshi Town and talk to the Bishop. He knew, of course, that the students were not going to return after the mid-term break, but he had not told us. During our meeting, the Bishop repeatedly said, "Don't worry. You are still our employees, and you should keep going to Njema even if there are no students to teach. We will take this issue all the way to the President's Office to make sure you are paid."*
>
> *At first, we believed him, but then as the months went by, we asked the Bishop to get our official termination letters so we could go to the NSSF [National Social Security Fund] to get our contributions, but the Bishop said the church was taking care of things and repeated that we should not be worried about our jobs. This is what really irritates me. You know, we're educated people and can understand things if they were explained to us. But the church leaders never even called a meeting to console the staff about the situation—nothing, nothing, nothing.*
>
> *Finally, we went to the Labor Office to report that we had still not gotten our letters of termination to take to NSSF and claim the contributions we made over the years. We needed to pay for things like our children's school fees. The Labor Office was sympathetic but told us these church officials are difficult and refuse to*

come to meetings. The problem is that the government has no legal right to sue the church, so we are only waiting as this process of mediation continues.

During our visit, Amina and I were told several different reasons for the closure of Njema, including poor academic administration, a dispute over land ownership, a conflict between the opposition and ruling political parties, and competition from the nearby ward school. Most thought it was a tragedy that the school had closed, though there was a vocal group of residents who wanted this private school turned over to the government as a public O-level institution or converted to a vocational school. All agreed, however, that the education system in the country was failing many young people, who struggled to find decent jobs after Standard 7 or Form 4. These parents and grandparents concurred that *kuhakikisha maisha*, the effort to make life certain, was becoming a more distant dream as salaried employment grows increasingly scarce, agriculture becomes more difficult due to climate change and land scarcity, and political tensions mount under the country's authoritarian president.

The strain of uncertainty surrounding the fate of the school was inscribed on the bodies of my former colleagues, their thinner frames and whiter locks leading me to wonder about a community being collectively worn down. Berlant's notion of "slow death" came to mind as I listened to these repeated efforts, which have continued to the present, to find justice for those caught between church and state (2007: 754).

Many residents of Old Moshi may be suffering, but this framing does not sufficiently capture the productive dimensions of the uncertainty surrounding their futures. The staff pressed for their back pay; women in the neighborhood moved into new markets; and, in the case of the teachers, many of them found positions at other schools, including Mr. Mweka. "The productivity of indeterminacy is not a given condition," as Di Nunzio wrote in reference to his research with youth in Ethiopia, but it often sparks action across a "terrain of possibility" (2015: 153). Schooling as uncertainty speaks not only to the indeterminate future education may afford us as beings marked by gender, race, class, and nationality; it also reminds us that schools themselves are social institutions deeply embedded in communities whose optimistic attachment to them may lead to immiseration or whose loss may propel new possibilities.

*****

It is Amina's story, however, that may best exemplify the dual nature of schooling and uncertainty. She could have very easily failed secondary school after her mother's death because the odds were never with her to succeed. She might not have completed university as she was dealing with a very complicated pregnancy and birth during her final semester. And she was tightly attached to schooling as a deeply desired object, and its nonattainment could have been a cruel indictment of the unrealistic optimism of youth from very poor families to radically change their circumstances.

Yet succeed she did, through intelligence, grit, *and* social relationships that have enabled her to continue in school when other bright young women from difficult background could not. We have shared many moments in each other's lives, and this "co-temporality" as we have navigated challenging circumstances has become part of our intimate lexicon whereby one of us says, or sends in a text, the word *changamoto* (challenges) and the other finishes the phrase: challenges of motherhood, challenges of doing research, and, most recently, challenges of building a house as we have spent the past six months constructing adjoining homes on the slopes of Mount Kilimanjaro (Fabian 2014: 205).

Amina is no longer the fifteen-year-old girl who yearned to go to secondary school any more than I am still the thirty-one-year-old graduate student and new mother finding her way in the academy. Maybe our serendipitous meeting was *mpango wa Mungu*, God's plan; we will never know. Yet I'm convinced that it has been our shared experiences of uncertainty and support provided to each other that has enabled us, in our very different social worlds, to make our lives a little more secure.

Notes

Figures

1   My thanks to Jules Wight for his assistance in formatting the photographs used throughout the book.

Introduction

1   The terms *education* and *schooling* are often used interchangeably, but it is important to keep in mind the distinction between them. Cremin (1978) defined education as the "deliberate, systematic, and sustained effort to transmit, evoke, or acquire knowledge, attitudes, values, skills, or sensibilities, and any learning that results from the effort, direct or indirect, intended or unintended" (701). Schooling more narrowly describes these efforts in one particular institution: the school. Although I will frequently use the term *education* in this broad sense, my primary goal is to explore beliefs about schooling and educative practices in schools.

2   Appendix A provides details on the various research and teaching projects in which I was involved from 1992 to 2017, the period from which most of the examples and arguments in this book are drawn.

3   See Appendix B for details on the Tanzanian education system.

4   Dewey's view of uncertainty is remarkably similar: "We survey conditions, make the wisest choice we can; we act, and we must trust the rest to fate, fortune, or providence" (1929: 7).

5   I have used this pseudonym for the school in my past publications and retain it here for the sake of consistency even though readers familiar with the region will undoubtedly be able to identify it due to its historical significance. I have also used a pseudonym for the college where I taught from 2006 to 2007, again due to using this name in previous publications.

6   I have opted for pseudonyms for my colleagues and friends in Tanzania to protect their confidentiality because some of the stories I recount contain painful moments or politically sensitive matters. The only exception to this rule is the late Mr. Ramos Makindara, the son of the last chief of Old Moshi, whom I discuss in Chapter 2 and whose identity I could not easily conceal. I have used the actual names of my US

friends and family members only when they have given me permission to do so, and I have used pseudonyms in other cases.

7   There are important exceptions to this view that have informed my thinking on this matter, especially Bartlett, Dowd, and Jonason (2015) and Sayed and Ahmed (2015).

Chapter 1

1   Dar es Salaam is considered the commercial capital of Tanzania even though Dodoma, located in the center of the country, is the official capital. In fact, Tanzania and Zimbabwe are not adjacent but rather are separated by Zambia, Malawi, and Mozambique.

2   The country known today as the United Republic of Tanzania was formed in 1964 by the union of Tanganyika, the mainland, and the islands of Zanzibar and Pemba. Thus, President Nyerere was initially the leader of Tanganyika before the formation of the union three years later.

Chapter 2

1   For a more detailed account of the history of Moshi and Old Moshi, see Vavrus (2003 and 2016a).

Chapter 4

1   More recent studies uphold this trend, but most point toward a delay in fertility and to intermediary factors that affect how schooling may affect childbearing (see Ezeh, Mberu, and Emina 2009; Shapiro and Gebreselassie 2013). For instance, the correlation may not hold as strongly, or even at all, once women finish their schooling. Other factors affect fertility, too, such as access to or use of contraception (Bongaarts 2010; Musick et al. 2009), religious affiliation (Zhang 2008), social networks of which women are a part (Colleran et al. 2014), and uncertainty about the economy or their relationships (Musick et al. 2009).

2   By contrast, the figure for the United States in the mid-1990s was less than 1 percent in either age category for both Black and white children (United Nations Development Programme 2017; Ventura et al. 1997). In recent years, Tanzania has made tremendous improvements in these areas, with the infant mortality rate

dropping to 4.3 percent and the under-five rate down to 6.7 percent for the period from 2010–2011 to 2015–2016 (Ministry of Health 2016).

3   It is important to note the striking racial differences in infant mortality rates in the United States that persist to the present: As of 2017, the rate was 2.3 times higher for African Americans at 11 infant deaths per 1,000 live births compared to 4.7 for non-Hispanic white infants (Office of Minority Health 2017).

4   Asthma rates in the United States vividly illustrate racial health disparities in this country as African Americans have a 20 percent higher rate for the disease than the nationwide average, and the costs for steroid inhalers have skyrocketed (Rosenthal 2013). Moreover, severe and moderate asthma conditions may increase the risk of serious illness from COVID-19 (Centers for Disease Control and Prevention 2020).

Chapter 5

1   *Chagga* and *Chaga* are both acceptable spellings for the ethnic group that predominates on Mount Kilimanjaro and in the Kilimanjaro Region. The research for this book was conducted as part of Raum's PhD in anthropology at the London School of Economics, where Raum, who had grown up in Moshi as the son of German Lutheran missionaries, studied with giants in the field like Bronislaw Malinowski and Audrey Richards ("Short Portrait: Otto Raum" 2012).

Chapter 6

1   In 1996, the female students commuted to school each day because the girls' dormitory had not yet been completed. They all lived within walking distance, though for some a long walk, to Njema, and they were required to come to campus on a rotation to clean the school during the Christmas holiday. They also had this responsibility during the school year and often stayed after school and came in on Saturdays to do so. In this case, some of the girls did not show up to clean during the December holiday, and their punishment was administered in March for reasons that were never made clear. I surmised that it had to do with the period when students were needed to help prepare the school farm for planting. From my field notes, I can discern an uptick in punishment involving work on the school farm during March and April.

2   Bold in the interview transcripts indicates a word or phrase uttered with emphasis by the interviewee. Interviews conducted in English, such as this one, have not been edited to make them conform to Standard American English.

Chapter 7

1 For a fuller discussion of Amina's life and the strategies Tanzanian youth employ to stay in school, see Vavrus (2015).

2 James was using a phrase common among youth in Kilimanjaro at the time to mean that contracting AIDS is a stroke of bad luck, similar to having an accident and not something one could foresee or prevent (see Setel 1999).

3 A similar analysis can be found in Berlant's (2011) discussion of obesity in the United States and what she termed "interruptive agency," an illustration being when obese persons are "lectured at, shamed, and exhorted to die" and yet "these exhortations go unheard" (114–15). She argued that refusing to follow advice to make oneself healthier is a feature of "slow death," whereby the poor and working classes, in particular, are "wearing out" (95).

Chapter 8

1 These are terms used widely in the demographic and health literature to describe a child who has lost one parent (a single orphan) or both parents (a double orphan) (Guest 2001). In Tanzania, however, any child who has lost one parent or two is referred to as *mtoto yatima*, an orphaned child.

Chapter 9

1 The typical time for the tenure review is during the junior faculty member's sixth year at her institution. This is based on the guidelines established by the American Association of University Professors (AAUP 2014a). However, the "tenure clock," as it is known, can be stopped for a semester, year, or longer owing to childbirth, adoption, illness, or other factors.

2 In subsequent years, Lesley Bartlett and I have published three books, one monograph, seven articles, and four book chapters together, and she was a critical partner in the Teaching in Action program discussed in Chapter 11.

3 Research 1 (or R1) is the top category on the Carnegie Classification of Institutions of Higher Education system used in the United States. R1 denotes a university granting at least twenty different doctoral degrees (excluding professional doctoral degrees such as MD) and "highest research activity" (Indiana University Center for Postsecondary Research 2017a). "Research activity" is calculated via indices of aggregate and per capita measures, including expenditure on research, staffing, and doctoral degrees conferred (Indiana University Center for Postsecondary Research 2017b).

Chapter 10

1   I have used the designation inter/national in previous publications to indicate that the distinction between policies formulated by international financial institutions, such as the World Bank and the IMF, and the national policies of heavily indebted poor countries like Tanzania is often quite blurry (Vavrus 2005).

2   The interviews with my former students were conducted in English, and these are verbatim excerpts from the transcripts.

Chapter 11

1   Tanzania receives grants and borrows money from domestic and international lenders to cover the shortfall in its revenue collection while still paying salaries and purchasing supplies in sectors that include education and infrastructure. Overseas development assistance alone accounts for more than 25 percent of the country's budget (Tripp 2012). Therefore, funding from the central government for municipal projects like this one may come from domestic tax revenue or foreign aid.

2   My description of these meetings is an illustration of turning field notes into a vignette, a story based closely on short notes taken during an event and then fleshed out at a later time (Emerson, Fretz, and Shaw 1995).

3   I would like to acknowledge the primary members of the TIA team during the years in which I was most involved with the program, namely, 2007–2011: Lesley Bartlett, Theresia Boniface, Angelista Joseph, Edward Kileo, Denis Mbilinyi, Augustina Mtanga, Allen Rugambwa, Brent Ruter, Victorini Salema, and Bethany Wilinski. Matthew Thomas was an especially important member of this team as he helped with workshop facilitation and data management, and he continued to work with some members of the team well beyond 2011.

4   These two examples are presented in modified form in Thomas and Vavrus (2019).

Chapter 12

1   The cut off score for entrance to public universities has changed over time depending on the number of available spots and funding through the government's student loan program. Since the late 1990s, women have gained admission and access to loans with lower scores than men to address the gender imbalance in higher education (for instance, more than 60 percent of the students at the University of Dar es Salaam are male) (Kilango, Qin, Nyoni, and Senguo 2017).

A Division 3 (on a scale of 1—highest—to 4, the lowest besides an outright fail) would have been sufficient for Grace to enter the university.

2   The national participation rate in higher education institutions was 2.4 percent in 2013–2014, and the Tanzania Commission for University's (TCU) 2015/16–2019/20 Strategic Plan seeks to increase this figure to 4 percent by 2020. It also intends to increase the percentage of female students at colleges and universities from 36 percent (2012–2013) to 50 percent by 2020 (Tanzania Commission for Universities 2016).

3   If this study had been conducted in the United States, race would certainly have been on this list of forces affecting opportunities for higher education. For instance, three-quarters of the students at the nation's top 468 colleges and universities are white, and 34 percent of Black and Latino youth are attending college compared to 42 percent among their white peers (Marcus 2018).

4   The latest *Education and Training Policy* (MOEVT 2014) marks a significant change in the education system because it states: "The government shall establish procedures for a compulsory ten (10) years basic education from Standard 1 to Form 4," and that this basic education will be "fee free" (19–20). Six years later, it is still not clear how comprehensively this policy is being implemented across the country.

5   I do not include any former students from Mbali in this chapter because they were the least likely to continue in school beyond the primary level, and there were only a few focal youth from Mbali—both young men—who had been interviewed in 2007 and could be located again in 2012. Instead, I include two youth, one woman (Grace) and one man (Baraka), from Sokoni Primary School because of the parallel nature of their post-primary school stories, one woman from Bonde (Furaha), and one man from Miti (Jackson).

6   Children typically attend the public primary school closest to their home, and this was the case for the students in this study. Thus, the families of the children who attended Sokoni, for instance, usually lived in the southernmost stratum on the mountain while the families of children attending Mbali lived in the northern part of Old Moshi. See Vavrus (2003, 2016a) and Vavrus and Moshi (2009) for details on the longitudinal study.

7   At this time, children typically began Standard 1 between the ages of 6 and 7. The 2014 *Education and Training Policy* stipulates that children should begin primary school between ages 4 and 6, which is significantly younger than in previous policies (MOEVT 2014).

8   The School of Education recently moved to a new, spacious building on the edge of the Mlimani campus.

Appendix A: Summary of Research and Teaching Activities in Tanzania

Dates	Primary Activities	Primary Participants
1992–1993	- "Hanging out" and studying Swahili - Teaching at Njema Secondary School	- Neighbors and Tim - Form 2 and 4 students, teachers, and administrators
1996	- Dissertation research in Old Moshi: - Participant-observation - Interviewing - Surveying - Archival research in Dar es Salaam - "Hanging out" in Old Moshi	- Students, teachers, and administrators at Njema and six other schools in the Kilimanjaro and Arusha Regions - Education officials in Kilimanjaro and Dar es Salaam - Out-of-school girls in Moshi and Old Moshi - Tim, Hannah, Amina, and other neighbors
2000	- First round of data collection in longitudinal study in Old Moshi - Mail-in survey	- 277 parents/guardians and students in Standards 6 and 7 at four primary schools in Old Moshi; Mr. Mweka - 225 former students at Njema and Safi Secondary Schools in Old Moshi
2001	- Second round of data collection in longitudinal study - Focus group discussions	- 128 parents/guardians of students who were in Standard 7 in 2000; Mr. Mweka - 20 former students at Njema and Safi Secondary Schools in Old Moshi
2002	Data presentations and discussions	- Parents/guardians, teachers, and school heads at the four primary schools in the longitudinal study; Mr. Mweka
2003	Development Policy in Practice course	- 10 graduate students from Teachers College, Columbia University; Amina and Mr. Mweka

Dates	Primary Activities	Primary Participants
2004	- "Hanging out" in Old Moshi - HIV/AIDS study of grandparents	- Tim, Gus, Oscar, Amina, and Mama Ephraim - 12 grandparents
2005	Development Policy in Practice course	- 12 graduate students from Teachers College and Columbia University's School of International and Public Affairs
2006–2007	- Fulbright Scholar at Badiliko Teachers College - Third round of data collection in longitudinal study - Development of Teaching in Action workshop with Badiliko colleagues	- Students and faculty at college - Tim, Gus, and Oscar - Parents/guardians of former Standards 6 and 7 students; Mr. Mweka - 36 youth and 6 former Badiliko student interviews - 5 interviews with colleagues at Badiliko
2008	Teaching in Action workshop	Badiliko faculty, Tanzanian secondary school teachers, and 4 US facilitators
2009	Teaching in Action workshop	Badiliko faculty, Tanzanian secondary school teachers, and 4 US facilitators
2010	Teaching in Action workshop and launch of research project with participants	Badiliko faculty, Tanzanian secondary school teachers, and 7 US facilitators
2011	Teaching in Action workshop and research conference at Badiliko Teachers College	Badiliko faculty and students, Tanzanian secondary school teachers, and 3 US facilitators
2012	- Teaching in Action workshop - Fourth round of data collection in longitudinal study	- Badiliko faculty, Tanzanian secondary school teachers, and 1 US facilitator - Parents/guardians of former Standards 6 and 7 students; Mr. Mweka - 20 interviews with former students; Amina
2014	- Teaching in Action workshop - Life history interviews	- Badiliko faculty, Tanzanian secondary school teachers, and 2 US facilitators - 4 young women from Bonde Primary School; Amina

Dates	Primary Activities	Primary Participants
2015	Teaching in Action workshop	- Badiliko faculty, Tanzanian secondary school teachers, and 2 US facilitators - Faculty at a second teachers college developing their own version of the workshop
2017	- Participation in National Conference on Teacher Training in Tanzania - Focus group discussions about the closure of Njema Secondary School	- Ministry of Education, Science and Technology and international and national NGOs - Former neighbors and teachers at Njema; Amina
2019	- Meetings with faculty and administrators of 5 colleges and universities in Dar es Salaam and Moshi to discuss new initiatives for pre- and in-service teacher education	- Amina - Mr. Mweka

Appendix B: Overview of the Tanzanian Education System

Level	Approximate Age of Students	Grades
Preprimary	5–6 years old	–
Primary	7–13 years old	Standards 1–7
Lower secondary	14–17 years old	Forms 1–4
Upper secondary	18–19 years old	Forms 5–6
Post-secondary	20–22 years old	Certificate (1–2 years)
		Diploma (2 years)
Tertiary	20–30 years old	Bachelor's degree (3 years)
		Master's degree (1–2 years)
		PhD (3+ years)

Information based upon Ministry of Education and Vocational Training (n.d). Available online: https://www.scholaro.com/pro/Countries/Tanzania/Education-System

References

Abowitz, K. K. (2016), "Imagining Democratic Futures for Public Universities: Educational Leadership against Fatalism's Temptations," *Educational Theory*, 66 (1–2): 181–97.

Abrahams, P. (1963), *Mine Boy*, Lawrence, KS: University Press of Kansas.

Adichie, C. N. (2009), "The Danger of a Single Story," *TED Talk*, July. Available online: https://www.ted.com/talks/chimamanda_adichie_the_danger_of_a_single_story (accessed November 14, 2016).

Agarwal, M. and D. Satish (2017), *Bridge International Academies*, Telangana, India: IBS Center for Management Research.

Ainsworth, M. and I. Semali (2000), *The Impact of Adult Deaths on Children's Health in Northwestern Tanzania*. (Policy Research Working Paper 2266), Washington: World Bank Publications.

Ainsworth, M., K. Beegle, and A. Nyamete (1995), "The Impact of Women's Schooling on Fertility and Contraceptive Use: A Study of Fourteen Sub-Saharan African Countries," *The World Bank Economic Review*, 10 (1): 85–122.

Althusser, L. (1971), *Lenin and Philosophy and Other Essays*, New York: Monthly Review Press.

American Association of University Professors (1940), *1940 Statement of Principles on Academic Freedom and Tenure*. Available online: https://www.aaup.org/report/1940-statement-principles-academic-freedom-and-tenure (accessed July 17, 2018).

American Association of University Professors (2014a), *Recommended Institutional Regulations on Academic Freedom and Tenure*. Available online: https://www.aaup.org/report/recommended-institutional-regulations-academic-freedom-and-tenure (accessed July 17, 2018).

American Association of University Professors (2014b), *Tenure and Teaching-Intensive Appointments*. Available online: https://www.aaup.org/AAUP/comm/rep/teachertenure.htm#b5 (accessed July 18, 2018).

Anderson, L. W. and D. R. Krathwohl, eds. (2000), *A Taxonomy for Learning, Teaching, and Assessing: A Revision of Bloom's Taxonomy of Educational Objectives*, New York: Pearson.

Apple, M. (1990), *Ideology and Curriculum*, London: Routledge.

Bagachwa, M. S. and E. Cromwell (1995), *Structural Adjustment and Sustainable Development in Tanzania*, Dar es Salaam: Dar es Salaam University Press.

Bahn, K. (2014), "Faking It: Women, the Academy, and the Imposter Syndrome," *The Chronicle of Higher Education*, March 27. Available online: https://chroniclevitae.

com/news/412-faking-it-women-academia-and-impostor-syndrome (accessed July 15, 2018).

Bartlett, L. and F. Vavrus (2019), "Rethinking the Concept of 'Context' in Comparative Research," In R. Gorur, S. Sellar, and G. Steiner-Khamsi (eds), *Comparative Methodology in the Era of Big Data and Global Networks: World Yearbook of Education*, 187–201. London and New York: Routledge.

Bartlett, L., A. J. Dowd, and C. Jonason (2015), "Problematizing Early Grade Reading: Should the Post-2015 Agenda Treasure What Is Measured?" *International Journal of Educational Development*, 40: 308–14.

Bartlett, L., G. Oliveira, and L. Ungemah (2018), "Cruel Optimism: Migration and Schooling for Dominican Newcomer Immigrant Youth," *Anthropology and Education Quarterly*, 49 (4): 444–61.

Beck, U. (1992), *Risk Society: Towards a New Modernity*, London and Thousand Oaks, CA: SAGE Publications.

Beckmann, N. (2015), "The Quest for Trust in the Face of Uncertainty: Managing Pregnancy Outcomes in Zanzibar," In E. Cooper and D. Pratten (eds), *Ethnographies of Uncertainty in Africa*, 59–83. London: Palgrave Macmillan.

Behar, R. (1991), "Death and Memory: From Santa María del Monte to Miami Beach," *Cultural Anthropology*, 6 (3): 346–84.

Behar, R. (1996), *The Vulnerable Observer: Anthropology That Breaks Your Heart*, Boston: Beacon Press.

Benbow, R. (2011), "With Hope for the Future: Privatization, Development, and the New University in Tanzania," PhD dissertation, University of Wisconsin-Madison.

Bender, M. V. (2013), "Being 'Chagga': Natural Resources, Political Activism, and Identity on Kilimanjaro," *The Journal of African History*, 54 (2): 199–220.

Berlant, L. (2006), "Cruel Optimism," *Differences: A Journal of Feminist Cultural Studies*, 17 (3): 20–36.

Berlant, L. (2007), "Slow Death (Sovereignty, Obesity, Lateral Agency)," *Critical Inquiry*, 33: 754–80.

Berlant, L. (2011), *Cruel Optimism*, Durham, NC: Duke University Press.

Besousa, M., M. Bousquet, L. Barnes, C. Nelson, M. Newfield, J. Nienow, and K. Thompson (2014), "Tenure and Teaching Intensive Appointments," Available online: https://www.aaup.org/AAUP/comm/rep/teachertenure.htm#2 (accessed July 20, 2018).

Blakely, J. (2017), "A History of the Conservative War on Universities," *The Atlantic*, December 7. Available online: https://www.theatlantic.com/education/archive/2017/12/a-history-of-the-conservative-war-on-universities/547703/ (accessed July 21, 2018).

Bledsoe, C. (1990), "'No Success Without Struggle': Social Mobility and Hardship for Foster Children in Sierra Leone," *Man*, 25 (1): 70–88.

Bledsoe, C. (2002), *Contingent Lives: Fertility, Time, and Aging in West Africa*, Chicago: University of Chicago Press.

Bloom, D., D. Canning, and K. Chan (2006), *Higher Education and Economic Development in Africa*, Washington: World Bank (Africa Region).

Bongaarts, J. (2010), "The Causes of Educational Differences in Fertility in Sub-Saharan Africa," *Vienna Yearbook of Population Research*, 8 (1): 31–50.

Bourdieu, P. (1977), *Outline of a Theory of Practice*, Cambridge: Cambridge University Press.

Bourdieu, P. and J. C. Passeron (1990), *Reproduction in Education, Society, and Culture*, London and Thousand Oaks, CA: SAGE Publications.

Bourdieu, P. and L. J. D. Wacquant (1992), *An Invitation to Reflective Sociology*, Chicago: University of Chicago Press.

Brice, A. (2017), "Celebrating 'Barefoot Anthropology'—A Q and A with Nancy Scheper-Hughes," *Berkeley News*, April 28. Available online: https://news.berkeley.edu/2017/04/28/celebrating-barefoot-anthropology-nancy-scheper-hughes/ (accessed June 2, 2020).

Broucker, B. and K. De Wit (2015), "New Public Management in Higher Education," In J. Husiman, H. de Boer, D. D. Dill, and M. Souto-Otero (eds), *The Palgrave International Handbook of Higher Education Policy and Governance*, 57–75. London: Palgrave Macmillan.

Bruner, J. (1991), "The Narrative Construction of Reality," *Critical Inquiry*, 18: 1–21.

Burawoy, M. (2003), "Revisits: An Outline of a Theory of Reflexive Ethnography," *American Sociological Review*, 68 (5): 645–79.

Bureau of Statistics (1993), *Tanzania Demographic and Health Survey 1991/1992*, Dar es Salaam: Bureau of Statistics and Columbia, MD: Macro International.

Calkins, S. (2016), *Who Knows Tomorrow? Uncertainty in North-Eastern Sudan*, New York and Oxford: Berghahn Books.

Centers for Disease Control and Prevention (2020), *Coronavirus Disease 2019 (COVID-19)*, Available online: https://www.cdc.gov/coronavirus/2019-ncov/need-extra-precautions/asthma.html (accessed June 2, 2020).

Central Intelligence Agency (2018), *The World Factbook: Africa: Tanzania*. Available online: https://www.cia.gov/library/publications/the-world-factbook/geos/print_tz.html

Chakrabarty, D. (2000), *Provincializing Europe: Postcolonial Thought and Historical Difference*, Princeton: Princeton University Press.

Chen, K. H. (2010), *Asia as Method: Toward Deimperialization*, Durham, NC: Duke University Press.

Chipindi, F. and F. Vavrus (2018), "The Ontology of Mention: Contexts, Contests, and Constructs of Academic Identity among University of Zambia Faculty," *FIRE: Forum for International Research in Education*, 4 (3): 135–50.

Colleran, H., G. Jasienska, I. Nenko, A. Galbarczyk, and R. Mace (2014), "Community-Level Education Accelerates the Cultural Evolution of Fertility Decline," *Proceedings of the Royal Society of London B: Biological Sciences*, 281 (1779): 2732.

Collins, R. and A. Gallinat (2010), *The Ethnographic Self as Resource: Writing Memory and Experience into Ethnography*, New York and Oxford: Berghahn Books.

Cook, D. and D. Rudabiri (1971), *Poems from East Africa*, Oxford: Heinemann Educational Publishers.

Cooper, E. and D. Pratten, eds. (2015), *Ethnographies of Uncertainty in Africa*, London: Palgrave Macmillan UK.

Cramer, K. J. (2016), *The Politics of Resentment: Rural Consciousness in Wisconsin and the Rise of Scott Walker*, Chicago and London: University of Chicago Press.

Cremin, L. (1978), "Family-Community Linkages in American Education: Some Comments on the Recent Historiography," *Teachers College Record*, 79 (4): 683–704.

Colwell, A. S. C. (2001), "Vision and Revision: Demography, Maternal and Child Health Development, and the Representation of Native Women in Colonial Tanzania," PhD dissertation, University of Illinois at Urbana-Champaign.

"Crying It Out," (2014), *What to Expect*, August 25, 2014. Available online: https://www.whattoexpect.com/first-year/crying-it-out.aspx (accessed September 9, 2016).

Dandeker, C. (1994), *Surveillance, Power, and Modernity*, Cambridge: Polity Press.

Dean, M. (2010), *Governmentality: Power and Rule in Modern Society*, Thousand Oaks, CA: SAGE Publications.

Deem, R. and K. J. Brehony (2005), "Management as Ideology: The Case of 'New Managerialism' in Higher Education," *Oxford Review of Education*, 31 (2): 217–35.

Deininger, K., M. Garcia, and K. Subbarao (2003), "AIDS-Induced Orphanhood as a Systemic Shock: Magnitude, Impact, and Program Interventions in Africa," *World Development*, 31 (7): 1201–20.

DeJaeghere, J., J. Josić, and K. McCleary, eds. (2016), *Education and Youth Agency: Qualitative Case Studies in Global Contexts*, New York: Springer.

DeJaeghere, J. G. (2017), *Educating Entrepreneurial Citizens: Neoliberalism and Youth Livelihoods in Tanzania*, New York: Routledge.

Deloitte (2016), "*Tanzania Economic Outlook 2016: The Story behind the Numbers*," Available online: https://www2.deloitte.com/content/dam/Deloitte/tz/Documents/tax/Economicpercent20Outlookpercent202016percent20TZ.pdf (accessed September 9, 2018).

Dewey, J. (1925), *Experience and Nature*, New York: W. W. Norton.

Dewey, J. (1929), *The Quest for Certainty: A Study of the Relation of Knowledge and Action*, New York: Minton, Balch and Co.

Diamond, I., M. Newby, and S. Varle (1999), "Female Education and Fertility: Examining the Links," In C. H. Bledsoe, J. B. Casterline, J. A. Johnson-Kuhn, and J. G. Haaga (eds), *Critical Perspectives on Schooling and Fertility in the Developing World*, 23–48. Washington: National Academy Press.

Dinerstein, J. (2011), "To Realize You're Creolized: White Flight, Black Culture, Hybridity," In N. Inayatullah (ed.), *Autobiographical International Relations: I, IR*, 118–35. New York and London: Routledge.

Di Nunzio, M. (2015), "Embracing Uncertainty: Young People on the Move in Addis Ababa's Inner City," In E. Cooper and D. Pratten (eds), *Ethnographies of Uncertainty in Africa*, 149–72. London: Palgrave Macmillan UK.

Douglas, M. and A. Wildavsky (1982), *Risk and Culture: An Essay on the Selection of Technological and Environmental Dangers*, Berkeley and Los Angeles: University of California Press.

Duckworth, A. (2016), *Grit: The Power of Passion and Perseverance*, New York: Scribner.

Dundas, A. (1924), *Beneath African Glaciers*, Livingston: Witherby.

Dweck, C. (2016), *Mindset: The New Psychology of Success*, New York: Ballantine Books.

Edwards, F., H. Lee, and M. Esposito (2019), *Risk of Being Killed by Police Use of Force in the United States by Age, Race–Ethnicity, and Sex*, Washington: Proceedings of the National Academy of Sciences of the United States. Available online: https://www.pnas.org/content/116/34/16793 (accessed June 15, 2020).

Emerson, R. M., R. I. Frentz, and L. L. Shaw (1995), *Writing Ethnographic Fieldnotes*, Chicago: University of Chicago Press.

Erickson, F. (2014), "Scaling Down: A Modest Proposal for Practice-Based Policy Research in Teaching," *Education Policy Analysis Archives*, 22 (9). doi: 10.14507/epaa.v22n9.2014 (accessed August 15, 2016).

Ezeh, A. C., B. U. Mberu, and J. O. Emina (2009), "Stall in Fertility Decline in Eastern African Countries: Regional Analysis of Patterns, Determinants and Implications," *Philosophical Transactions of the Royal Society B: Biological Sciences*, 364 (1532): 2991–3007.

Fabian, J. (2002), *Time and the Other: How Anthropology Makes Its Other*, New York: Columbia University Press.

Fabian, J. (2014), "Ethnography and Intersubjectivity: Loose Ends," *HAU: Journal of Ethnographic Theory*, 4 (1): 199–209.

Ferguson, J. (1994), *The Anti-Politics Machine: "Development," Depoliticization, and Bureaucratic Power in Lesotho*, Minneapolis and London: University of Minnesota Press.

Ferguson, J. (2006), *Global Shadows: Africa in the Neoliberal World Order*, Durham, NC: Duke University Press.

Fieldler, K. (1996), *Christianity and African Culture: Conservative German Protestant Missionaries in Tanzania, 1900–1940* (Vol. 14), Leiden: Brill.

Ford, T., S. Reber, and R. Reeves (2020), "Race Gaps in COVID-19 Deaths Are Even Bigger than They Appear," Washington, DC: The Brookings Institution, June 16. Available online: https://www.brookings.edu/blog/up-front/2020/06/16/race-gaps-in-covid-19-deaths-are-even-bigger-than-they-appear/ (accessed June 22, 2020).

Franklin, C. G. (2009), *Academic Lives: Memoir, Cultural Theory, and the University Today*, Athens, GA: University of Georgia Press.

Freeman, D. (1983), *Margaret Mead and Samoa: The Making and Unmaking of an Anthropological Myth*, Cambridge, MA: Harvard University Press.

Freire, P. (1970), *Pedagogy of the Oppressed*, New York: Continuum.

Gardner, H. (2011), *Frames of Mind: The Theory of Multiple Intelligences*, New York: Basic Books.

Geertz, C. (1995), *After the Fact: Two Countries, Four Decades, One Anthropologist*, Cambridge, MA: Harvard University Press.

Gluck, S. B. and D. Patai (1991), *Women's Words: The Feminist Practice of Oral History*, New York: Routledge.

Gottlieb, A. (2000), "Where Have All the Babies Gone? Toward an Anthropology of Infants (and Their Caretakers)," *Anthropological Quarterly*, 73 (3): 21–132.

Gottlieb, A. (2004), *The Afterlife Is Where We Come From: The Culture of Infancy in West Africa*, Chicago and London: University of Chicago Press.

Gottlieb, A. and J. S. DeLoache (2017), *A World of Babies: Imagined Childcare Guides for Eight Societies*, 2nd edn, Cambridge, UK: Cambridge University Press.

Gottlieb, A. and P. Graham (1993), *Parallel Worlds: An Anthropologist and a Writer Encounter Africa*, Chicago: University of Chicago Press.

Gottlieb, A. and P. Graham (2012), *Braided Worlds*, Chicago and London: University of Chicago Press.

Grossman, M. (2005), *Education and Nonmarket Outcomes* (NBER Working Paper No. 11582), Cambridge: National Bureau of Economic Research.

Guest, E. (2001), *Children of AIDS. Africa's Orphan Crisis*, London and Sterling, VA: Pluto Press.

Gutmann, B. (1926), *Das Recht der Dschagga*, Munich: Beck'sch Verlagsbuchhandlung.

Hamermesh, D. (2018), *Why are Professors "Poorly Paid"?* (NBER Working Paper No. 24215), Cambridge: National Bureau of Economic Research.

Hancock, A.-M. (2016), *Intersectionality: An Intellectual History*, New York: Oxford University Press.

Hanushek, E. A. and L. Woessmann (2015), *The Knowledge Capital of Nations: Education and the Economics of Growth*, Cambridge: MIT Press.

Heckman, J. (2013), *Giving Kids a Fair Chance (A Strategy That Works)*, Cambridge: MIT Press.

Hornqvist, M. (2011), *Risk, Power and the State After Foucault*, New York: Routledge.

Human Rights Watch (1999), *Spare the Child: Corporal Punishment in Kenyan Schools*. Available online: https://www.hrw.org/reports/1999/kenya/index.htm#TopOfPage (accessed June 18, 2020).

Human Rights Watch (2017), '*I Had a Dream to Finish School': Barriers to Secondary Education in Tanzania*, New York: Human Rights Watch.

Hutchinson, S. (1996), *Nuer Dilemmas: Coping with Money, War, and the State*, Berkeley and Los Angeles: University of California Press.

Ibhawoh, B. and J. I. Dibua (2003), "Deconstructing *Ujamaa*: The Legacy of Julius Nyerere in the Quest for Social and Economic Development in Africa," *African Journal of Political Science*, 8 (1): 59–83.

Ihucha, A. (2005), "Moshi Community Wants Mangi Meli's Skull Returned," *The Guardian* (Tanzania), October 18. Available online: http://web.

archive.org/web/20070928064942/ and http://www.ippmedia.com/ipp/
guardian/2005/10/18/52083.html (accessed June 16, 2018).

Iliffe, J. (1969), *Tanganyika under German Rule, 1905–1912*, Cambridge, UK:
Cambridge University Press.

Inayatullah, N., ed. (2011), *Autobiographical International Relations: I, IR*, New York
and London: Routledge.

Indiana University Center for Postsecondary Research (2017a), *Basic Classification
Description*. Available online: http://carnegieclassifications.iu.edu/classification_
descriptions/basic.php (accessed September 19, 2018).

Indiana University Center for Postsecondary Research (2017b), *Basic Classification
Methodology*. Available online: http://carnegieclassifications.iu.edu/methodology/
basic.php (accessed September 19, 2018).

International Budget Partnership (n.d.), *Quality of Education Reforms: The HakiElimu
campaign of 2005–2007*. Available online: https://www.internationalbudget.org/wp-
content/uploads/LP-case-study-HakiElimu-one-page-summary.pdf (accessed May
20, 2020).

Johnson, S., M. Monk, and M. Hodges (2000), "Teacher Development and Change in
South Africa: A Critique of the Appropriateness of Transfer of Northern/Western
Practice," *Compare*, 30 (2): 179–92.

Johnson-Hanks, J. (2006), *Uncertain Honor: Modern Motherhood in an African Crisis*,
Chicago and London: University of Chicago Press.

Karr, M. (2015), *The Art of Memoir*, New York: HarperCollins.

Katz, C. (2004), *Growing Up Global: Economic Restructuring and Children's Everyday
Lives*, Minneapolis: University of Minnesota Press.

Kenner, A. (1991), "Death and Memory: From Santa María del Monte to Miami Beach:
Supplemental Material," *Fieldsights: Society for Cultural Anthropology*, August 1, 1999.
Available online: https://culanth.org/fieldsights/death-and-memory-from-santa-
marpercentC3percentADa-del-monte-to-miami-beach (accessed June 18, 2016).

Kent, M. M. (2010), *Fertility and Infant Mortality Declines in Tanzania*, Washington:
Population Reference Bureau.

Kilango, N. C., Y. H. Qin, W. P. Nyoni, and R. A. Senguo (2017), "Interventions That
Increase Enrolment of Women in Higher Education: The University of Dar es
Salaam, Tanzania," *Journal of Education and Practice*, 8 (13): 21–7.

Kilbride, P. L. and J. C. Kilbride (1990), *Changing Family Life in East Africa: Women
and Children at Risk*, University Park, PA: Pennsylvania State University Press.

Kilimanjaro Christian Medical Center (KCMC) (2017), *Background Information*.
Available online: https://www.kcmc.ac.tz/?q=background (accessed June 14, 2018).

Klees, S. J., M. Ginsberg, H. Anwar, M. B. Robbins, H. Bloom, and C. Busacca (2020),
"The World Bank's SABER: A Critical Analysis," *Comparative Education Review*,
64 (1): 46–65.

Lancy, D. F. (2015), *The Anthropology of Childhood: Cherubs, Chattel, Changelings*,
Cambridge: Cambridge University Press.

Lawuo, Z. E. (1984), *Education and Social Change in a Rural Community: A Study of Colonial Education and Local Response among the Chagga between 1920 and 1945*, Dar es Salaam: University of Dar es Salaam Press.

Lema, E., M. Mbilinyi, and R. Rajani, eds. (2004), *Nyerere on Education/Nyerere kuhusu Elimu*, Dar es Salaam, Tanzania: HakiElimu.

Lemov, D. (2010), *Teach Like a Champion: 49 Techniques That Put Students on the Path to College*, San Francisco: Jossey-Bass.

LeVine, R. A. (2007), "Ethnographic Studies of Childhood: A Historical Overview" *American Anthropologist*, 109: 247–60.

LeVine, R. A. and S. E. LeVine (1988), "Parental Strategies among the Gusii of Kenya," In R. A. LeVine, P. M. Miller, and M. Maxwell West (eds), *Parental Behavior in Diverse Societies* (special issue of *New Directions for Child Development*), 40, 27–36, San Francisco: Jossey-Bass.

LeVine, R. A., S. E. LeVine, S. Dixon, A. Richman, P. H. Leiderman, C. H. Keefer, and T. B. Brazelton (1994), *Child Care and Culture: Lessons from Africa*, Cambridge, UK: Cambridge University Press.

Levinson, B. A., D. E. Foley, and D. C. Holland (1996), *The Cultural Production of the Educated Person: Critical Ethnographies of Schooling and Local Practice*, Albany: SUNY Press.

Lieberman, A., S. Hanson, J. Gless, and E. Moir (2011), *Mentoring Teachers: Navigating Real World Tensions*, San Francisco: Jossey-Bass.

Lloyd, C. B., C. E. Kaufman, and P. Hewett (2000), "The Spread of Primary Schooling in Sub-Saharan Africa: Implications for Fertility Change," *Population and Development Review*, 26 (3): 483–515.

Lugalla, J. L. (1997), "Economic Reforms and Health Conditions of the Urban Poor in Tanzania," *African Studies Quarterly*, 1 (2): 17.

Luhmann, N. (1993), *Risk: A Sociological Theory*, New York: de Gruyter.

Lyima, D. (2017), *40 Years of Immunization Program in Tanzania*. Available online: http://ehealth.go.tz/admin/rmo_materials/Day1/IVD-Chanjopercent20-percent20Dr.percent20Dafrosa.pdf (accessed June 14, 2018).

Mafuru, W. L. (2011), "Coping with Inadequacy: Understanding the Effects of Central Teacher Recruitment in Six Ward Secondary Schools in Tanzania," PhD dissertation, University of Groningen.

Malekela, G. A. (1983), "Access to Secondary Education in Sub-Saharan Africa: The Tanzanian Experiment," PhD dissertation, University of Chicago.

Marcus, J. (2018), "Facts about Race and College Admission," *The Hechinger Report*, July 6. Available online: https://hechingerreport.org/facts-about-race-and-college-admission/ (accessed June 10, 2020).

Mason, M. A., M. Goulden, and K. Frasch (2009), "Why Graduate Students Reject the Fast Track," *AAUP*. Available online: https://www.aaup.org/article/why-graduate-students-reject-fast-track#.WzT3s6inGUk (September 14, 2018).

Mason, M. A., N. H. Wolfinger, and M. Goulden (2013), *Do Babies Matter? Gender and Family in the Ivory Tower*, New Brunswick, NJ: Rutgers University Press.

McTighe, J. and G. Wiggins (2013), *Essential Questions: Opening Doors to Student Understanding*, Alexandria, VA: ASCD.

Meneley, A. and D. J. Young (2005), *Auto-Ethnographies: The Anthropology of Academic Practices*, Ontario: Broadview Press.

Mgaiwa, S. J. (2018), "The Paradox of Financing Public Higher Education in Tanzania and the Fate of Quality Education: The Experience of Selected Universities," *Sage Open*. doi: 10.1177/2158244018771729

Ministry of Education (1991), *Basic Education Statistics in Tanzania*. Dar es Salaam: Ministry of Education.

Ministry of Education and Culture (2004), *Education Sector Development Programme (SEDP), 2004-2009*, Dar es Salaam: United Republic of Tanzania.

Ministry of Education and Vocational Training (2010), *Secondary Education Development Programme II (July 2010–June 2015)*, Dar es Salaam: Ministry of Education and Vocational Training.

Ministry of Education and Vocational Training (2014), *The Education and Training Policy* (translated English version), Dar es Salaam: Ministry of Education and Vocational Training.

Ministry of Health, Community Development, Gender, Elderly and Children (2016), *Tanzania Demographic and Health Survey and Malaria Indicator Survey (TDHS-MIS) 2015–16*, Dar es Salaam: Ministry of Health, Community Development, Gender, Elderly and Children.

Moore, S. F. (1986), *Social Facts and Fabrications: "Customary" Law on Kilimanjaro, 1880–1980*, Cambridge and New York: Cambridge University Press.

Moore, S. F. and P. Puritt (1977), *Chagga and Meru: Ethnographic Survey of Africa*, London: International African Institute.

Morris, E. (2018), "Performing Graduates and Dropouts: The Gendered Scripts and Aspirations of Secondary School Students in Zanzibar," PhD dissertation, University of Minnesota.

Mosha, R. S. (2000), *The Heartbeat of Indigenous Africa: A Study of the Chagga Educational System*, New York: Garland Publishing.

Mulkeen, A., D. W. Chapman, J. G. DeJaeghere, and E. Leu (2007), *Recruiting, Retaining, and Retraining Secondary School Teachers and Principals in Sub-Saharan Africa*, Washington: The World Bank.

Mushi, P. A. K. (2009), *History and Development of Education in Tanzania*, Oxford: African Books Collective.

Musick, K., P. England, S. Edgington, and N. Kangas (2009), "Education Differences in Intended and Unintended Fertility," *Social Forces*, 88 (2): 543–72.

Nagar, R. (2014), *Muddying the Waters: Coauthoring Feminisms Across Scholarship and Activism*, Urbana, Springfield, and Chicago, IL: University of Illinois Press.

Nagar, R. (2019), *Hungry Translations: The World Through Radical Vulnerability*, Urbana, IL: University of Illinois Press.

National Bureau of Statistics (2019), *Tanzania in Figures 2018*, Dodoma: National Bureau of Statistics.

National Bureau of Statistics and Office of Chief Government Statistician (2015), *Thematic Report on Fertility and Nuptiality: 2012 Population and Housing Census Volume IV*, Dar es Salaam: National Bureau of Statistics.

Nencel, L. (2014), "Situating Reflexivity: Voices, Positionalities and Representations in Feminist Ethnographic Texts," *Women's Studies International Forum*, 43: 75–83.

Newfield, C. (2011), *Unmaking the Public University: The Forty Year Assault on the Middle Class*, Cambridge: Harvard University Press.

Ngatara, L. A. (2001), "Doomsday for Kilimanjaro People in Sight," *The Guardian* (Tanzania), March 17. n.pag.

Niyozov, S. (2017), "Understanding Pedagogy: Cross-Cultural and Comparative Insights from Central Asia," In K. Bickmore, R. Hayhoe, C. Manion, K. Mundy, and R. Read (eds), *Comparative and International Education: Issues for Teachers*, 2nd edn, 88–118. Toronto: Canadian Scholars Press.

Nyerere, J. (1967), "Education for Self-Reliance," *The Ecumenical Review*, 19 (4): 382–403.

Nyerere, J. (1973), *Freedom and Development: Uhuru na Maendeleo* [Freedom and Development]. *A Selection from Writings and Speeches 1968–1973*, New York: Oxford University Press.

Nyerere, J. (1974), *Ujamaa: Essays on Socialism*, Dar es Salaam: Oxford University Press.

Nyerere, J. (1985), "Education in Tanzania," *Harvard Educational Review*, 55 (1): 45–53.

Office of Minority Health (2017), *Infant Mortality and African Americans*, Washington: US Department of Health and Human Services. Available online: https://minorityhealth.hhs.gov/omh/browse.aspx?lvl=4andlvlid=23 (accessed June 8, 2020).

Organisation for Economic Co-operation and Development (2018), "*The Future of Education and Skills: Education 2030*," Available online: https://www.oecd.org/education/2030/E2030percent20Positionpercent20Paperpercent20_05.04.2018_.pdf (accessed June 4, 2020).

Parkman, A. (2016), "The Imposter Phenomenon in Higher Education: Incidence and Impact," *Journal of Higher Education Theory and Practice*, 16 (1): 51.

p'Bitek, O. (1967), *Song of Lawino and Song of Ocol*, Oxford: Heinemann Educational Publishers.

Pillow, W. (2003), "Confession, Catharsis, or Cure? Rethinking the Uses of Reflexivity as Methodological Power in Qualitative Research," *International Journal of Qualitative Studies in Education*, 16 (2): 175–96.

Prout, A. and A. James (2005), "A New Paradigm for the Sociology of Childhood? Provenance, Promise and Problems" *Childhood: Critical Concepts in Sociology*, 1: 56–80.

Rabinow, P. (1977), *Reflections on Fieldwork in Morocco*, Berkeley: University of California Press.

Raum, O. F. (1940), *Chaga Childhood: A Description of Indigenous Education in an East African Tribe*, Oxford: Oxford University Press.

Riessman, C. K. (2008), *Narrative Methods for the Human Sciences*, Los Angeles: SAGE Publications.

Rogers, M. L. (2007), "Action and Inquiry in Dewey's Philosophy," *Transactions of the Charles S. Peirce Foundation*, 43 (1): 90–115.

Rogers, S. G. (1972), "The Search for Political Focus on Kilimanjaro: A History of Chagga Politics, 1916–1952, with Special Reference to the Cooperative Movement and Indirect Rule," PhD dissertation, University of Dar es Salaam.

Rosaldo, R. (1989), *Culture and Truth: The Remaking of Social Analysis*, Boston: Beacon Press.

Rosenthal, E. (2013), "The Soaring Cost of a Simple Breath," *The New York Times*, October 12. Available online: https://www.nytimes.com/2013/10/13/us/the-soaring-cost-of-a-simple-breath.html (accessed August 8, 2016).

Ryan, C. (2012), *Field of Degree and Earnings by Selected Employment Characteristics: 2011*. Available online: https://www.census.gov/prod/2012pubs/acsbr11-10.pdf (accessed June 4, 2020).

Samimian-Darash, L. and P. Rabinow, eds. (2015), *Modes of Uncertainty: Anthropological Cases*, Chicago: University of Chicago Press.

Samoff, J. (1979), "Education in Tanzania: Class Formation and Reproduction," *The Journal of Modern African Studies*, 17 (1): 47–69.

Sandburg, C. (1916/1992), "Chicago," In W. Harmon (ed.), *The Top 500 Poems*, 912–13. New York: Columbia University Press.

Sayed, Y. and R. Ahmed (2015), "Education Quality, and Teaching and Learning in the Post-2015 Education agenda" *International Journal of Educational Development*, 40: 330–8.

Scheper-Hughes, N. (1992), "Death without Weeping," In A. C. G. M. Robben (ed.), *Death, Mourning, and Burial: A Cross-Cultural Reader*, 179–93. Oxford: Blackwell Publishing.

Scheper-Hughes, N. (1995), "The Primacy of the Ethical: Propositions for a Militant Anthropology," *Current Anthropology*, 36 (3): 409–40.

Schultz, T. W. (1961), "Investment in Human Capital," *The American Economic Review*, 51 (1): 1–17.

Schweisfurth, M. (2013), *Learner-Centred Education in International Perspective: Whose Pedagogy for Whose Development?* London and New York: Routledge.

Secondary Education in Africa Initiative (2007), *At the Crossroads: Choices for Secondary Education in Sub-Saharan Africa*. Unpublished synthesis report.

Setel, P. (1999), *A Plague of Paradoxes: AIDS, Culture, and Demography in Northern Tanzania*, Chicago: University of Chicago Press.

Seuss, Dr. (1990), *Oh the Places You'll Go*, New York: Random House.

Shapiro, D. and T. Gebreselassie (2013), "Fertility Transition in Sub-Saharan Africa: Falling and Stalling," *African Population Studies*, 23 (1): 3–23.

Shirazi, R. (2017), "How Much of This Is New? Thoughts on How We Got Here, Solidarity, and Research in the Current Moment," *Anthropology and Education Quarterly*, 48 (4): 354–61.

Shore, C. (2008), "Audit Culture and Illiberal Governance: Universities and the Politics of Accountability," *Anthropological Theory*, 8 (3): 278–98.

Shore, C. and S. Wright (1997), *Anthropology of Policy: Critical Perspectives on Governance and Power*, London and New York: Routledge.

"Short Portrait: Otto Raum," (2012), *Interviews with German Anthropologists*. Available online: http://www.germananthropology.com/short-portrait/otto-raum/258 (accessed August 18, 2017).

Smith, B. L. (2012), "The Case against Spanking," *American Psychological Association Monitor on Psychology*, 43 (4). Available online: http://www.apa.org/monitor/2012/04/spanking.aspx (accessed September 8, 2017).

Spock, B. and R. Needlman (2011), *Dr. Spock's Baby and Child Care*, 9th edn, New York: Simon and Schuster.

Sriprakasha, A., L. Tikly, and S. Walker (2020), "The Erasures of Racism in Education and International Development: Re-reading the 'Global Learning Crisis,'" *Compare*, 50 (5): 676–92. doi: 10.1080/03057925.2018.1559040

Stacki, S. and S. Baily, eds. (2015), *Educating Adolescent Girls Around the Globe: Challenges and Opportunities*, New York: Routledge.

Stahl, K. M. (1964), *History of the Chagga People of Kilimanjaro* (Vol. 2). The Hague: Mouton.

Stambach, A. (2000), *Lessons from Kilimanjaro: Schooling, Community, and Gender in East Africa*, New York: Routledge.

Steiner-Khamsi, G. (2013), "What Is Wrong with the 'What-Went-Right' Approach in Educational Policy?" *European Educational Research Journal*, 12 (1): 20–33.

Strauss, V. (2015), "It's 2015. Where Are All the Black College Faculty?" *The Washington Post*, November 12. Available online: https://www.washingtonpost.com/news/answer-sheet/wp/2015/11/12/its-2015-where-are-all-the-black-college-faculty/?utm_term=.4d95fdc42e0f (accessed June 8, 2020).

Sumra, S. and R. Rajani (2006), *Secondary Education in Tanzania: Key Policy Challenges*. Available online: http://hakielimu.org/files/publications/document34secondary_edu_tz_policy_challenges_en.pdf (accessed August 10, 2016).

Swadener, B. B. (2000), *Does the Village Still Raise the Child?: A Collaborative Study of Changing Child-Rearing and Early Education in Kenya*, Albany: State University of New York Press.

Takayama, K. (2020), "An Invitation to 'Negative' Comparative Education," *Comparative Education*, 56 (1): 79–95. doi: 10.1080/03050068.2019.1701250

Tanzania Commission for Universities (2016), *The TCU Rolling Strategic Plan 2015/16–2019/20*, Dar es Salaam: Tanzania Commission for Universities.

Tao, S. (2015), "Corporal Punishment, Capabilities and Well-Being: Tanzanian Primary School Teachers' Perspectives." In J. Parkes (ed.), *Gender Violence in Poverty Contexts: The Educational Challenge*, 84–100. London and New York: Routledge.

Thomas, M. A. M. (2018), "Research Capacity and Dissemination among Academics in Tanzania: Examining Knowledge Production and the Perceived Binary of 'Local' and 'International' Journals," *Compare*, 48 (2): 281–98.

Thomas, M. A. M. and A. Rugambwa (2011), "Equity, Power, and Capabilities: Constructions of Gender in a Tanzanian Secondary School," *Feminist Formations*, 23 (3): 153–75.

Thomas, M. A. M. and F. Vavrus (2010), "Lessons from Teaching in Action: Developing, Implementing, and Sustaining a Teacher-Training Development Program," In M. Desforges and P. V. Lyimo (eds), *Supporting Quality Education in East Africa: VMM Partnership Programmes*, 135–51. Liverpool: VMM England.

Thomas, M. A. M. and F. Vavrus (2019), "The Pluto Problem: Reflexivities of Discomfort in Teacher Professional Development," *Critical Studies in Education*. doi: 10.1080/17508487.2019.1587782

Tikly, L. (2004), "Education and the New Imperialism," *Compare*, 40 (2): 173–98.

Tough, P. (2016), *Helping Children Succeed: What Works and Why*, New York: Houghton Mifflin Harcourt.

Tripp, A. M. (1997), *Changing the Rules: The Politics of Liberalization and the Urban Informal Economy in Tanzania*, Berkeley: University of California Press.

Tripp, A. M. (2012), "Donor Assistance and Political Reform in Tanzania," Unpublished working paper, United Nations University World Institute for Development Economics Research, Helsinki, Finland.

Tsing, A. L. (2005), *Friction: An Ethnography of Global Connections*, Princeton: Princeton University Press.

Turner, S. (2015), "'We Wait for Miracles': Ideas of Hope and Future among Clandestine Burundian Refugees in Nairobi," In E. Cooper and D. Pratten (eds), *Ethnographies of Uncertainty in Africa*, 173–91. London: Palgrave Macmillan.

Turshen, M. (1999), *Privatizing Health Services in Africa*, Piscataway, NJ: Rutgers University Press.

UNAIDS (2018), *United Republic of Tanzania 2018: Country Factsheet*. Available online: https://www.unaids.org/en/regionscountries/countries/unitedrepublicoftanzania (accessed June 8, 2020).

United Nations Development Programme (2017), *Human Development Reports: Under Five Mortality Rates*. Available online: http://hdr.undp.org/en/content/under-five-mortality-rate-1000-live-births (accessed June 7, 2020).

UNESCO (2018), *United Republic of Tanzania*. Available online: http://uis.unesco.org/en/country/tz (accessed June 7, 2020).

UNICEF (2000), *The Progress of Nations 2000*, New York: UNICEF.

UNICEF (2004, June 11), "Efforts against Child Labour Often Overlook Domestic Workers," Available online: https://www.unicef.org/media/media_21576.html

UNICEF (2006), *Africa's Orphaned and Vulnerable Generations: Children Affected by AIDS*, New York: UNICEF.

United Nations General Assembly (1989), *Convention on the Rights of the Child*. Available online: https://www.ohchr.org/en/professionalinterest/pages/crc.aspx

University of Minnesota (2013), *Guidelines for Standards, Policies, and Procedures for Promotion and Tenure Review of Faculty.* Available online: https://faculty.umn.edu/sites/faculty.umn.edu/files/olpd.pdf (accessed September 20, 2016).

US Census Bureau (2008), *HIV/AIDS Profile: Tanzania.* Available online: https://www.census.gov/content/dam/Census/library/publications/2008/demo/tanzania08.pdf (accessed October 8, 2016).

Vandemoortele, J. and E. Delamonica (2000), "The 'Education Vaccine' against HIV," *Current Issues in Comparative Education*, 3 (1). Available online: http://www.tc.columbia.edu/CICE/articles/jved131.htm (accessed October 14, 2003).

Vavrus, F. (2003), *Desire and Decline: Schooling amid Crisis in Tanzania*, New York: Peter Lang.

Vavrus, F. (2005), "Adjusting Inequality: Education and Structural Adjustment Policies in Tanzania," *Harvard Educational Review*, 75 (2): 174–201.

Vavrus, F. (2006), "Girls' Schooling in Tanzania: The Key to HIV/AIDS Prevention?" *AIDS Care*, 18 (8): 863–71.

Vavrus, F. (2009), "The Cultural Politics of Constructivist Pedagogies: Teacher Education Reform in the United Republic of Tanzania," *International Journal of Educational Development*, 29 (3): 303–11.

Vavrus, F. (2013), "The Emergence of an International Teacher Education and Research Collaboration," In F. Vavrus and L. Bartlett (eds), *Teaching in Tension: International Pedagogies, National Policies, and Teachers' Practices in Tanzania*, 23–38. Rotterdam: Sense Publishers.

Vavrus, F. (2015), "More Clever than the Devil: *Ujanja* as Schooling Strategy in Tanzania," *International Journal of Qualitative Studies in Education*, 28 (1): 50–71.

Vavrus, F. (2016a), "Topographies of Power: Critical Historical Geography in the Study of Education in Tanzania," *Comparative Education*, 52 (2): 136–56.

Vavrus, F. (2016b), "*When 'What Works' Doesn't: Comparative Pedagogies and Epistemological Diversity*," Sydney Ideas Dean's Lecture, Faculty of Education and Social Work, University of Sydney, Australia, November 9, 2016.

Vavrus, F. and L. Bartlett (2012), "Comparative Pedagogies and Epistemological Diversity: Social and Materials Contexts of Teaching in Tanzania," *Comparative Education Review*, 56 (4): 634–58.

Vavrus, F. and L. Bartlett, eds. (2013), *Teaching in Tension: International Pedagogies, National Policies, and Teachers' Practices in Tanzania*, Rotterdam: Sense Publishers.

Vavrus, F. and C. Kwauk (2013), "The New Abolitionists? The World Bank and the 'Boldness' of Global School Fee Elimination Reforms," *Discourse: Studies in the Cultural Politics of Education*, 34 (3): 351–65.

Vavrus, F. and G. Moshi (2009), "The Cost of a 'Free' Primary Education in Tanzania" *International Journal of Educational Policy, Research, and Practice*, 8: 31–42.

Vavrus, F. and M. Seghers (2010), "Critical Discourse Analysis in Comparative Education: A Discursive Study of 'Partnership' in Tanzania's Poverty Reduction Policies," *Comparative Education Review*, 54 (1): 77–103.

Vavrus, F. and U. Larsen (2003), "Girls' Education and Fertility Transitions: An Analysis of Recent Trends in Tanzania and Uganda," *Economic Development and Cultural Change*, 51 (4): 945–75.

Vavrus, F. and V. Salema (2013), "Working Lives of Teachers: Social and Material Constraints," In F. Vavrus and L. Bartlett (eds), *Teaching in Tension: International Pedagogies, National Policies, and Teachers' Practices in Tanzania*, 75–92. Rotterdam: Sense Publishers.

Ventura, S. J., K. D. Peters, J. A. Martin, and J. D. Maurer (1997), "Births and Deaths: United States, 1996," *Monthly Vital Statistics Report*, 46 (1 suppl 2): 1–40.

Vumilia, P. L. (2010), "Teacher Training and Quality Education: Diploma Science in Tanzania," In M. Desforges and P. V. Lyimo (eds), *Supporting Quality Education in East Africa: VMM Partnership Programmes*, 108–26. Liverpool: VMM England.

Wagner, D. (2018), *Learning as Development: Rethinking International Education in a Changing World*, New York and London: Routledge.

Wagner, D. and N. Castillo (2014), "Learning at the Bottom of the Pyramid: Constraints, Comparability and Policy in Developing Countries," *Prospects: Quarterly Review of Comparative Education*, XLIV (44): 627–38.

Ward, K. and L. Wolf-Wendel (2012), *Academic Motherhood: How Faculty Manage Work and Family*, New Brunswick, NJ: Rutgers University Press.

Weber, E. (2007), "Globalization, 'Glocal' Development, and Teachers' Work: A Research Agenda," *Review of Educational Research*, 77 (3): 279–309. doi: 10.3102/003465430303946

Wedgewood, R. (2005), *Post-Basic Education and Poverty in Tanzania*, Unpublished working paper, Centre of African Studies, University of Edinburgh.

Weller-Ferris, L. (1999), "Working Conditions," In A. Menlo and P. Poppleton (eds), *The Meanings of Teaching: An International Study of Secondary Teachers' Work Lives*, 117–47. Westport, CT: Bergin and Garvey.

Whyte, S. R. (1997), *Questioning Misfortune: The Pragmatics of Uncertainty in Eastern Uganda*, Cambridge, UK: Cambridge University Press.

Whyte, S. R. and G. E. Siu (2015), "Contingency: Interpersonal and Historical Dependencies in HIV care," In E. Cooper and D. Pratten (eds), *Ethnographies of Uncertainty in Africa*, 19–35. London: Palgrave Macmillan.

Wiggins, G. and J. McTighe (2005), *Understanding by Design*, Alexandria, VA: ASCD.

The World Bank (1999), *Tanzania: Social Sector Review*, Washington: The World Bank.

The World Bank (2013), *What Matters Most for Teacher Policies: A Framework Paper*, Washington: The World Bank.

The World Bank (2017), *Tanzania: GDP Per Capita*. Available online: https://data.worldbank.org/country/tanzania (accessed June 19, 2018).

The World Bank (2018), *GNI Per Capita, Atlas Method (Current $)—Tanzania*. Available online: https://data.worldbank.org/indicator/NY.GNP.PCAP.CD?locations=TZ (accessed June 19, 2018).

The World Health Organization (2004), *The World Health Report 2004: Changing History*. Available online: https://www.who.int/whr/2004/en/report04_en.pdf?ua=1 (accessed August 20 2016).

Worldometer (2020), *Tanzania Population*. Available online: https://www.worldometers.info/world-population/tanzania-population/ (accessed June 8, 2020).

Zeichner, K. M. and D. P. Liston (1996), *Reflective Teaching: An Introduction*, Mahwah, NJ: Lawrence Erlbaum Associates.

Zhang, L. (2008), "Religious Affiliation, Religiosity, and Male and Female Fertility," *Demographic Research*, 18 (8): 233–62.

Index